ENDANGERED SPECIES:
A SURLY BEAR IN THE BIBLE BELT

endangered species
A SURLY BEAR IN THE BIBLE BELT

JEFF MANN

Lethe Press
Amherst, MA

Published by Lethe Press
lethepressbooks.com

Copyright © 2019 Jeff Mann

ISBN: 9781590217016

No part of this work may be reproduced or utilized in any form or by any means, electronic or mechanical, including photocopying, microfilm, and recording, or by any information storage and retrieval system, without permission in writing from the Author or Publisher.

Library of Congress Cataloging-in-Publication Data available on request

Cover photograph by Jakk Blood
Cover and Interior design by Inkspiral Design

For John, and for my clan.

Acknowledgments

MANY THANKS TO Steve Berman and Lethe Press for supporting my work for so many years. And many thanks to Paul J. Willis and Amie Evans for giving the world the Saints and Sinners Literary Festival.

A number of these essays appeared in these journals and anthologies:

"Romantic" appeared in *Who's Yer Daddy? Gay Writers Celebrate Their Mentors and Forerunners*, ed. by Jim Elledge and David Groff (Madison: Terrace Books/University of Wisconsin Press, 2012).

"Country Queer" appeared in *Floyd County Moonshine* 2.1 (Fall 2009).

"Letter to my Sixteen-Year-Old Self" appeared in *Glitterwolf Magazine* 8 (April 2015).

"Surly Bear in the Bible Belt" appeared in *Chelsea Station* 3 (2012).

"Thomas" appeared in *The Other Man: 21 Writers Speak Candidly About Sex, Love, Infidelity, and Moving On*, ed. by Paul Alan Fahey (Glen Allen, Virginia: JMS Books, 2013).

"The Painters" appeared in *Chelsea Station* (12 June 2014).

"The Bells of Bruges," a poem included in "Lending the Outlier Pluck," first appeared in *Chiron Review* 81 (Winter 2005).

"The Feast Hall, the Arsenal, and the Mirror" appeared in *Appalachia in the Classroom: Teaching the Region*, ed. by Theresa L. Burriss and Patricia M. Gantt (Athens, Ohio: Ohio University Press, 2013).

"A Leather Bear in the Big Easy" appeared in *My Gay New Orleans*, ed. by Frank Perez and Jeffrey Palmquist (Bedford, Texas: LL-Publications, 2016). Included in this essay are sections of "Ode to a Dick Dancer," a poem that first appeared in *Velvet Mafia: Dangerous Queer Fiction* (8 June 2009), and "The Angel of Royal Street," a poem that first appeared in *Blue Fifth Review* 10.2 (March 2010).

"Offensive Hillbilly Queer" appeared in *Walk Till the Dogs Get Mean: Meditations on the Forbidden from Contemporary Appalachia*, ed. by Karen Salyer McElmurray and Adrian Blevins (Athens, Ohio: Ohio University Press, 2015).

"Amy" appeared in *Chelsea Station* (13 March 2015).

"Two Mountain Weddings" appeared in *Equality: What Do You Think About When You Think of Equality?* ed. by Paul Alan Fahey (Melbourne, Australia: Vine Leaves Press, 2017).

"Big Queer Convocations" appeared in *Unbroken Circle: Stories of Cultural Diversity in the South*, ed. by Julia Watts and Larry Smith (Huron, Ohio: Bottom Dog Press, 2017).

Author's Note

THE MAJORITY OF these essays were not originally written to appear together in one volume. Instead, they were published in assorted literary journals and anthologies between 2009 and 2017.

Since all of them are autobiographical personal essays, and since all of them deal with the experience of being gay in Appalachia, expect to see some overlap. Thanks go to my husband, John Ross, for helping me remove as much repetition as possible. Some I've left, so as to retain the integrity of each individual essay and to make more sense to readers who choose to read the essays out of order.

In some of the older essays, I've updated assorted references and facts.

CONTENTS

1	ROMANTIC
13	COUNTRY QUEER
19	LETTER TO MY SIXTEEN-YEAR-OLD SELF
25	SURLY BEAR IN THE BIBLE BELT
39	THOMAS
53	THE PAINTERS
59	LENDING THE OUTLIER PLUCK
69	THE FEAST HALL, THE ARSENAL, AND THE MIRROR
87	DAVID
93	A LEATHER BEAR IN THE BIG EASY
113	COUNTRY BOY
119	OFFENSIVE HILLBILLY QUEER
131	AMY
147	TWO MOUNTAIN WEDDINGS
159	COMPARING TATTOOS
163	WHOREMONGER
185	BIG QUEER CONVOCATIONS
201	CONFEDERATE
249	SCRAPPLE
253	MUSLIM FOOD
271	A FEROCIOUS DRAG QUEEN
299	WATCH OUT! THAT QUEER'S GOT A GUN!

Daddy's love of Emerson and Thoreau he transmitted to me, and their doctrines of individualism and nonconformity have come in hugely handy. From them, I learned to do as I please.

romantic

I. Daddy

MY FATHER TURNED NINETY THIS month, March of 2011. On the way home from an Appalachian Studies conference in Kentucky, where I'd read some poems and spoken on gay life in the Mountain South, my partner John and I swung through Summers County, West Virginia, for an afternoon of birthday celebration at my sister Amy's rural homestead. Outside, the first daffodils gleamed in the chilly afternoon; the vegetable garden lay gray-brown and fallow, soon to be prepared for another season of my father's enthusiastic planting and harvesting. Inside, a wood fire glowed. We drank red-eyes, a country concoction of cheap beer and tomato juice (tastier than it sounds, I promise). Amy made a wonderful meal—Swedish meatballs over noodles, broccoli casserole, deviled eggs, and German chocolate cake—supplemented by the bread my father had baked. Daddy gave John and me a loaf to take home; I gave Daddy a big bottle of Bushmill's Irish whiskey as a birthday present.

We're all about good food and drink, my father and I. But we're also devoted to literary pursuits. Daddy and I talked about our recent writing endeavors—he's published another essay on gardening in *The Charleston Gazette*, I've published a batch of poems in *The Southern Poetry Anthology, Volume 3: Contemporary Appalachia*—and our recent reading—he's moving through Mark Twain's voluminous autobiography, I'm perusing a Confederate soldier's memoir, *Life in the Army of Northern Virginia 1861-1865*.

That late-winter afternoon's combination of hillside farm, strong drink, fresh bread, down-home food, and conversations about reading and writing pretty much summarizes my father's legacy. Though we've had our conflicts—both of us possess strong streaks of self-absorption, stubbornness, and selfishness—when it comes to intellect and the creative life, he's been the perfect role model, continuing to educate himself, to read and write, into his ninth decade. I can only hope to emulate him in this regard, and I certainly would never have become a writer without his influence. I would also never have become the kind of writer I am. When I examine my peculiar literary passions and ornery obsessions, I can trace a goodly number of them to those formative years with Daddy, walking the woods with him, reading the books he suggested.

A carping critic once dismissed my poetry as romantic. He meant such an adjective to be derogatory, but I claim the term as a compliment. I can thank my father for this predilection. He brought me up to love nature, imaginative literature, and the past; to read Wordsworth and Keats; to listen to Beethoven, Brahms, Rachmaninoff, and Puccini. Today, browsing the lengthy introduction to romanticism in *The Norton Anthology of English Literature: The Major Authors*, I find myself and my writing effectively summarized: a love of history, the supernatural, and the Gothic; a defiant individualism; a dedication to the natural world; an emphasis on powerful feeling and lyrical autobiography; and a fascination with the local, the rural, the regional, and the commonplace. Such definitions help me make as much sense of my literary influences as my familial ones: Ralph Waldo Emerson, Henry David Thoreau, the English Romantics, Robert Frost, Joni

Mitchell, Sylvia Plath, Anne Sexton, Walt Whitman, and assorted gay or Appalachian poets.

II. History and the Gothic

IN COVINGTON, VIRGINIA, where I spent my first decade, one of my earliest memories is walking with my father to the public library. There, my initial enthusiasms were King Arthur and his exploits, as well as Greek and Roman mythology, and so I developed a taste for heroic adventure and its depictions in literature. To this day, I'm an occasional reader of the classics in translation—Marcus Aurelius, Ovid, Hesiod, Homer, Sappho—and in the last ten years I've expanded my interests to the mythologies of my bloodlines, Celtic and Germanic. From these readings has come my third book of poems, *Ash: Poems from Norse Mythology*, as well as a passion for such tasty video fare as *Gladiator*, *300*, and *Spartacus*.

The supernatural elements of mythology and legend—gods, monsters, enchanters, and suchlike—also bred in me a fascination with the occult. Watching the supernatural soap opera *Dark Shadows* as a boy only contributed to this. From such influences spring my own enjoyable dabblings in erotic horror: my Appalachian vampire character, Derek Maclaine, has appeared in a novella, a novel, and several short stories. As an academic, I'm sharply aware of how complete is the dominance of realism in contemporary literary fiction—many of my colleagues regard "genre fiction" such as horror, historical fiction, and literotica as inferior fare—but the achievement of tenure has made me comfortably uncaring of such attitudes.

Romantics also have a fascination with distant places and the past. I'm no different in this regard. One of the few things I'm willing to spend a lot of money on is travel, and writing travel essays is my way of making sense of those wanderings. As for the past, my father attended Washington and Lee for his bachelor's degree in English and later for law school, and so spent time in Lexington,

Virginia, where Southern idols Robert E. Lee and Stonewall Jackson lived and are buried. When I visited the campus of W&L to pay my respects at those men's graves in the summer of 2010, I had vivid flashes of memory: being a very young boy there, my father showing me the garage which once had been the stable for Lee's famous horse, Traveller. I could almost hear Daddy's reverent tones again. No surprise, then, that my latest projects all involve the Confederate experience in the War of Northern Aggression. At the very least, I'll get two novels, a novella, a book of poetry, and a collection of short stories out of my recent readings of Civil War history. From my native region I have also inherited a sense of fatalism and the tragic: as Appomattox proves, a man may fight and fight and sacrifice everything, yet still suffer defeat.

III. Individualism and Nonconformity

SOMEWHERE AMONG THE boxes of papers my husband's always after me to sort through and throw out is a mimeographed copy of Ralph Waldo Emerson's essay "Self-Reliance" that my father gave me during my high school years, as well as a paperback copy of *Walden* I devoured during high-school study hall. Daddy's love of Emerson and Thoreau he transmitted to me, and their doctrines of individualism and nonconformity have come in hugely handy. From them, I learned to do as I please; to care little for public opinion; to follow my own passions, however eccentric; and to prize solitude and independence. These attitudes have made it easier to take risks in my writing, to deal with topics—adultery, despair, queer lust, BDSM, rage—that I might not otherwise have had the guts to write about, much less publish. My most recent collection of personal essays, *Binding the God*, I find sometimes almost wincingly frank. Like myself, it's a crazy amalgam of disparate elements—salaciously detailed erotic memoir, West Virginia folklore, a reverence for the Confederate experience and the Confederate flag, my futile lust for a country-music star, my attempt to reconcile pagan mythology with sadomasochism. In other words, it's a collection likely to bemuse or repulse many. It makes me feel uncomfortably exposed. But then I think of my father, who was fired from a high-school teaching job for attacking racist policies in Virginia schools in the 1960s. I think of fine queer writers like Dorothy Allison and Patrick Califia, the risks such predecessors have taken; I think of Emerson and Thoreau. And I promise myself to be as defiantly myself as possible.

IV. Nature

ALL THOSE WOODLAND walks my father and I took have had a great shaping power over my work. One attendee at a poetry reading I once gave claimed that he'd have to study botany to fully enjoy my poems. From Daddy, I learned not only the basics of gardening and wood-cutting (both of which this sedentary academic has avoided for years), but how to identify trees, recognize birds, and read the landscape. An extensive study of Robert Frost's work during my senior year of high school, followed by my undergraduate years at West Virginia University—devouring Wordsworth's verse in my British literature classes and studying for undergraduate degrees not only in English but in Nature Interpretation—contributed to these interests.

Rural dwellers are often encouraged to believe that the big city is where all important activities occur—this would be especially true for gays in small towns and the country, many of whom dream of escape to queer-friendly urban areas—but Frost and Wordsworth helped me understand early on that writing poems about sugar maples and milkweed pods is entirely valid. I realize that much gay poetry has focused on city life—Frank O'Hara comes to mind—but that poetics is one I have never shared. As a small-town/country-dweller and as a Wiccan (a faith which, like most neo-pagan religions, finds a sense of the divine in nature), I'm not interested in the artificial—and the city is the apotheosis of that—but in the natural. Certainly, when I reach for a metaphor, I find it most often in the natural world: tree, bird, sky, rock, stream.

V. Emotion and the "I"

WORDSWORTH DESCRIBES POETRY as "the spontaneous overflow of powerful feeling." Yes, indeed. Poetry that's distanced and intellectual has never appealed to me a whit. The current popular poetry of ironic wit I find to be tiresome, a waste of time and paper. It seems to me cowardly, as if the poet were afraid of expressing honest emotion for fear of being mocked. The poetry I want to read has a sense of emotional urgency. In such works, it's clear that the poet *needed* to write the poem.

When I discovered Joni Mitchell's album *Hejira* in high school, her lyrical explorations of powerful emotion and of self impressed me tremendously. My ongoing love of her work not only inspired me to teach myself how to play piano, acoustic guitar, and Appalachian dulcimer, but she's served as a fine role model over the last three and a half decades. Though at present she seems to have retired from the music world (much to my regret), the poetic intensity of her love songs, her risky honesty, as well as her stubborn determination to ignore fad and fashion and create as she pleases, have encouraged me to do the same.

So much about romanticism is about intensity, I think: wanting to burn, as often as possible, with Walter Pater's "hard, gemlike flame." During my years at WVU, I found such enviable intensity in the love poems of John Keats and W.B. Yeats, as well as the sonnets of Shakespeare. When I discovered Sylvia Plath's poetry during my senior year, and later, that of Anne Sexton, I found more contemporary models: how to use "powerful feeling," such as despair, desire, loneliness, sorrow, and rage as fuel for art.

The autobiographical nature of such poetry also appealed to me. Though I have since come to appreciate the persona poems of Robert Browning—at this age I'm weary enough of myself and my issues to seek relief from all that by writing poems in others' voices—the verse that feels most authentic to me is personal poetry that speaks, honestly and powerfully, from the revealed self.

I had encountered Walt Whitman's poems here and there in high school and college, but it wasn't until my first year in graduate school at WVU, working for an M.A. in English, that I read extensive amounts of *Leaves of Grass*. Whitman's use of nature was attractive, true, but it was his attempt to make the personal universal that I found especially inspiring, as well as the frank homoeroticism of the *Calamus* poems. When I read "When I Heard at the Close of the Day," I was astounded. Here was a man in the middle of the nineteenth century describing male love in a natural setting. Here was the kind of life, the kind of love, the kind of poetry I aspired to. I had a similar frisson of excitement encountering Constantine Cavafy's poetry years later, and Hart Crane's work, as well as the homoerotic poems of Ian Young and Gavin Dillard. All of these men showed me that man-on-man love and erotic experience could make for graceful, poignant lyrics.

One note on the risks of autobiographical art. A few years ago, I visited a colleague's creative writing class. The students had read some of my poems; the professor had prompted them to have questions ready. One woman asked me how it felt to publish material that was so utterly, often painfully, personal, how it felt to know that readers knew so much about me: my love life, my erotic eccentricities, my insecurities, resentments, and fears. My first, flip response: "I don't think I *have* that many readers, so it's not really a concern." The real response: that's the kind of candid art that has moved me most deeply as a reader, the kind of art that has deepened my empathy and reduced my isolation, so that's the kind of art I try to create. Being honest about one's life—even during times when autobiographical poetry is out of style—can make one's audience feel less alone. When I receive letters and e-mail messages from readers like me—queers, mountain folks, sufferers from depression or unrequited love—and those folks tell me that reading my work has helped them make sense of themselves, well, I know that, despite the relative lack of critical acclaim, I must be doing something right.

VI. The Commonplace

FINALLY, ROMANTICISM REVERES the commonplace and the rustic. It's here that reading other mountain writers has helped me. As Appalachian novelists Denise Giardina and Lee Smith have pointed out, the influence of mass media leads young artists in Appalachia to believe that their lives are not worth the gravity of art. In film and television, mountaineers and Southerners are so often depicted as ridiculous. Who wants to read about hicks?

I was lucky. The first living writer I encountered was an Appalachian poet, a West Virginia poet. Muriel Miller Dressler spoke to my high school when I was in the ninth grade. She read a poem, "Appalachia," that so inspired me that I borrowed my English teacher's mimeograph and copied it by hand. In "Appalachia," Dressler mentions family graveyards: how they are so often located on hilltops. *My* family has a graveyard, on a hilltop in Summers County. By the tenth grade, I was to realize that I was gay and to begin dreaming of a better, a queerer life, in some distant city, and it would be many years before I was to come to terms with my Appalachian identity, many years before I discovered that cities were not for me, but hearing Dressler's poem was the first time I realized that one's local environs, one's region, and all the distinctive commonplaces that come with that place, could be the subject of art.

At WVU, I had no interest in taking the course on Appalachian literature—Appalachia was, for me, a fundamentalist-infested region I wanted to flee as soon as possible—but a West Virginian friend introduced me to the poetry of Maggie Anderson. Anderson was from West Virginia too; she had studied under the same WVU teachers only a decade before me. I bought her first book, *Years That Answer*, and was reminded of what Dressler had shown me before: you can make art from home.

When, after a brief and unsuccessful sojourn in the Washington, D.C., area, I returned to the mountains, determined to somehow claim both gay and Appalachian identities, Anderson's poetry, and later, that of her compatriot, the late Irene McKinney (the former Poet Laureate of West Virginia), showed me how rich Appalachian literary tradition is. Since then, I've taught courses in Appalachian Studies and Appalachian Literature at Virginia Tech and have encountered—on the page and face to face, at readings and at conferences—a multitude of fine mountain writers. Thus, I've been encouraged to use my own experiences as a mountaineer and a lover of Appalachian folk culture as source material in my writing. At this point, I would be hard pressed to compose something devoid of mountain flora, fauna, cuisine, or custom.

VII. The Individual Talent

I'VE HAD SEVERAL friends over the last thirty years who seem to be exceptional changelings. They are smart, liberal, and creative, yet their kin are average at best; at worst, backwards, plodding, conservative trolls. I look at these friends and wonder how they came to be. They appear to have sprung into the world fully formed, like Athena from Zeus's brow. They are not at all logical products of their environment.

But, oh god, I am very clearly a logical product of mine. This essay has given me a chance to study where I've come from, and there's nary a trace of my hopelessly convoluted personality and literary work that can't be explained by my region, my father's scholarly romanticism, and my early readings. (Well, no one can explain my penchant for leather-sex and my ardor for hairy, butch, bearded men, but Eros is always a mystery, thank the gods.)

I have not mentioned T. S. Eliot yet, and it is with him that I want to end. I loved him in graduate school. I read book-length analyses of *The Waste Land* so as to fully appreciate that long, difficult poem. I savored his despair, imagery, and lyrical music, his echoes of mythology. A pagan, still I relished the exquisite Christian loveliness of *Four Quartets*. A very personal poet, still I found his wide-ranging intelligence downright delectable, despite his attack on personal poetry in "Tradition and the Individual Talent." I hope he would forgive such a queer/autobiographical/hillbilly poet for quoting from that same essay: "No poet, no artist of any art, has his complete meaning alone. His significance, his appreciation is the appreciation of his relation to the dead poets and artists. You cannot value him alone; you must set him, for contrast and comparison, among the dead."

Well, as I write this, I'm fifty-three. I will be dead soon enough. It is often disheartening to be a writer in the face of the world's vast indifference. It is often hard to continue. Gathering my forerunners about me, even if only in an essay like this, helps considerably. It is as if I were surrounded by warrior-kin. I know beyond a shadow of a doubt that they suffered what I have suffered, that many of my passions have been theirs. If I am to be set anywhere, set me among that family: the mountain regionalists, the nature poets, the love poets, the wild-eyed, self-absorbed, perfervid romantics.

What I am? I reach for simple identities— leatherman, bear, country boy, scholar, artist—and none of them's sufficient.

country queer
or I Was Brokeback When Brokeback Wasn't Cool

Do I contradict myself?
Very well then I contradict myself,
(I am large, I contain multitudes.)
—*Song of Myself*, Walt Whitman

"Whoso would be a man must be a nonconformist," says Ralph Waldo Emerson in "Self-Reliance." I couldn't have been much more than ten years old when my father handed me a copy of that essay. I guess he figured I'd need it. He was more right than he knew.

For reasons I can't unravel, my identity has always been predicated on dissent, defiance, and resistance. I've never fit comfortably into any context. I've never entirely belonged. Being gay certainly isolated me during my high school years growing up in a small town in West Virginia. (Being a Wiccan and an intellectual certainly didn't help.) But when I got to college, eager to fling myself into queer life, I realized, to my surprise and disappointment, that I didn't fit into the gay community very well at all. I was too dark, too serious, too hairy, too country, too kinky, too shy. This displacement has only continued as, aging, I've become more and more of what I am.

What I'm not: a city queer, one of those upon whom so many stereotypes are based. I'll visit Chelsea, Dupont Circle, the Castro, but will never, ever live there. I own no Cher or Streisand CDs. I don't enjoy the dance club or the ballet. I hate to shop. I find the fashion industry trivial and effete. I don't resemble one of those over-groomed, hopelessly urbane clones created by *Queer Eye for the Straight Guy*, nor am I attracted to neatly domesticated men like that. I'm not interested in fabrics or window treatments, colors that hurt the somber eye, drinks the color of Key West sunsets. I regard faddish, refined foods like sushi with the same disapproving dubiousness with which I eye shaved chests and plucked eyebrows. I'm not, in other words, a fan of delicacy and artifice.

What I am? I reach for simple identities—leatherman, bear, country boy, scholar, artist—and none of them's sufficient. I collect swords and daggers, drink a good bit of bourbon, occasionally indulge in a cigar. My 4X4 pickup truck makes me feel more endowed than I really am; the hunting knife hidden beneath my truck seat makes me feel safe. I can strum the mountain dulcimer, make the punching bag swing while imagining a certain politician's chimp-like face. I can identify trees by their twigs, leaves, and bark. I read, with the same avid interest, BDSM literotica, contemporary poetry, Hesiod, Ovid, and Icelandic sagas. Summer is cheap beer, hot dogs, and baseball at nearby Calfee Park; fall is West Virginia University Mountaineer football games. Puccini's sweet, but I'd rather be four-wheeling mountain backroads listening to country music by Lee Brice or Tim McGraw (or, better by far, shacked up in a spruce-shadowed cabin with Lee, Tim, and lots of rope, gags, lube, bondage tape, and moonshine). Like many men who grew up in small hill towns, I'm partial to boots—lumberjack, cowboy, harness-strap. I move through the day in jeans, T-shirts, Western dusters and leather jackets. My patron deities are the Celtic Cernunnos, Horned God of forest and mountain, body hair and semen, and the Nordic Thor, Storm Lord of drunken feasts, fighting, and fucking. My totem is the bear: protective with friends and kin, fierce with enemies. I want Appalachian family history on my tongue: Germany, England, Scotland, Ireland: wilted lettuce, brown beans and cornbread, chowchow and creecy greens, fried apple pies and potato cakes. Beard shadow heats me up, and dark goatees, big pecs, tattooed biceps, wife-beaters, and torn jeans. Men like mountains. Men like me.

Pulaski, Virginia, this town where today I write, is small and isolated, very much like my West Virginia hometown. I have a partner of twenty-one years, a passel of cats. I need no gay bar, no disco, no beltway rumble. My gay community's composed of distant friends; e-mails from San Francisco, New York, and LA; the occasional queer writers' festival; the occasional well-feted houseguest. I've stayed in Appalachia for the silence, and, beyond that, the rumble of trains at night, the New River's whitewater shush, cedar waxwings whistling in the holly trees. I've stayed for these hills composing my horizon; for the farmer's market with its onion sets, sausage biscuits, beets, and rhubarb; for snow in the pastures, spring peepers in the creek, fields of rippling sweet corn, forests full of autumn's maple-flame.

Like Whitman, I contradict myself. *Cocksucker, redneck, hillbilly, faggot.* By now my beard's the color of wood-ash, but I'm a little wild still yet. I've learned to contain the multitudes I must, make my peace with several selves, in this burly, clumsy, furry body finally to belong.

Today, mid-February in the mountains of Southwest Virginia, the mourning dove's returned. It sobs in snow flurries, in bare crabapple boughs. Candlemas has passed, the light creeps back. Soon Bradford pears will spill the young flesh of flowers. Their white petals will swarm the driveway, scattering my pickup bed like perfumed snow. Today's bleak and cold, but I see, far ahead, in future's forest, two cowboy hats hung on budding maple twigs, in green-gold light two sets of cowboy boots shucked off. The god's moist armpits smell like forest moss, like cumin and prayer. Path's end, naked in warm needle-beds, we lie together in the pines. Cheek pressed against his chest, I hear the hairy growth of grass, the restless ache of magma. Belly pressed against his back, I enter earth's rough and seething heart.

you'll give yourself

the youth you wanted

but never had.

letter to my sixteen-year-old self

HEY, BUDDY,

I know you're lonely. The wonderful lesbian teacher who lent you *The Front Runner*, the novel that helped you realize you're gay, she's left town, and so have your lesbian buddies, Bill and Brenda. You've got another year of high school to endure before you flee small, conservative Hinton, West Virginia, and head for college. You're wondering how you're going to make it through, hiding your homosexuality from your parents and your peers, yearning after handsome classmates you can't have.

You'll never be this isolated and lonely again, I promise you. You have a lot of things to look forward to. Here are a few:

Your straight buddy, Mike, the one who's about to join the Marines? The guy with the dark beard, muscular body, and hairy chest, so sexy he could be a porn star? Model your sense of masculinity after him. He'll teach you how to be a strong man who protects his people and stands up for what he believes in. For the rest of your life, you'll be attracted to furry, solidly built, bearded country boys who resemble him. He'll help you define what's erotic.

That poetry you write about

Mike and other good-looking boys at school? Those long entries you scrawl in your journal? You're not wasting your time. Keep that up. By the time you're fifty-six, you'll have published fourteen books. In one of your novels, you'll give yourself the youth you wanted but never had: you'll meet Mike again, and he'll want you as much as you want him, and the two of you will become fervent teenaged lovers.

Those confusing fantasies you have about tying Mike up, gagging him, beating him, ravishing him roughly and then holding him tenderly? They don't mean you're psycho. They only mean that one day, when you're nineteen, you'll read another novel, *The Beauty Queen*, and realize that other men share your fascination with kinky sex. A few years later, you'll step into a leather bar in Washington, D.C., sip a glass of Scotch, look around the room, and feel like you belong.

That despairing sense you have that no one will ever want you? Boy, you'll have so many men over the next four decades that you'll lose count. A few will break your heart, but at least you'll feel deeply, as deeply as dark, passionate Heathcliff, your first literary role model. Every time your heart is broken, you'll write more poems. And one day, after many, many years of frustrated bachelorhood, you'll meet John, a man who'll want to stay with you despite your hot temper, prickly ego, and wandering eye. Eventually—I know this is almost impossible to believe—the laws will change so dramatically that the two of you will get married.

Your pudgy body? Your pimply face? Your hairless torso? Those will change too. In a few decades, you'll have a bushy beard, a furry chest, strong arms, and an assortment of tattoos. The homophobes you're so afraid of now will think twice about crossing you then.

Those lesbian friends you're missing so badly? They're only the first of many. Your love life might be difficult and frustrating for decades to come, but your friends, especially your lesbian friends, they'll save your life. When beautiful men let you down and leave you full of self-doubt and grief, women will help you survive.

Finally, that hometown you're wanting so badly to escape? The Appalachian culture in which you've been raised has shaped you in profound ways you can't yet begin to realize. When you do leave West Virginia, you'll see how much of a Southerner and a mountain man you actually are, and you'll head back to the hills in a hurry. Learning to balance your identities as an Appalachian and a gay man will be the hardest thing you'll ever do. It'll take decades. But you'll do it. By the time you've come to be me, you'll be living with your husband in a wonderful house in Pulaski, Virginia, a mountain town much like Hinton. You'll also own the Hinton house you grew up in, and you'll go back to visit your family as often as you can, and there you'll listen to the New River and look up at the surrounding mountains and tuck into good country food and be thankful that you've had the life you've had and become the man you've become.

Bearhugs,

Jeff

I call lean, bearded, longhaired young men "little Jesuses," and they— along with what current gay parlance would call bear cubs— are among my favorite bottoms to truss, torture, and ravish.

surly bear in the bible belt

I. "Tits Up!"

I WAS TRYING TO BE ALTRUISTIC, BUT then it all went sour. "Pear-shaped! Tit's up!" as the Brits would say. In other words, all to hell.

During the spring of 2011, Pulaski, Virginia, the little mountain town where my husband John and I have lived for several years, was hit by a tornado; one of the poorest neighborhoods was devastated. Some community-minded local folks decided to organize a poetry reading at the Pulaski Theater to raise money for afflicted families. John and I are very busy, keep to ourselves, and socialize little. Thus, few people in Pulaski know or care that I'm a published writer. Fewer know how widely my books range, from stories of Civil War-era soldiers fleeing both battlefield bloodshed and a society offended by their love, to poetry featuring not only my great fondness for Southern food, but also my less conventional appetite for burly men hogtied on the bed. But the sweet lady who runs the independent bookstore in town carries some of my work, so she passed on my name to the organizer.

I was invited to read, and I agreed. Truth be told, I don't give free readings anymore. Well, I do at bookstores and at literary festivals, but if universities want to host me, I mention my reading fee (most published writers ask for an honorarium; many ask for much larger amounts than I). But this poetry event was a benefit, to help people. It was not about me, not about promoting my literary career. I was glad to read gratis. A week before the benefit, we had a practice in the theater, so that the sound man could adjust the mikes to our voice levels and the organizer could decide on the most effective ordering of readers. Seven people each read three poems. I chose three of mine about Appalachian cooking; I figured the audience would savor those more than my frank verse about country boys with hairy chests. If folks were going to be kind enough to come to the event and pay the five-dollar entrance fee, I would entertain rather than disturb. I'm a Southerner: I was brought up not to be confrontational, not to give offense. I save my in-your-face queer politics for more appropriate contexts.

Things went fine until the very end. "Now Ed will finish with a prayer," said the organizer. Up shuffled the elderly man who'd earlier read several heavily rhymed poems. This poem was much the same, except for many references to Jesus Christ. I bristled. As often happens, my good manners went to war with my prickly nonconformity. A few years back, I would have simmered and said nothing. By age fifty-one, however, I've finally achieved some solid sense of self. This time the irascible pagan queer beat out the polite Southerner. After the practice was done, I spoke to the organizer, as calmly as my considerable annoyance would allow. "I don't mean to cause trouble, but I'm not a Christian, and I don't think ending with a Christian prayer is appropriate. I thought this was supposed to be an inclusive event." She seemed to understand my concerns—I had expected her to ruffle with Sunday pew indignation. Yet, after I'd said my piece, as I walked home, the gathering thunderclouds matched my mood. Once again, I'd been transformed from a man who feels very much at home in his native mountains to one alienated, like an outsider.

At home, my husbear poured me a welcome martini. I raged

for a while. One martini became three. We ran out of olives. "How dare they assume everyone in the room is Christian?" I snarled between sips. "*Goddamn* them. Let the Rapture come soon, so they'll all be sucked up into their boring version of an afterlife and leave this planet to us. Good riddance to bad rubbish! Fuckers! I wish I could step back in time and throttle the baby Jesus in his crib. *That'd* snip those pests off at the root!" "Uh, Christians have created some beautiful buildings, art, and music," John said. After fourteen years together, he knows not to get in the way of my rants. "I know...." I sighed between pacing. "Some Christians, I know they're compassionate people, they've done a lot of good, but the rest of them.... Dammit, I need another drink!" "Well, you know we're living in Jesus Land here..." "So, I shouldn't be surprised? Hell, I know. I grew up in these mountains. I'm *not* surprised. But that doesn't mean I have to like it. Or not be pissed! Look! See!" I pointed triumphantly out the window at the lightning storm and downpour that had descended on the town. "Even Thor is angry!"

Eventually my tantrum subsided. The evening improved, happily enough: a good gin buzz and leftover country-fried steak to gobble up. (I don't share the religious views of my fellow Bible-Belt denizens, but I match their taste in down-home cooking.) Somewhere between the caloric meal and watching television in bed, I'd decided. When the organizer e-mailed the participants about the order of the readers, I'd be asking her about that prayer, whether it was still included in the program. If they'd remove the prayer, I'd read. If they wouldn't, I wouldn't. As John implied, perhaps I should be used to this sort of thing, having spent just about my entire life in the mountains of Virginia and West Virginia, but no, that long familiarity has only made my resentments against Bible-Belt religion passionate and deep. Conservative Christianity remains the element of my native Appalachia I most despise. The constant pressures of that regionally ubiquitous religion and my reactions to it have shaped me in numerous complex ways.

II. Bible-Belt Butch

SOME OF THE effects are relatively innocuous. One is my love affair with masculinity.

The conservative faiths of the South encourage—nay, insist upon—traditional gender-role behavior. As I grappled with my first sexual attractions, the blue-collar and rustic men in Summers County, West Virginia, where I spent my formative years, shaped my erotic aesthetic, my sense of what's desirable. Butch country boys continue to be the men I find most arousing: brawny bodies, hairy chests, beards and goatees, jeans and boots. ("Ruffian beauties," a city friend calls them.) Refined and urbane do nothing for me; give me scruffy and rough redneck rural any day.

That same aesthetic has shaped my own personal style; I'm in many ways indistinguishable from the men I lust after. I wear similar clothes—jeans, boots, ball caps; I drive a pickup truck and listen to country music. (In the last few decades, the bear movement has, to my delight, helped create gay and thus more accessible versions of the manly heterosexual beefcake I hankered for in my youth.) This attraction to and emulation of the butch has, therefore, caused me to admire and relate to conventional masculinity more than many queers, especially those who think of such manliness as dangerous and politically suspect. (I'm no more interested in their disapproval of masculinity than I am in a Baptist's disapproval of my sodomitic lust.)

III. "The Pore Kinky Thang Cain't Even Flirt!"

INEVITABLY, SHAME ISSUES crop up when a boy knows that his desires, if revealed, would be regarded as freakish or monstrous. This shame—combined with the fact that expressing same-sex attraction in such a Baptist-lousy town might have gotten me ostracized, beaten, or even killed—meant that I learned early to conceal my desires for other men. Such desire felt like dangerous weakness, vulnerability. Hiding it became a protective instinct, a habit. When I finally found myself, during my college years, in gay-friendly places, I seemed unable to turn off this cautious veiling. To this day, I joke about being unable to flirt unless the object of my lust signs a document declaring his attraction to me and then has a Notary Public stamp it.

My shyness and insecurity have made finding sexual partners exceedingly difficult. Earlier this month, a sexy bear I was flirting with on e-mail after we'd met at a literary festival told me that I'd been so cool around him in person he'd been convinced I didn't find him attractive. Truth be told, he was one of few men at the festival I wanted to throw onto the bed. The hotter the man, the more aloof I become. Those early years of self-doubt, shame, and small-town isolation not only spawned my erotic interest in bearded, butch men and my reluctance to express it, they also shaped my BDSM inclinations. As the play *Equus* points out, why certain things are eroticized, "magnetized," for each of us remains mysterious. As a top, perhaps I want to tie and gag a man before I make love to him because, on some unconscious level where shame lingers, I assume my desire for him would be unwelcome and thus he must be made helpless and forced to surrender. As a bottom, perhaps I want to be trussed up before submitting to another man because powerlessness absolves me of responsibility. If I'm bound, then I have an excuse; it's not my fault; I can feel like one of those hyper-masculine, roped-up TV cowboys or comic-book superheroes who so aroused me in my pubescence. In this fetish-rich world, any sort of mock-resistance or mock-force—a captive fighting his bonds, shouting into his gag till his captor has to subdue him—only heightens the heat.

Though I'm a pagan now, I suspect I can thank Christian guilt for such erotic delight. I can also thank those many images of a nearly naked, suffering Christ—bound, bleeding, whipped, crucified—for coloring my sadomasochism. I call lean, bearded, longhaired young men "little Jesuses," and they—along with what current gay parlance would call bear cubs— are among my favorite bottoms to truss, torture, and ravish, if opportunity presents itself. In addition, when I write erotic fiction, I come back again and again, almost despite myself, to images of Christ's flagellation and crucifixion, albeit as reflections of such pre-Christian sacrificed gods as Osiris and Tammuz. Somehow, I doubt that most Christians would be pleased to hear about the ways in which their handsome Savior functions in my fantasies.

IV. Alien Monster

MY PARENTS HAD absolutely no use for orthodox religion. In fact, my father has scorned and baited the devout all his life. His contempt for them has ranged from a savage humor I relish—his recommendation, for instance, that a local rabid preacher be given a habanero enema—to years of op-ed essays he's published in West Virginia newspapers, pointing out Christian bigotry and hypocrisy. Such an upbringing was to prove a blessing, in that I was left free to choose my own spiritual path—eventually adopting Wicca and then an even broader neopaganism that embraces the divinities of my Germanic and Celtic bloodlines. This freedom from local faiths also made coming to terms with my homosexuality far less stressful, since I didn't have Christian condemnation to struggle with, in my parents or in myself, when I came out. (I didn't know how lucky I was till I got to West Virginia University, made lots of gay and lesbian friends, and heard their horror stories. Several of their pious parents regarded homosexuality as willful sin and had rejected them outright.)

My family's unorthodoxy was also something of a curse, for it set me apart. I can remember the regular hassles I got from fellow students, especially the sanctimonious brats in Hinton High School's Bible Club. My family was known for never attending church; we were regarded as atheists at best and Satanists at worst. In fact, when my father ran for prosecuting attorney back in the

1970s, he actually felt the need to run a political ad in the town paper explaining that, despite rumor, he was not an atheist. Those Christians of my hometown did not tolerate difference. Theirs was the "one way." The rest of us were sinners heading straight to hell. They were interested not in New Testament love but Old Testament judgment. My response to this unfriendly state of affairs was, and always has been, antipathy and anger.

Most human beings take a deep comfort in feeling as if they belong, as if they're safe and welcome in their immediate surroundings. In many respects, I've been denied that. Sometimes I feel like a complete alien in my native region. When I walk the streets of Pulaski, where I live now, and Hinton, where I grew up, I look like just another brawny, bearded redneck. In many ways I am that. In many ways I belong, and this is home—I love the landscape, the quiet, the music, food, and folk culture of Appalachian living. All that is my heritage, and I claim it with pride and pleasure. But as a gay man, pagan, and leather bear, I feel hemmed in, at the very same time, with potential hostility. Small towns in the Bible Belt have no use for monsters like me, and I've tried to developed a warrior's gruff toughness simply to survive here. (Leaving is not an option. I prefer conflict to homesickness.)

V. Bible-phobe

IN THE WRITING of this essay, I asked my partner his opinion of the ways growing up in the Bible Belt has shaped me. "You weren't so much directly influenced as you reacted," he said. Smart man. Reaction definitely explains my lack of knowledge when it comes to the so-called "Good Book."

I discovered something peculiar when I read John Milton in graduate school. *Paradise Lost* was full of footnotes, about half of them explaining Biblical references, the other half explaining allusions to Greek and Roman mythology. The pagan material I already knew; the Christian I was almost completely unaware of.

My parents, in my youth, did not encourage me to read the Bible. Instead, they recommended the classics: *Wuthering Heights,* the *Iliad,* the *Aeneid, Dracula, Jane Eyre.* When my paternal grandmother, a Christian, albeit not an obnoxious one, beseeched me in my teenage years to read the Bible, I resisted. By that age, my natural contrariness had made me a nonconformist, the bane of any small town. I countered the locals' hosannas by devouring books on mythology, magic, and Wicca. And I learned that for every persecuted saint, martyred for faith, a hundred women were burned or hanged for witchcraft. I could not have despised fundamentalist Christianity more, and I seethed at its hypocrisy.

VI. Swords, Hammers, and Axes

THE LOCAL BOGEYMEN appear at the door every so often: evangelists always dressed for Sundays.

When I open the door, I'm prepared. "Christians?" I smiled caustically at two gangly boys, each about eighteen, who stood on my stoop a few months ago with their Bibles clutched to their skinny chests. I loomed over them, and the contrast in our sizes pleased me. I'm 230 pounds, with a shaved head, solid arms and chest, a salt-and-pepper goatee, and loads of tattoos. The look's been honed to emulate men I savor. It also intimidates the ignorant.

"Yes, sir." One boy's disconcerted glance toward his fellow waif was delicious. "We'd like to talk to you about—"

"I'm a homosexual and a pagan. I really have nothing to say to you. I have no use for your religion."

Their eyes widened. *We have met the enemy and he is a bear.* If only I could sprout horns and fangs at will. Perhaps they would have nightmares about me. Didn't all Southern church boys fear and loathe (and ache for) a *virile* homosexual? And yet, I quickly felt pity for them. They were baby copperheads, but they were also unnerved little boys.

"Uh, sorry, sir." Sensing that discretion was the better part of valor, they clutched their Bibles closer and hastily departed.

"Y'all take care now," I drawled after them. The entire exchange had taken less time than it would to make a cup of coffee. I spare no more time for proselytizers than that.

Being surrounded by such aggressive religiosity all my life has given me somewhat of a siege mentality. In public settings, I'm often wary, on my guard, as if someone hostile might read my mind, recognize my many radical differences, and challenge me. With my family and friends, I'm compulsively protective. Those who cross them I detest, sometimes to the point of snarling vengefulness, almost always with a complete incapacity to forgive. This clannish sense of siege is probably one reason why I've developed a hot appreciation for swords and daggers and am thinking about buying a Viking axe. It's impractical, romantic weaponry, not the more useful guns beloved of many fellow country boys, but what such a collection bespeaks is my conviction that my surroundings are unfriendly and at some point might have to be dealt with.

VII. Perhaps This Is Why My Publisher Is A Gay Jew

THERE IS AN innate tribal need, I think, to suspect, hate, and fear the other, to regard the different with suspicion. From such a need all racism and xenophobia spring. I've sought to resist such an impulse. Unlike many folks bred in homogeneous small towns, I relish cultural difference and variety. But aggressive, intolerant monotheism (Judaic, Islamic, or Christian, though the latter is, of course, the dominant version in my Highland South) I regard with the hate and suspicion that racists feel for those with differently hued skins.

It's a hate—this is very clear to me—born of fear. I've been surrounded by that hostile majority all my life. As tough as I try to appear and to be, there are infinitely more of them. They are numerous, and they are powerful. To borrow from their favorite book, they are legion, a hydra-headed monster that dominates these mountains I love.

My best friend Cynthia Burack has published a book called *Sin, Sex, and Democracy: Antigay Rhetoric and the Christian Right*. Her analyses of Christian fundamentalists' rise to political power and their ongoing attempts to block pro-LGBT legislation, as well as her conviction that such religious attitudes are the basis for most manifestations of homophobia, have only heightened my fear and hate. When I drive around Pulaski and see "Jesus fish" on car bumpers, or the pink "Prayer Infirmary" down the street, or the Christian bookstore, or another empty storefront taken over by some damned ministry, my snarls are sharper than they were in adolescence, when I hated local Christians simply for their supercilious sense of superiority and their insistence that everyone become like them or pay the price. My surly detestation is political now: these are the people who want to deny my kind our rights. Some of them would, if they could, wipe us out. Sometimes I think, had I the power, I would try to do the same to them. Sometimes, in my darker moods, I entertain dark fantasies: swords, heroism, blood, victory. These are only vicarious dreams, true. On the other hand, the righteous, intolerant, homophobic, and devout had best stay out of my way. The considerable mean streak I possess is due in large part to them.

VIII. Awake

THE AFOREMENTIONED SIEGE mentality tips quite easily into unreasoning paranoia. When, day after day, I got no e-mail message from the poetry organizer announcing the order of readers, I assumed the worst. I brooded; I cursed. "They've all conspired, taken a vote, decided to cut me out of it and go on with the prayer. Damn them then! If they prefer a tedious old religious rhymester to me, well, then, to hell with them all." It takes very little for me to assume the world's malevolence and return the same.

Well, no, none of those feverish assumptions was accurate. When I finally called the organizer, mere hours before the reading, ready to bow out if I didn't hear what I wanted to hear, she said the theater board had been split right down the middle over the issue but had finally decided to replace the prayer with an uplifting story about communal unity.

And so the surly bear was (briefly) mollified. And so, on that hot June evening, I reluctantly relinquished cargo shorts and tank top for linen dress clothes. I drank some wine at the pre-reading reception; I quietly salivated over a hot little country boy in the audience and entertained a few abduction fantasies; I refrained from scowling at the old man, who indeed did not regale us with his prayer; and, at evening's end, after reading my poems, I wrote a check for one hundred dollars to help the tornado victims, then shot out of there, as the saying goes, "like a bat out of hell."

As I left, it was clearer to me than ever how so many of my eccentricities—both strengths and weaknesses—can be attributed to Appalachia's rampant fundamentalism. In my fifties, I'm not slack, stale, soft, comfortable, and complacent. I'm still edgy, passionate, protective, defiant, determined, and awake. Resisting Christian self-righteousness—the homophobic bastards of the Bible Belt—keeps me strong, makes me younger than my years. For these reasons at least, I am thankful for such foes. Their intolerance has hardened me, honed me, and given me a fighter's edgy fortitude, a protector's prickly grit.

I would wake before him, lift the sheet, and study his nakedness with silent reverence, thanking the gods that such a gift had been bestowed on me.

thomas

WE SAID OUR GOODBYES TWENTY years ago today. As poorly as I remember numbers, I remember that date: the nineteenth of September. The day of my greatest loss, really. Still, my memory is as unreliable as anyone else's, so, for the sake of accuracy, I've dug through dusty boxes of old journals for confirmation. Yes, my entry for September 20, 1991, reads:

Washington, DC. 6:50 am. He's gone. For all intents and purposes. Leaving Monday. I refused—unable to see him privately again—to hang around this weekend, to put on the ultimate acting job and see him with Dick. My sense of time is disjointed. Can it be only seventeen hours since he came into my office at two p.m. yesterday to tell me Dick got the job in Boston? That time between now and then seems not short, not long, just somehow nonexistent. Hours on the road, for the most part. Fleeing. When I return, he will be gone. Soon I will have lived with this for twenty-four hours. Somehow that amazes me, as the work traffic thickens along Connecticut Avenue, as the coffee dews my wild-length moustache, as dawn spreads across an almost cloudless and completely indifferent and unchanged sky over D.C.

"We said our goodbyes twenty

years ago today." It's the sort of coincidence and symmetry we writers relish, and an attention-grabbing way to start this essay. Still, trying to read the scrawled notes my much younger self made so long ago, I'm stung, even after two decades, by that old pain: loving Thomas, conducting that hot, hot, furtive affair for six months behind his partner's back, then having to say goodbye.

TODAY, THE NINETEENTH of September 2011, is unremarkable. I took notes for this essay. I drove John, my partner of fourteen years, downtown to get his car serviced. After lunch, I started this essay. Later, I'll try to lift weights in our basement gym, if my aging back permits. Then, come five p.m., we'll get a good buzz on with a couple of martinis, followed by some leftover Chinese delivery and Netflix. This is a typical day for me: routine, unexciting, the placid life of a middle-aged writer/academic.

That nineteenth of September—the afternoon Thomas came to my Virginia Tech office to tell me his partner Dick had been offered a job in Framingham, Massachusetts, and they were already packing—that was another matter, one of those momentous days that change everything. Its significance seems so far removed from my present existence that it feels like some other man's history, some other man's sorrow. Still, much of what I've become is because of that day's leave-taking.

THOMAS AND I were introduced by a mutual friend in Virginia Tech's War Memorial Gym in February 1991. He was twenty-seven, partnered, a graduate student in horticulture; I was thirty-one, single, an English instructor. We shared eccentric interests in neopaganism and the occult. I grew fond of both him and Dick, sharing relaxed evenings with them drinking, cooking, watching television. My attraction to him grew powerful, but I refused to act on it since he was coupled. Then one April evening, we attended a reading Allen Ginsberg gave at Radford University. Dick had campus connections, and afterwards we split several pitchers of beer at BT's, a student pub, with the famous author. When Thomas's leg brushed mine beneath the table, my leg rubbed his in return. Immediately my focus shifted from Ginsberg to less literary concerns.

The next day, Thomas and I confessed our reciprocal desire. Soon a secretive sexual relationship began. We made love roughly once a week, in a woodland cabin an acquaintance lent us. That summer, we even managed a getaway together, to Washington, D.C., and a conference of his at Penn State. Finally we were able to take our time, make love without watching the clock, and sleep all night side by side. In the mornings, I would wake before him, lift the sheet, and study his nakedness with silent reverence, thanking the gods that such a gift had been bestowed on me.

After years of almost constant celibacy, I was thoroughly besotted. I knew the pair was planning to leave Blacksburg once Thomas had finished his master's degree in horticulture and they'd found jobs elsewhere. Rather than encouraging me to be cautious and retain some detachment, this knowledge only made me love him harder, more deeply, more desperately. Somehow I sensed that I'd never encounter such a passion again, and I was determined to live it to the hilt as long as I could, despite the guilt I felt in deceiving Dick, despite the looming loneliness bound to come. My desire for Thomas and our imminent parting inspired me to write poem after poem, all of them longing, erotic, and elegiac. There I was, in the grand tradition of the love poets I admired: Yeats, Keats, Shakespeare. It was a once-in-a-lifetime ardor and inspiration, I thought. I was right.

THOMAS WAS MY erotic ideal, a short, muscular, scruffy-faced, hairy butch bottom. To my gratitude and delight, he shared my predilection for kink, meaning that our sex usually involved rope and gags. Making love to him was perverse, delicious, and intoxicating. To see him naked, bound spread-eagle to the bed, gnawing the bandana knotted between his teeth, ready to submit to whatever I chose, was, for me, beauty beyond compare. To rest my face in the thick brown fur between his substantial pecs was as close to an earthly paradise as I've ever known. To give him up left me in the midst of a pain worse than any I've felt before or since.

To this day, despite the many, many men I've known carnally, despite my solid relationship with John, Thomas remains the great passion of my life. John—steady, orderly, meticulous—grounds, protects, and supports me. He makes for us a comfortable, beautiful home, a life where we can pursue our busy professional careers and profoundly relax once those overfull days are done. He is the perfect mate for my middle years. Thomas—fascinating, impish, mercurial—maddened, haunted, and stimulated me. He was the perfect muse for my youth. Though I may yet surprise myself by falling into a midlife affair equally as foolish as that long-ago relationship with Thomas, I think not. My fervid love for him seems to have burnt out in me the capacity to feel so deeply.

MY JOURNAL PROVIDES me with details of that September parting I had forgotten. Reading my own words, I feel deep pity for the self I used to be, the hopeful boy with the beard much blacker than the one I wear today, the boy about to descend into that terrible sense of loss, bodilessness, and abandonment, about to pay the price for loving someone already spoken for.

Thomas is wearing jeans and a blue button-down shirt, over the top button of which curls brown chest hair. I lock the door behind him; we sit face to face. I'm quietly terrified, knowing that Dick has recently had a job interview in New England. Realizing how bereft I'm soon to be, Thomas tries to play down his excitement over moving to the Boston area, but soon enough he's chattering about the leather bars, the gargoyle store, the occult bookshop. No chance of another tryst or one last lovemaking, he explains. He and Dick will be too busy packing.

I break down, leaning against him, pressing my face against his chest, finally resting my head in his lap. With great effort, I choke back sobs. I'm the top, the big butch mountain man; I should be strong and stoic in the face of this! My tears flow nevertheless. He holds me, without words, stroking my hair. His eyes are dry, but he swallows hard again and again. When I start fumbling for a Kleenex, he pulls one from his pocket, ever prepared. "Is this what you're looking for?"

Even in such extremity, I'm verbose. I want him to know what our too-brief connection has meant to me. I talk about the poetry he's inspired, how he's helped me escape the unlived life Henry James warns against in *The Ambassadors*. It's all been about touching beauty, I say, finally finding someone worthy, feeling more deeply than ever before, knowing this pain is just part of it. "With you, will all your gifts withdraw?" I quote from one of my own poems. No, no, some gifts will remain; I've got to believe that. He's the most exciting, intelligent, complex, desirable man I've ever known; I've learned so much…

Finally I say it, what he surely knows but what I've never verbalized: "I love you." To my stunned amazement, he replies, "I love you, too." It seems unbelievable, finally to hear it, but to hear it mere minutes before we part.

We agree to keep in touch. He'll call collect sometimes, so that the call won't show up on a bill that Dick might see. I wipe my eyes. One last hug before I unlock my office door. He looks up at me with what I take to be beaming fondness. I look down at him with a devotion I can only hope he doesn't perceive as pathetic. "With those boots on, you look ten feet tall!" he jokes. We shake hands on the steps of my office building. Seductively, cruelly, he tickles the inside of my palm with his middle finger. He strides across the Drill Field, and I watch him go. He looks back once, then disappears behind a line of trees. I stand in the sun, panting in the warm scent of junipers, trying to remember the smell of his armpits after vigorous lovemaking.

My eyes are red from crying, so I teach my next class wearing sunglasses. That evening, desperate for some kind of consolation, I drive to Washington, D.C., listening to Nanci Griffith's *Late Night Grande Hotel* again and again. When I cry, tear spots spatter my glasses, like the salt stains left on winter pavement. The broken lines in the middle of the interstate say *subtraction subtraction subtraction*. I spend a few days with my best friend Cindy. She's given me advice during the last six months of my up-and-down feelings, my stint as The Other Man, loving someone I can cherish only for hurried assignations. She understands.

I WANTED NO one else for a long time. No one else measured up. Men who resembled him—who possessed his compact form, high brow, or wavy brown hair—only honed my grief. We kept in touch as promised, via letters and the rare phone call. He sent me gifts that helped me cling to the hope that he might one day leave Dick and come to me: an onyx pentagram ring, a Valentine's Day bear with devil horns. (Appropriate, since I'd always called him my demon lover, my Mephistopheles, making me, of course, a Faustus willingly bargaining his soul.) Upon the bear was imprinted the words I was so frantic to hear and to see: "I Love You."

Truth be told, September 19, 1991 was the day of our first goodbye. There were actually two other partings, an admission that dilutes the epic importance of the first. In March 1992, I drove to Framingham to visit Thomas and Dick. I had become a consummate actor and liar by then; ethics and honor meant nothing in the face of the passion I felt. While Dick was at work, Thomas and I enjoyed more ardent lovemaking. We shared a matchless erotic chemistry that, to this day, sad to say, I've found with no one else. Being with him again was sheer rapture, but in the end it only reminded me of all I was missing and how much more I wanted. I was in too much pain to continue the contact, I told him. The next day, I left the couple to their life together and drove back to Virginia and a bitter celibacy.

In the aftermath, I listened to Melissa Etheridge's lovelorn early albums and sad country music like Vince Gill's "Never Knew Lonely." I took walks in the rain. I drove mountain back roads, wishing I had the strength to drive into a hillside. I was, obviously, a romantic cliché. Thomas's absence was all-devouring. To have had such a passionate, beautiful lover and then not to have him, not to have anyone? For some deity to have allowed my body to awaken to such pleasure only to rob me of it seemed to me cosmic sadism without excuse. (At age fifty-two, I can barely comprehend my own past suffering, though, writing this, I can feel the slightest edge of it.) Family, friends, work, the simple pleasures of eating and drinking, none of them dulled that pain, though they were sufficient, just barely, to keep me from suicide, which I contemplated regularly, albeit lazily.

In 1995, Thomas wrote me, telling me that he and Dick had moved to Falls Church, Virginia. He missed me, he said; he wanted to see me. I fell back into it. We shared two weekends in February and May while Dick was out of town. I remember more amazing lovemaking, working Thomas' nipples with clamps, fucking him on his back, his thighs locked about my waist. I remember a stroll on Roosevelt Island, an evening concert at the Kennedy Center, the silver beginning in his beard. I remember fights, caused, I suspect, by my desperate desire to feel closer to him, feel indispensable, achieve a truer intimacy, and his profound need to keep some distance, guard himself, not get in too deep.

Finally, I remember one last lovemaking in Cindy's Cleveland Park apartment, a sweaty July afternoon after I'd returned from a sojourn in the British Isles. Thomas and I drank mead from quaichs I'd brought from Scotland. I licked Atholl Brose liqueur from his chest hair and the tip of his cock. "You're a wonderful lover," he panted in our semen-sticky aftermath. As young, obsessive, and fervent as I was, I suspect he was right. I desired him more than any man before or since, and that focus must have translated into inventive and enthusiastic ways to give him pleasure.

After that, things fell irredeemably apart. The autumn of 1995, we quarreled over petty things via the new medium of e-mail. Then he and Dick broke up, and Thomas did what I could never forgive: After all I'd suffered loving him, he took a new boyfriend rather than come to me. Eventually, he and Dick got back together. By then I'd decided, after nearly five years of such agonizing ardor, that I'd finally, finally, finally had enough. His last e-mail message was flirtatious, telling me about his new black leather jacket, how good it looked with his full beard and chest hair.

Many of the poems inspired by my love for him I published, in literary journals, then in chapbooks and full-length collections. When I read those poems in public, I often joke about how artistically productive sleeping with someone else's spouse can be, though the emotional repercussions make the poems hardly worth it. I'm not likely to write so many lyrics about any one man again. My love poetry is inspired by conflict and the crazing inability to possess beauty and the beloved, and so my immoderate passion for Thomas created the ideal confluence of inspirational elements: yearning, remorse, sorrow. I don't expect to encounter such a "perfect storm" again. I say this with both regret and relief.

I got more than tortured poetry and a bevy of publications from Thomas. I learned a great deal: that my heart is attracted to complex, emotionally distant men, men who might inspire in me grand passion but who are, in the long run, not good for me; that I contributed as much to my own sad fate as Thomas did; that many people will take from you as much as you are willing to give; that suffering in the aftermath of a lost love maims you, perhaps irreparably, but opens your heart to others' suffering, thus making you more compassionate and more deeply human. That love and that loss were among the grand experiences of my life. I would do it all again, if only for the poems and the emotional growth.

I'VE SEEN HIM once since that final farewell. In January 2007, my publishers arranged a dual reading for famed author Patrick Califia and me in a San Francisco bookstore. There were two men already sitting in the foldout chairs when I arrived. One, a short, gray-bearded guy, gave me a huge smile. It wasn't until I was in the restroom that I realized who it was. Much of the old feeling came back. Had I been younger, less solid in my sense of self, I would have panicked. As it was, I wanted to stay in the bathroom and cry. Instead, I came out, acted as if everything were fine, and then very deliberately read material, both prose and poetry, based on my affair with Thomas. I did a fine job, if I may say so myself. The event I had dreaded for years had come to pass—crossing paths with him again—yet I was composed.

After I read, I joined the audience while Patrick took his turn. Anyone watching me would have assumed I was listening. Certainly my partner John, sitting only a few feet from me, had no idea how stunned I was. Actually, I was studying Thomas. He was no longer the beautiful young man I had loved so wildly, for whom I had suffered such sorrow. He was no longer in his late twenties. He was in his mid-forties. He was plump, even grayer than I. I felt pity for him, and pity for myself, and pity for all mortal, aging beings. That was the last gift that loving him gave me, that sweeping, oceanic compassion. Thomas, the man with whom I had hoped to share my life, sat beside John, the man with whom I've shared my life. I studied them both, heart swelling, and knew how soon our generation would lay down its turn at passion and shuffle off into the shadows.

After the reading, he approached me. "I'm Thomas!" he blurted. "Oh, I know who you are," I said, mustering the defense of a sardonic tone. He introduced me to his new partner, who ironically turned out to be a fan of my writing, and then to Dick and his new partner. Thomas and Dick had broken up at last, long after it would have done me any good. After all the deceit, Dick still came to my reading. Obviously, he had a much greater capacity for forgiveness than I ever would. And he had the last laugh, in a manner of speaking. He hadn't aged at all.

I fled after that. Southerners are pretty good at summoning false facades, and the affair with Thomas had honed my natural talent for duplicity, but my calm composure was splintering fast. "That was Thomas," I said to John as he and I headed across Market Street with Patrick and his adorable boy for a few drinks. "*That* Thomas?" John gasped.

I drank a lot of Tullamore Dew that night. When John and I returned to our romantic guesthouse, I watched the gas fire flicker and couldn't sleep. Back home, I got an e-mail from Thomas, saying, among other chatty things, "I hoped you would have gotten over it long ago and would have been up for a beer and catching up."

I fell into a depression of several months' duration. My sex drive left me. I had no desire to be touched. Seeing Thomas had robbed me of my last illusion: that he, were we ever to meet again, would admit what a mistake it had been to leave me, how much he'd loved me, how much I haunted him. No. The relationship that had meant so much to me I'd always feared had meant very little to him, and now I knew that to be true.

SEPTEMBER 19TH WAS not the first Thomas-anniversary of 2011. The first was February 5th, twenty years since the day we met. This date I couldn't remember and had to look up in my journals. I spent that Saturday with pleasant distractions, visiting my old friend, Cindy, and her wife, Laree, in D.C. To Cindy, I explained the significance of the day. John I spared. In the first months of our relationship, he'd heard so much about Thomas that he'd politely but firmly asked me to stop talking about him. Seemed fair. I've honored that, except for rare and passing references to "The Demon Seed," "The Mythical Thomas," or "He Whose Name Must Not Be Mentioned." The letters, the empty bottles of mead and Atholl Brose, the devil-bear and pentagram ring, a pair of worn underwear, and a photo album, I keep discreetly packed away.

A couple of weeks after that twenty-year mark, I had lunch with a friend, Donnie, at the Radford bar BT's. It was the first time I'd been there since the night Thomas and I played footsie beneath the table after the Ginsberg reading. When Donnie arrived, I was reminded of how much he resembles a young Thomas. In fact, Donnie's about the age Thomas was when we met in 1991. He's short, butch, black-bearded, muscular, and very, very hairy.

I'm intimately acquainted with his lush body hair because sometimes, when John's out of town, Donnie shares my bed. Turns out I'm no more capable of monogamy than Thomas was, a fact John grudgingly tolerates. After I top Donnie, I lie there, that furry, handsome, burly boy in my arms, and watch him sleep. It's almost as if the miserly universe, after making me wait for two decades, finally decided to honor the fidelity of my feelings by giving me some version of Thomas back.

At BT's, Donnie and I split a plate of chicken wings. He had worries; I gave him advice. He's a son of sorts, one of my boys, someone I want to take care of and protect. I'm not in love with him, though I love him. The desperate need and half-addled longing I felt for Thomas aren't there, just warm fondness, and gratitude, that an old daddy bear like me has such a buddy, a young man who's willing to share his beautiful body.

In the parking lot we hugged before Donnie headed back to classes. I drove home, listening to my favorite country-music star Tim McGraw singing "Everywhere." Something about that convergence—a young version of Thomas at BT's—had allowed for resolution. A tension in my heart eased up and laid down its bitterness, as if deciding that twenty years of mourning were finally enough. What I was left with, on that sunny February day, after all my fervid passions and attachments, my long history of deep loving, was a welling sense of thanks.

Jim and Mike are sweltering in the home office, applying a kind of greige.

the painters

I WONDER WHAT THEY SAY ABOUT US behind our backs. What my spouse John and I say about them in their absence is what a good job they're doing, how friendly they are, and how much nicer it would be if they worked naked. Both of them are good-looking, well-built young guys, both Southwest Virginia natives like me. It's a small erotic thrill to have them in our house, painting our living room, bedroom, and home office. As if a cock-tease pastry chef has come to visit, displaying Napoleons, cream puffs, and éclairs you can pay to see but not to eat. One of them, Jim, is a younger version of myself, with dark beard, bald head, stocky physique, and tattoos flowing out of his T-shirt sleeves. (Turns out we even have the same tattoo artist.) The other's Mike, a lean, pale, clean-shaven, very buff boy, whose cargo shorts are ripped to expose a hairy right thigh, whose cargo shorts barely fit him, hanging precariously off his round butt, hanging low to expose a strip of underwear, sky blue.

TODAY MIKE'S CHEWING A TOOTHPICK. I want to think that's evidence of an oral fixation, but I'm probably projecting. For that bubble butt, the usual fruit metaphors occur—peach, apricot, nectarine, those fragrant pink edibles that splash the mouth with juice, whose raison d'être is the tentative lap of tongue, the slow sink of teeth—or receptacles that need filling—wineglasses, quaichs, the knuckle-deep (or is it pecker-deep?) hole in moist mountain earth where one nestles three kernels of corn. His cargo shorts teeter, slowly slip down, are all too frequently tugged back up. It's the suspense of icicles edging eaves in the first gusts of spring. John and I both are fascinated. In middle age, men long together become, sad to admit, less lovers, more cruise buddies. Today Mike's on his hands and knees, working in the living room, butt in the air. I come up with excuses to leave this laptop and check on his progress. Distracting sound of sandpaper on spackle. Beauty's abrasive, skinning the daily of its gloss. John and I are trying to concentrate at separate (I accidentally wrote "desperate") desks. How can a handsome man be both a downpour in drought and sandpaper on skin?

THEY'RE PAINTING LATE today, trying to finish up the bedroom. What I want to say is, "Why don't y'all stay for hummus, mint juleps, chiles rellenos?" What I want to say is, "I bet you boys are pretty sweaty. How about we all hit the shower stall? It's big enough for four." I've spent my life not saying what I want to say, not making love to men I desire. Thus this essay.

SPEAKING TO A straight man? I'm good at it. (The stereotypically gay topics have always bored me anyway.) Tattoos, food, pickup trucks, who grew up where. Celtic, tribal; sausage balls, Cajun alfredo sauce, red velvet cake; F150s, Toyota Tacomas; Hinton, Lexington, Catawba. When I speak to them, they must stand relatively still. They must stand relatively close. Close enough to touch. (Not quite close enough to smell; after hours of work, their pits must be spicy-ripe.) When I speak to them, they must look at me and not the brush, the drop cloth, the roller, the walls, which, over a matter of days, beneath their hands, have taken on hues of brown, gray-blue, greige, the boring ubiquitous tan of these walls disappearing beneath something "deeper and more vibrant," to use HGTV lingo. I must, painfully polite, look at their faces and not their biceps, crotches, the points of their nipples visible beneath the moist fabrics of T-shirts, their bellies—Jim's like mine, furry and slightly curved with good food and beer; Mike's white, hairless, flat—bellies exposed when they stretch up to roll the ceiling, flex stiff joints, or simply, lazily, scratch a navel. While they're here, the world glistens again, with that shattered-quartz late-spring sunlit radiance that heralds the beginning of a rich beer buzz. While they're here, in me there's something eager, bestial, reined in. Cat chittering at birds outside the window. Angler fish waiting in the ocean floor's darkness, waving its glowing lantern, jaws dripping teeth like grotto stalactites.

"HEY, GUYS, COULD you turn up the air-conditioning? It's really hot in here." Jim and Mike are sweltering in the home office, applying a kind of greige. (Who knew that was a word?) John and I look at one another and grin. Surely the world is more satisfying if you're not this highly sexed. Or maybe not. How high would we have to crank the heat before they stripped to the waist? I'm guessing Jim's got a light coat of hair black as his beard across his big soft chest. Mike's pecs are pale as November flurry or serviceberry petals, his nipples are apple buds, he's so muscled it's as if he's smuggling round chunks of semiprecious stones beneath his skin.

WHEN YOU'RE THIS settled, any chaos is heady for a while. Pine pollen dusts the carpets. Peony petals scatter the mantelpiece. The hard gusts of a thunderstorm fill the study and rifle the papers. Rain spatters the windowpanes. Wind nudges the back door open; the silver tabby escapes, crazy for the smell of grass, dirt, prey.

WE'RE BOTH HAPPIER, John and I. More frequent smiles, easier conversation. As if youth were bacterial, airborne, contagious. This is what painters are meant to do: add color. Like the wisteria twining the back deck. We cut it back, having heard that old growth only blooms when it's disturbed. Cut it back to sticks, what looked dead, irrecoverable. But here are new leaves, fresh flowers in which I bury my face—perfumed racemes, evanescent, generous, sky blue.

One reason to hate humanity: the way it mars near-perfect moments.

lending the outlier pluck

I.

In 1976 a shaggy-headed seventeen-year-old boy, riffling through the record bins of a department store in small-town Hinton, West Virginia, studied the eye-catching black and white cover of Joni Mitchell's album *Hejira*. Up till then, his taste in music had tended toward the Partridge Family, the Carpenters, and Neil Diamond. He'd never heard Mitchell's music, though he'd heard Judy Collins' rendition of "Both Sides, Now" and so recognized Mitchell's name. Despite having very little money to buy anything, despite having no idea of what kind of music that album might contain, he took a chance and bought *Hejira*.

Thirty-nine years later, on the third of July, 2015, he found himself—which is to say, I found myself—in the United Kingdom, an ocean away from West Virginia. Significantly less shaggy-headed—gray-bearded and bald, in fact—I spoke as part of "Court and Spark: An International Symposium on Joni Mitchell," held at the University of Lincoln. What I said there is the basis for what follows.

II.

JONI MITCHELL'S LYRICS AND MUSIC have profoundly pervaded my life and given me the resilience to continue. I'm immeasurably grateful for that.

I've needed to be resilient. At age sixteen, I figured out I was gay. I had a support system of lesbian friends during my junior year of high school, but by the time I discovered *Hejira* in the fall of 1976, they'd graduated and moved on to West Virginia University. I found myself painfully isolated, afraid to share my true self with anyone. Southern Appalachia, then and now, is full of devout Christians who regard homosexuality as a grave sin, so I knew it was crucial that I keep the secret of my same-sex attractions to myself or face serious consequences: social ostracism and physical violence. Silence, it seemed clear, was the better part of valor.

Still, I badly needed to articulate my inchoate desires in order to comprehend them. My father had brought me up on English and American literature—Wordsworth, Keats, Frost, Emerson, Thoreau—and I'd written my first poem in the seventh grade, so already I had a private outlet for feeling: the journals in which I regularly scribbled attempts at poetry. But to write poetry about love? About how handsome Robbie and Keith and Randy and Billy were, about how much I studied their faces and bodies and ached to touch them?

I can't recall if I managed to write my first poem about another boy before or after I listened to *Hejira*, but the love songs on the album certainly helped me continue in that vein, as did the songs on *Court and Spark*, which I bought soon thereafter. Other than West Virginia author Muriel Miller Dressler, Joni Mitchell was the first contemporary poet I'd ever encountered. I lay on my bed in the dark and listened to "Coyote," "Amelia," "Hejira," "Down to You," and "The Same Situation" over and over, admiring the power of the lyrics and fascinated by the analyses of romantic love. Here, I realized, was a woman who had ached and yearned just as I was aching and yearning, a woman who had made music out of that passion and that suffering. Her verse about the vagaries of ardor gave me permission to write my own love poems. And in her depictions of romantic consummation, complexity, and loss, I glimpsed my future, a future in which I might escape homophobic Hinton and find a place where the men I desired might conceivably desire me back.

In 1977, I fled to Morgantown, West Virginia (rumored to be the inspiration for Mitchell's "Morning Morgantown") to attend West Virginia University and experience the gay community there. During those undergraduate years, my Joni Mitchell album collection grew. Her remarkably innovative music inspired me to learn how to play piano, acoustic guitar, and Appalachian dulcimer. Her astute lyrics helped me make sense of my quest for erotic and romantic fulfillment and endure my first painful experiences of unrequited love. When I encountered Sylvia Plath's poetry, my regard for her work, combined with my enthusiasm for Mitchell's, made me decide to follow the avocation of poet, and so I attended graduate school at WVU from 1982 to 1984, reading Plath's *Ariel*, listening to Mitchell's *Shadows and Light* and *Wild Things Run Fast*, and writing *The German Darkness*, a thesis of gay love poetry about men I'd courted and sparked and lost. Here's a poem from that collection.

POSSESSION

This summer night I watch you fall asleep
under me, our bellies still stuck together
with opalescence, the altar candle snuffed out.
Yours is the trust of a mammal belly up
beside its den-mates. Soft snores filter through
the bushy red-gold grill of your moustache, your
half-open lips, and I try to imagine you as a child
in Waynesburg, stealing chrysanthemums

off restaurant tables and demanding doughnuts
before the bakery windows. Tonight I am still young
and I want to reach somehow through the hard
muscles of your chest fogged with red curls of
hair and finally palm that seed you keep from me,
that crystal inside no one sees or touches,
the possession you fear most. Tonight
I sit cross-legged on the bed beside you,
stroking your torso and rubbing my beard,
and I dream of clutching that crystal, of
reading its facets with my fingertips all night
till the wood thrush begins singing in the fog
long before dawn, the hosta lilies open
under the window, and you wake to find your heart
in my hands and your body embedded in amber.

    Since graduate school and *Wild Things* so long ago, I've persisted in both completing my Joni Mitchell collection and cultivating my creative abilities. By now, with the help of wonderful editors, publishers, and a patient husband, I've published many books, five of them collections of poetry. Would I have become a poet without experiencing Mitchell's wonderful lyrics? I don't know. What I do know without a shadow of a doubt is that I have been able to persist as a gay Appalachian author because of Mitchell's example.

    Being a minority writer isn't easy, as some of you know. Being a writer who's drawn to controversial subjects isn't easy either. Being a writer who focuses on the often maligned and stereotyped regions of the American South and Appalachia is also difficult. Mainstream audiences tend to ignore most queer writing. They also tend to ignore regional writing, material that depicts small-town or rural people who make their lives far from the urban centers of power.

    I am, for better or worse, such a writer. In my often-autobiographical work, I frankly examine gay relationships, gay eroticism, transgressive sexuality, mountain people, "rednecks," and "hillbillies." Writing uncompromisingly about what I please with no regard for literary fad or fashion has had, as you might expect, certain negative consequences. Like many provocative and marginalized authors, I've paid the price for following my perverse muse so freely, so steadily, and so defiantly. Although my publications have received a few awards and limited acclaim, for the most part I write and publish, like authors the world over, in relative isolation and solitude, far outside the mainstream literary world, with little support or encouragement. It is, occasionally, disheartening. Deeply disheartening.

These disappointments have been frequent but relatively minor. More recently, I suffered a major professional blow. In the autumn of 2014, despite the eight books I'd published since my last promotion in 2007, my bid for Full Professor at Virginia Tech was turned down, for the most part because outside reviewers dismissed my four novels as "genre fiction." I was shocked, hurt, and furious. It was the biggest "Fuck You" I'd ever received in my career as a writer and university teacher.

How did I cope with this massive insult? Revenge fantasies, of course, and copious alcohol, and embittered reclusiveness. More helpfully, I began reading books about one of my greatest role models. I read *Gathered Light: The Poetry of Joni Mitchell's Songs; Joni: The Creative Odyssey of Joni Mitchell; Joni Mitchell: In Her Own Words; Will You Take Me As I Am: Joni Mitchell's* Blue *Period;* and *The Words and Music of Joni Mitchell.*

Again and again, those books reminded me of important facts and reassuring parallels. Mitchell has always been an individualist, a restless, strikingly unique musician who has followed her own path. Her artistic integrity is matchless. She's created what she's been driven to create with little concern for musical trends, and she's changed when staying the same would have been far more lucrative. She's unwaveringly resisted commercialism, and her career has suffered as a result. Despite legions of dedicated fans like this hillbilly queer, her overall popularity has dwindled since 1974's

Court and Spark. There have been the stupid, shallow responses to her sterling 1975 album, *The Hissing of Summer Lawns*; her disappearance from the radio airwaves after 1979's *Mingus*; and the negative critical response to *Dog Eat Dog* in 1985. My guess is that she regrets nothing and that, given the opportunity, she would do nothing differently.

I feel much the same about my own ornery and obscure writing career, and I offer myself today as a representative, one of countless outsider artists who've done their best to emulate Mitchell's rigorous and hard-won independence.

From my poetry collection, *A Romantic Mann*, here's a more recent love poem of mine, which, like many of the songs on *Wild Things Run Fast*, is not about love yearned for or love lost, but about love achieved.

THE BELLS OF BRUGES

There is no chamber pot to hurl.
Not a lack I would normally feel,

but this sleep-splintering clamor in the street,
this corbie-stepped setting suddenly put me

in mind of it. Such an easily lobbable item,
such a nastily simple way to express displeasure.

The earth is beautiful, its people
unaccommodating. Like Juvenal,

I hurl words instead, or would if
I could bring myself to leave our bed.

We've had a busy tourist-morning—
a climb up the bell tower, a boat tour

along medieval canals. For lunch, crepes
with *advocaat*, then this midafternoon nap.

Which returns me to the chamber pot,
the inconvenient absence of it.

Children are shrieking in the street below
our open window, garbage cans ruckus by.

One reason to hate humanity:
the way it mars near-perfect moments.

I am annoyed, half-awake, my snarl
only another marring, but your soft snores

keep course through it all, till a sudden hard rain
empties the street, till there is only

the shush of it, pewter simmering on the sill,
a veil chimes part at intervals.

Only bells and rain now, your breath and mine.
My chin on your clavicle, chest hair

tickling my nose, I watch the pulse beat
metronomic in the curve of your neck.

By my mother's deathbed I watched
the drumskin loosen, the heart unwind.

Today, sweet steadiness of youth,
your nakedness curls against mine,

    the bells of your blood do not falter,
    joining the distant carillons of Bruges,

    opening their silver flowers,
    tonguing melodies I cannot name.

 The excellence of Joni Mitchell's words and music inspire us. Her body of work seems to say, "Create. Continue to create. Create what you believe in. Say what you are compelled to say. Persevere despite neglect and adversity."
 Her example gives the outsider strength in despondent times. Her example lends the outlier pluck.

It took a virulent case of homesickness to make me realize that I was a country boy and an Appalachian, despite my sexual orientation and literary enthusiasms.

the feast hall, the arsenal, and the mirror
Teaching Literature to Students at Risk

I'M PRIMARILY A POET, ONLY SECondarily a teacher. So, when I think about teaching—which I do rarely, since my pedagogy is more intuitive than consciously considered—I think in metaphor. The metaphors I choose can't help but reveal, to some extent, who and what I am.

The Feast Hall

WHEN TEACHING LITERATURE, SOMEtimes I feel as if I'm giving students much-needed food. It seems inevitable that a man like me, descended from a family of hearty mountain cooks and gourmands, would compare a poem to a biscuit, a short story to a big slab of country ham. The writing that's helped me survive—in particular, that by Appalachians, gay men, lesbians, and the confessional poets—certainly has felt like nourishment. And, to continue the culinary analogy, a soul without meaningful connections and affirmations is likely to feel starvacious, to use a coined word I'm fond of. Good writing can make those connections and allow those affirmations.

The Arsenal

AS A LIBERAL, AN APPALACHIAN, A GAY man, and an environmentalist, I'm angered by much of what's going on in contemporary America, including rampant conservatism, mountaintop removal, and homophobia. Add to that my love of Greek, Roman, Nordic, and Celtic classics, plus an innate bellicose orneriness, and the other set of metaphors that occurs to me when I teach literature involves battle. Giving students resonant words they will cherish is like giving them armor, swords, and shields to protect their fragile individuality and self-esteem against an occasionally hostile world.

The Mirror

FINALLY, ALONG WITH food and weapons, analogies natural to my personality, I also return with great regularity to a metaphor borrowed from poet and feminist Adrienne Rich. In her essay "Invisibility in Academe," she says,

> When those who have power to name and to socially construct reality choose not to see you or hear you, whether you are dark-skinned, old, disabled, female, or speak with a different accent or dialect than theirs, when someone with the authority of a teacher, say, describes the world and you are not in it, there is a moment of psychic disequilibrium, as if you looked into a mirror and saw nothing. (199)

When I teach, especially when I am addressing students in Appalachian Studies courses or the Gay and Lesbian Literature course I created at Virginia Tech, I'm trying to save younger versions of myself from this lack of reflection, from the absences and omissions I encountered as a student, from hunger, helplessness, and invisibility. Such privations, if that is all you know, feel like one's natural state, one's deserved condition. One adapts, as cave salamanders have. One assumes that dark and wavering reflections are all there is, like Plato's chained prisoners in his Allegory of the Cave. So much of what I do as a teacher is shaped by what I once experienced as a student. Forgive, then, a few pages of my past.

West Virginia History, 1972-73

WHEN I WAS in the eighth-grade, I took a full school year's course in West Virginia history. I had a very good teacher; I absorbed fact after fact. *Harper's Ferry is the lowest point in the state. West Virginia became a state on June 20, 1863. Arch Moore is the governor. There are two sizeable Indian mounds in the state, at South Charleston and Moundsville. Etc. Etc.* Enflamed with one of my first grand ambitions—to achieve the coveted Golden Horseshoe award—I studied like mad, took the Golden Horseshoe Test and—one of my first rapturous successes—made the top score in the county. This meant that I got to go to the State Capitol in Charleston, West Virginia, have my shoulder sword-tapped by the State Superintendent of Schools, and become a Knight of the Golden Horseshoe. Hooray! Sir Jeff...it sounded good.

As I returned to Summers County triumphant, full of youthful hubris, I knew more about West Virginia than I ever had before or ever would again. However, I did not know enough to realize that I had never heard of Matewan or the Paint Creek/Cabin Creek strikes, Sid Hatfield's assassination, the Battle of Blair Mountain, the ruinous environmental effects of mining, the War on Poverty, or the economic consequences of absentee land ownership.

No Hillbillies Here, 1973-77

IN HIGH SCHOOL I eagerly took to literature just as my parents expected. I was one of the few students in the ninth grade to love Shakespeare's *Romeo and Juliet*, and in Study Hall I read *Dracula*, the *Iliad*, and the *Odyssey* just for fun. Emily Brontë's *Wuthering Heights* provided me with an early role model: one day, with luck, I'd be as smoldering, complex, passionate, and irresistible as Heathcliff. By the tenth grade I was devouring *Julius Caesar* in English class and, inspired by a Latin course, my pleasure reading was composed of historical novels about Rome. Eleventh grade was American lit., and I was right in my element, since my father had already gotten me hooked on Emerson and Thoreau, Dickinson and Whitman. By the twelfth grade, I'd realized I was gay, so my enthusiasm for *Hamlet*, *Macbeth*, and Robert Frost was mixed up with more pleasure reading, Mary Renault's historical novels about ancient Greece, which are full of men loving men.

All fine material, all authors to be admired and reread throughout my adulthood-to-come. But no Appalachian authors. There I was living in Hinton, West Virginia, a small mountain town along the New River, and the teachers at Hinton High School didn't expose me to mountain writers' works (except for one Jesse Stuart story I didn't really take to). Well, the faculty was no doubt under pressure to teach classics, and I loved classics. I loved just about every writer I was introduced to. Gay and lesbian writers, of course, I had to furtively discover on my own. Appalachian writers, well, even if I'd known of them, I wouldn't have been much interested anyway. Appalachia had no culture. Mass media had made that clear. It was a backward place that young intellectuals like me wanted to flee as soon as possible.

Only one event caused me briefly to rethink these certainties. During my ninth-grade year, the Appalachian poet Muriel Miller Dressler visited my high school. I'd never seen a live poet, certainly not a West Virginia poet writing about West Virginia. She read her poem "Appalachia," mentioning the ways in which mountain folks establish their family graveyards on hilltops (105-106). *Well, yes,* I thought. *Just like ours, the Ferrell family cemetery up at Forest Hill.* Something clicked, some deep and nourishing recognition. That part of me shaped by the mountains, by Appalachian culture, that part of me I wasn't even at that point aware of, felt itself mirrored.

Country Boy at College, 1977-1981

IT WAS MY second semester at West Virginia University. I hated dorm life—all those immature boys I had to pass for straight around—so I hung out at my lesbian friend Bill's a lot, in her tiny apartment in Sunnyside, Morgantown's student ghetto. That semester her roommate Allen was taking an Appalachian Literature course. Allen and I were both gay, both from southern West Virginia, so I felt a certain kinship with him. Why he would want to take such a course confused me, however. Maybe because his daddy was a coal miner. I picked up the class textbook, *Voices from the Hills*, and browsed through it. Other than Jesse Stuart, I recognized none of the names in the table of contents. Well, I knew I was fairly well read. These writers were not known to me; therefore, they must not have been important. How's that for a syllogism? I wanted to take courses in modern poetry and Shakespeare, read writers like W.B. Yeats and John Keats. I had no time for Appalachian literature.

In my senior year, I was almost done with degrees in English and Nature Interpretation. I had a friend from South Charleston, Robin, who matched me in several Southern traits, including the way we said "I," which had branded us as Southerners in the linguistics course we took together. She was reading *Years That Answer* by Maggie Anderson. "Maggie's from West Virginia, and she went to school here at WVU," Robin explained. By that point, deeply gripped by Sylvia Plath's work, I'd started fooling with the idea of writing poetry seriously, so it was a relief to know that someone from West Virginia could make it as a poet. I browsed through *Years That Answer* and started getting that click-click-click of recognition I had with Muriel Miller Dressler's work. Gardening, lots of gardening and vegetable poems. Green beans, cucumbers, melons. The arts and crafts fair at Ripley, West Virginia. Queen Anne's lace. Yep, yep. All the great themes of classic literature I'd been gobbling up for years, but also details specific and relevant to West Virginia. And to think that Maggie Anderson once studied under a professor of mine, Winston Fuller, from whom I was taking a great class, Contemporary American Poetry. The gap between the ambitious nobody I was and published poets like Maggie narrowed just a tiny bit.

"Country Roads, Take Me Home," 1982-1989

MY FIRST SEMESTER in the English graduate program at WVU, Fall 1982, I sat in on a poetry workshop taught by Winston Fuller and finally met Maggie Anderson. She read from her work and signed my copy of her book. If she represented Appalachian literature, well, that field was starting to look more valid, more appealing to me, despite my mainstream literary ambitions and interests. Maggie's poems expanded my ideas of what art could be made from, where inspiration could be found. When I read Maggie, my country roots seemed like something to be proud of rather than to be ashamed of, though, as a gay man, I couldn't imagine a successful love life anywhere except an urban area.

In Fall 1985, I landed a part-time position teaching freshman composition at George Washington University in Washington, D.C. Finally, I'd gotten away from the mountains and all those homophobic rednecks. But the city was one obnoxious annoyance after another. Rude people who didn't display the Southern manners I'm accustomed to. Noise. Traffic. Everything took too long or moved too fast or cost too much. Hearing John Denver's "Take Me Home, Country Roads" on the radio made me teary-eyed. The gay community didn't welcome me with open arms, unbuttoned shirts, or unzipped pants; I was too plain, poor, somber, and shy to be an erotic hit. It took a virulent case of homesickness to make me realize that I was a country boy and an Appalachian, despite my sexual orientation and literary enthusiasms. I read my first Appalachian novel, Thomas Wolfe's *Look Homeward, Angel*, and I took the title's advice. I was back in the mountains by Christmas, and in the mountains I planned to stay. Cities, I'd decided, are fit only for visiting, not living in.

There was a horrible year of teaching part-time at both Waynesburg State College in southern Pennsylvania and Fairmont College in northern West Virginia. I was a "gypsy instructor" with no money, car troubles, and too many frigging freshman composition papers to grade. Then I ended up back at WVU, teaching more composition and the deadly dull Business English. Folks around the department were talking about Breece D'J Pancake a lot. I picked up a copy of his stories and saw how well fiction can be spun from the mountain-familiar. Hell, I even recognized that very curve in the road on Gauley Mountain that Pancake mentions in "Time and Again" (83-88). Another recognition-click: exciting to see the world you know reflected in good fiction.

Soon after, Winston Fuller, then a colleague, invited me to join a literary supper club including Maggie Anderson, Winston, and their spouses. What an honor to socialize with someone whose writings I so admired! That first evening, gathering at the Middle Eastern restaurant Ali Baba's, I met another West Virginia poet, Irene McKinney, and soon thereafter was buying and reading her books. Being gay had seriously problematized my Appalachian identity—so much of gay life was urban, so much of Appalachia was colored by homophobic brands of Christianity—but reading Maggie, Irene, and Breece Pancake helped considerably. Their work gave me that feast hall, that arsenal, that mirror.

Those at Risk, 1989 to the Present
IN THE SUMMER of 1989, I finally left WVU to teach English at Virginia Tech in Blacksburg, Virginia: better money, and closer to my hometown and family. It didn't take me long to meet Alice Kinder, another instructor in the VT English Department. Those with similar accents gravitate together fast. She was in-your-face proud of her mountain background and even referred to herself as a hillbilly. Pretty soon she'd convinced me that personal experience was more important than any knowledge of scholarship, that I didn't need to have had a course in Appalachian Studies to talk about

mountain life. "You haven't studied it, but you've lived it," she urged. *Well, yes*, I realized—thinking about my father's gardens, my grandmother's mountain cooking, my great-aunt's tales and sayings, Johnny-house and coal bucket —*well, yes, I* have *lived it.*

Alice and I started giving presentations on Appalachian culture at Elderhostels in the region: Mountain Lake Resort, Smith Mountain Lake 4-H Camp. I read articles in *The Foxfire Books* to supplement or refresh my experiential knowledge, looked up old ballads, learned about the oral tradition, mountain tools, and foodways. When, thanks to Alice's recommendation, I was assigned to teach Humanities 1704/Introduction to Appalachian Studies—a welcome escape from teaching detested freshman writing—I dove wholeheartedly into books about the mine wars, novels by Denise Giardina and Lee Smith, poetry by Robert Morgan and James Still. As Giardina's character Carrie Bishop says in *Storming Heaven*, "There is enough to study in these hills to last a lifetime" (89). I regretted only that my studies in this regard started so late, as, almost twenty years after first flipping with disinterest through Allen's Appalachian lit. textbook, *Voices from the Hills*, I taught Appalachian Studies using that very same textbook.

So, full circle, the past student has become the present teacher (though the teacher, like anyone with an active mind, intends to keep learning all the way to the grave's muddy brink). This particular teacher is most interested in teaching students at risk. As a gay man and as an Appalachian, I've often felt dismissed, threatened, mocked, or ignored. To return to the metaphors with which I began, I've felt starved, which is to say without sustenance; vulnerable, which is to say without armor; and invisible, which is to say a monster or cipher without any accurate or discernible reflection in the mirror. Students who share these unpleasant experiences, those who are members of embattled minorities, most concern me, whether they're gay or lesbian, Appalachian, or members of ethnic minorities. I have found myself in a marginalized position of some sort just about my entire life, and it's the students in that same difficult position who engage my heart.

Teaching Appalachian Literature and Gay and Lesbian Literature for the English Department and Appalachian Studies for Humanities has been my way of trying to reach such students. A goodly number of the pupils in the Appalachian classes are mountain-raised, and about half of the students in gay and lesbian lit. classes I've taught have identified as LGBT. When I teach them about Denise Giardina or Maggie Anderson or Sappho or Cavafy, I'm giving them some of what they need to fight, stay strong, and live their lives in defiant independence.

Queer kids just about everywhere feel pretty much at risk and besieged, and this fact shouldn't surprise anyone. Appalachians, however, are not always recognized as a minority group, much less one that's oppressed and harassed. My years of teaching at Virginia Tech, however, have more than convinced me that queers and hillbillies are two of the few groups left about whom one may make jokes with relative impunity. In the following, I'll focus on how important it is for teachers to spread the word that Appalachia, rather than being a backwards and benighted place, is possessed of a valuable, unique, and rich culture all its own.

Virginia Tech has a widely varied student population. A majority of the students are from what residents of that region call NOVA; that is, Northern Virginia, which is to say the upper-middle-class suburbs of Washington, D.C. These students know little about rural life, and many of them are not pleased to be stuck in a "cow town" in Southwest Virginia for several years. In dramatic contrast, other VT students are locals: students from the mountainous areas of Virginia, and, to a much lesser extent (due to high out-of-state tuition), West Virginia. These two groups of students, the NOVA crew and the locals, are discernibly different, in accent and dress. Each recognizes The Other. Hostilities sometimes ensue.

In all of my classes, not just the Appalachian-themed ones, I make it clear to students that I'm a mountain man. (I also make it clear that I'm gay, but that's another "kettle o' feesh," as my aunt used to say.) What this often means is that Appalachian students warm up to me fast, even if some of them are initially hesitant because I'm so casually open about my unconventional sexual orientation. They feel safe with me, and so they tell me stories they aren't likely to share with other professors.

Where Are You From?!

"*I WAS IN another class the other day, and not only did my professor make fun of the way I talk, but another student asked me if he could record me on his tape recorder. He said I sounded 'cute.'*"

*

"*Me and some Giles County buddies were invited to a frat party a few weeks back. Great, we thought. Girls to flirt with, and free beer too! We were there only about half an hour when the frat guy who'd invited us came up to us, sort of embarrassed, and said, 'Sorry, boys, but you're gonna have to leave.' 'Why?' I ask, pissed off. 'Because my frat brothers think you talk funny.' I threw my beer bottle against the wall and we left. I've had a grudge against Virginia Tech ever since.*"

*

"*My daughter Nicole was on the Blacksburg town bus the other evening. She and some other girl were the last ones who hadn't gotten off. So, Nicole is talking to the driver—they graduated from the same high school—and the other girl looks at them and listens for a while and then rolls her eyes and says, like she can't believe what hicks they are, 'Where are you from?!' And Nicole, God bless her, doesn't miss a beat. She just turns right around and says, 'I'm from here. Where are you from!?'*"

I've gotten a few tastes of this kind of casual and thoughtless mockery myself (though my age, my carriage, and my bulk have probably spared me from a lot more, and for that, I'm grateful, since I'm easily offended and have a terrible temper). Once, in the late 1990s, some gay friends of mine and I entered a Mexican restaurant in Rehoboth Beach, Delaware. When the young maitre d' saw my West Virginia T-shirt, he made some remarks about brothers copulating with their sisters. Disbelieving, taken completely aback by such bad manners, by the time I convinced myself that he'd actually said what he'd said, the opportunity to tell him something along the lines of "You are cordially invited to go fuck yourself" had passed.

Others' scorn is something I can shrug off fairly easily. I'm in my fifties, have occasionally encountered homophobia, have heard many jokes about West Virginians and hillbillies, and have had many years to develop in response a strong sense of self, pride in my regional origins and my sexuality, and a rebellious determination to live my life as unconventionally as I please. I roll my eyes at such ignorance, mutter to myself, "Consider the source," or, in less forgiving moods, exude a bristling hostility that says, "You'd better just shut up and pass by. Do what's best for both of us and just pass by."

But most young people, college kids, are not yet so strong. Appalachian students at Virginia Tech are like most self-conscious youths: they want to belong, they want to be liked, they want to avoid being the brunt of jokes. So many do what Cinderella's sisters did in the Grimm brothers' version of the tale. They cut off parts of themselves in order to fit. They try to assimilate. They change their dress or try to modify their accents. And they take courses in Appalachian literature and Appalachian studies, hoping that, in those classrooms at least, they can be themselves, feel legitimate, and see mountain life reflected accurately.

"A Lot More Trouble to Roll Out Steel..."

The strength to say who you are, to grow as you will, respectfully but determinedly to refuse the pressures to assimilate and to conform—how does a teacher help a student find that strength? Here, in what space this essay has left, are a few rich and complex meals, sharp swords, sturdy shields, and glittering looking-glasses I use to help Appalachian students to develop pride and self-esteem and to teach non-Appalachian students how worthy of respect this region is.

"Appalachian Values" by Loyal Jones, a short essay included in *Voices from the Hills*, is a fine place to start. So many students, both flatlanders and hill kids, have heard a good deal from mass media about how flawed and backward Appalachian culture is, so Jones' essay is a healthy corrective. Furthermore, inviting mountain-bred students to talk about the ways in which they see such values as attachment to land and to family, self-reliance, and hospitality in their own backgrounds starts up lively discussion fast. I encourage honest response by first telling a few anecdotes that illustrate the ways in which I see in myself those values Jones lists: I'm a stoic fatalist, I don't like to be beholden, I like to do for myself, I remain in this region in order to remain close to my family. Mountain kids inevitably feel that thrill of recognition and always leave that day's class meeting feeling pretty good about being from the hills.

Every day, I point out to my classes, all of us must create some compromise between the persons we want to be and the persons the world wants us to be. What better work to discuss this conflict, the need to be ourselves versus the ache to belong, than Harriette Arnow's *The Dollmaker*? Students resist reading the novel in its very long entirety, but "Adjusting," the excerpt included in *Voices from the Hills*, is an effective way of beginning a class discussion about assimilation and the social pressure to conform. The novel's protagonist, Gertie Nevels, at a school open house, encounters her son Reuben's teacher Mrs. Whittle, who is clearly, to use one student's succinct summary, a "bitter old bitch," and who serves as the clear embodiment of that societal voice that demands that we abandon our individuality and "adjust." Mrs. Whittle mocks Gertie's dialect, complains about Reuben's sullen attitude, and explains condescendingly, "'That is the most important thing, to learn to live with others, to get along, to adapt one's self to one's surroundings.'" "'The trouble is,'" Mrs. Whittle accuses, "'you don't want to adjust—and Reuben doesn't either.'" Gertie's is one of the great individualist responses in literature: "'That's part way right...But he cain't hep th way he's made. It's a lot more trouble to roll out steel—an make it like you want it—than it is biscuit dough'" (274). It's at this point that, if reading the excerpt out loud, I try politely to suppress my natural response, a rapturously shouted, vigorous "*Hell*, yes!"

Harriette Arnow and James Still are often mentioned together as two monumental mid-twentieth-century Appalachian writers, so it's easy to segue from Arnow's *The Dollmaker* to Still's *River of Earth*. Most NOVA students are from middle-class and upper-middle-class backgrounds and have very little sense of what poverty is like, so it's a revelation for them to read a novel in which the characters are so poor that the next meal is often of uncertain origin. Students who have known poverty, on the other hand, are going to admire and relate to the strength with which the Baldridge family stubbornly endures.

One of James Still's poems I often use is "Heritage," in order to depict the ways in which natives of the Appalachian region have such a passionate attachment to place (another of the values that Jones mentions). "I will never leave these prisoning hills," swears the speaker (and note the concise way Still suggests ambivalence even in this paean of praise) (82). This poem always gets me a little wet-eyed when I read it out loud, so I often use a bit of comic relief afterwards by telling my students a joke, "Hillbillies in Heaven," from Loyal Jones' and Billy Edd Wheeler's *Laughter in Appalachia*, the basic gist of which is that hillbillies in heaven need to be kept chained up, or else "they'd go home every weekend" (30).

The coalfield novels of Denise Giardina are not only amazingly written, powerful, and unforgettable, but they can serve as a series of wonderful illustrations of those values that Loyal Jones mentions, from the self-reliance displayed by many of the characters in *Storming Heaven* to the stubborn attachment to place, the characters' refusal to leave the dying coalfields, in *The Unquiet Earth*. Most useful of all, however, is how Giardina, gracefully and without heavy-handed didacticism, portrays the ways in which Appalachians learn contempt for themselves through the false and exaggerated images of mass media and the ways in which poverty in central Appalachia is caused by greedy outside interests, absentee landowners, and the rapaciousness of the coal industry—the Colonialism Exploitation Model, as some Appalachian studies scholars call it. Students are full of stories about television shows and films that depict mountain folks as morons, and those from the coalfields can certainly relate to tales of unemployment and out-migration. There are, predictably, some heated debates between students from mining backgrounds and students who are passionate environmentalists. I do my best to remain neutral, so as not to alienate the former group, but I'm guessing that my environmental sympathies show through.

Appalachian folk culture is what I most relish about my region: the dialect, proverbs, stories, legends, superstitions, and foodways. Jan Harold Brunvand's *The Study of American Folklore* is a wonderful way to put Appalachian folk culture in a larger context. Brunvand's descriptions of oral, customary, and material culture are exceptionally clear, and they encourage students from other areas of America or other countries to share their own region's customs, place names, foods, and ghost stories. In such a context—almost anthropological—it's easy to convince students to take pride in the uniqueness of their native cultures and to look at difference and diversity as enriching, exciting, and delightful, not threatening. I even pull out a few details of gay folklore just to remind them of how every subculture, whether occupational, regional, or sexual, has its own myths, jargon, and oral tradition. Teaching Lee Smith's novels *Fair and Tender Ladies* and *Oral History* is an effective way of examining the specifics of Appalachian folk culture while also introducing the students to moving and poignant story lines. (I must add that Ivy Rowe, the protagonist of *Fair and Tender Ladies*, is a fine role model for anyone resisting convention and societal expectations.)

As a writer, I often feel ghettoized as either a gay or an Appalachian author. Many mainstream readers and publishers assume that writers like me who depict the experiences of sexual or cultural minorities have nothing of value to say to them, so we are relegated to the Regional Writers or Gay/Lesbian sections of the bookstore (if we're lucky enough to be published at all), and our work is discussed only in Appalachian Literature or Gay/Lesbian Literature courses (again, if we're lucky). I resist this pigeonholing by bringing the work of Appalachian writers, as well as gay and lesbian writers, to my creative writing classes. Neither group of authors is represented to any extent in creative-writing textbooks, so I simply ransack my personal library and begin many classes by reading poems or brief prose passages by any of the fine authors mentioned above. Mountain writers deserve wider recognition, I passionately believe, and if I can't do anything about my own publications' ghettoization, I can certainly take advantage of my position as a professor to spread the word about my fellow Appalachian writers. For instance, Maggie Anderson's "Long Story" is a gripping illustration of narrative poetry (21-23), I tell my pupils, and Irene McKinney's "At 24" is delicious in its sharp tone and insistence on personal freedom from gender-role expectations (91).

Other professors, those enamored of mainstream authors without minority identity or status, are welcome to sing their praises and encourage students to emulate them. I prefer the privilege of supporting members of my own clan, whether they be Appalachian or queer, writers or students. What I admire most are lives and words like Arnow's steel: courageous, complex, marginalized, and at risk; refusing to be passively shaped like malleable biscuit dough; troublesome, rough-edged souls who are defiantly themselves.

a smiling idea stripping beside my bed, a beefy, fur-dusted impossibility.

david

I haven't thought of you in years. In the late seventies, you loved and lived with a college friend of mine, till Jeb—a narcissistic neurotic who never deserved you—grew bored and threw you away, like eggshells and melon rinds lobbed out to compost.

If I try to tally the scattered minutes, you and I spent, on the whole, less than two hours in one another's company. I remember your thick brown moustache, how you loved the Pacific Northwest, how muscular your shoulders, chest, and arms were, despite a professed disinterest in the weight-training I was already devoted to. I so wanted to be well-built and beautiful like you, to bed well-built and beautiful men like you.

There was one afternoon in Morgantown, chatting by a line of blooming Bradford pears, waiting for Jeb to choose from among his plethora of fussy outfits. There was one night in Pittsburgh, after you two had moved there—the dance floor at Pegasus and a late-night diner with friends, followed by a quick drive around the block, just the two of us, in your new Triumph Spitfire. Or was that after Jeb dumped you, when, grieving, bereft, you turned desperately promiscuous and solaced your sorrow by sleeping around? With looks like that, you must have had a long litany of lovers.

That was the last time I saw you. I was in love with you a little. You were solid and fine, butch and kind, the sort of man I ached to touch and yearned to become. Word was you grew ill and died with all the others, ground down to ash by history. So much time has passed that I can't recall where you grew up, even if I ever knew. Pennsylvania? West Virginia? Where are you buried? Did you live to see thirty? Was there someone there to help you with your dying?

TONIGHT, I'M THINKING of your youth and mine, brooding over a Facebook photo I stumbled upon today, two older men treating a younger to dinner at Antoine's in New Orleans.

Here's John, my patient partner. Here's Erik, the spoiled, fuckable boy whose self-absorption we tolerated for a time because he was luscious and gave himself to us. Christ, what a face, what a hairy chest, what a splendid, edible ass, what a thick, uncut prick. For a few months, carnal miracle, he wanted John and me despite our ages.

And here's me, with my bald head and graying beard, hereditary bags growing darker and deeper beneath my eyes, satchels weighed down with half a century, my middle-aged spread barely disguised by the suit jacket Antoine's dress code requires. Old, old, standing beside a boy so young and desirable the contrast's shocking. As if, even in my twenties, I were ever as delicious as you or he.

Tonight, insomniac, I lie in midlife's banal bed, wincing, regretting, remembering. You're shifting gears at my elbow, making that hot little stud-car spark through the 2 a.m. streets of Pittsburgh. My hope's unspoken, that we might leave our friends, find a room, make love, but that's what-will-never-be, that's what-might-have-been. I'm too inexperienced, too young, too commonplace for you to want that way. It's 1979, and no one knows what contagion's to come, how soon bevies of infected beauties will wither and die, while the plain and unpopular survive, to wane away the decades in slow, less tragic ways.

And now it's 2010, and now at last you've come, a smiling idea stripping beside my bed, a beefy, fur-dusted impossibility, resting your young, warm weight atop me after thirty years apart. You kiss my brow, caress my beard, and scold the vain self-pity from my head, whispering, *Sweet boy, grizzled ingrate, fool. Lucky, lucky, living all those years, living long enough to look this old.*

Nothing inspires me more to write a poem than studying a hot man I know I can't have.

a leather bear in the big easy

(for Paul J. Willis and
Amie M. Evans)

I. Foreplay

THE NOVELS OF ANNE RICE FIRST brought me to New Orleans. Having read *Interview with the Vampire* and *The Witching Hour*, I was eager to see the city. In 1996, when two lesbian friends invited me to drive down to Louisiana and spend a few days in a family timeshare, I excitedly agreed. The drive from southwest Virginia was a miserable fourteen hours, and the timeshare turned out to be in Abita Springs, across Lake Pontchartrain from New Orleans, but we had a grand time nevertheless. We checked out the Abita brewery, wandered around the French Quarter, visited the Robert E. Lee Monument, explored the Garden District, where Anne Rice lived at the time, and Lafayette Cemetery, where Rice's Lestat slept away the days, and took a swamp tour. One afternoon, Dixie beers in hand, we attended the Maple Leaf Bar Poetry Series, and I got up the nerve to read a few of my poems. One early evening, I wedged resentfully into a linen suit, dress shirt, and tie (we country boys aren't much on dressing up) and enjoyed a solitary meal at the legendary Galatoire's while my friends went shopping.

Every night, the three of us stayed in our free accommodations, the timeshare way across the lake, so I was denied the pleasures of cruising the fabled French Quarter gay bars. Too bad. At thirty-six, I was single and perennially horny, and I was still fairly young. I might, despite my habitual shyness, have had a few tasty adventures searching for bears, cubs, and leather guys interested in sharing perverse frolic. Instead, I drank beer with my friends, marveled over the Louisiana humidity, and listened to the deafening night-noise of summer insects congregating in the pine forests outside Abita Springs.

Just about a year after that initial trip, I met John at a faculty development workshop at Virginia Tech, where I've been teaching since 1989, and he and I began our present relationship, thus ending my many decades of bachelorhood. Thus, I was feeling very middle-aged and very married in March of 2001, when next I made it to the Crescent City, this time for John's family reunion. He and I spent just about the entire time with his extended family, including a meal in the Mystery Room of Antoine's, where all nineteen of us were served a many-course feast (including a showy baked Alaska) and all the female family members wore feather masks that John had created. Again, no delving into the multitudinous queer delights of the city, though we did manage to attend a Ghost and Vampire Tour.

In 2002, I made it to New Orleans for the Associated Writing Programs Conference, but since I was traveling with Virginia Tech creative writing colleagues, salacious gay adventures in the Big Easy were denied me yet again. The wildest I got was smoking a cigar on the street and dancing with a female colleague in Oz, a raucous gay bar on Bourbon Street. (Most of my other colleagues, dubious, remained outside.)

In 2003, my relationship with New Orleans—up to then distant and infrequent, a form of frustrating foreplay—changed forever for the better. The wonderful Paul J. Willis began the Saints and Sinners Literary Festival. I don't recall how I even heard about it, but there

I was, standing shyly in the corner of a French Quarter courtyard, a name-tag lanyard around my neck. Writers and publishers I had long admired but never met laughed and congregated, the brittle leather of fallen magnolia leaves crackling beneath their feet. I'd grown up in the mountains of Southwest Virginia and West Virginia, and most of my life I'd lived in Appalachia, far from urban queer enclaves, so in a big city like New Orleans, I expected to feel out of my element. Instead, standing smack dab in the middle of the gay and lesbian literary scene, I began to feel very much at home.

I loved that sense of queer community. I've attended Saints and Sinners every year since, and my gratitude for the support I've found there is boundless. Meeting publishers, editors, and other queer writers has benefited my own writing career immeasurably, and I'm sure that's just as true for a plethora of other authors. Attending the annual festival has also given me the time—finally!—to experience gay life in New Orleans and participate in its pleasures. Now, as I compose this essay, I'm reliving many a vignette, many carnal, one mournful.

II. Ode to a Dick-Dancer

HE'S SHIRTLESS, IN ripped-up jeans that are more tattered holes than fabric, dancing on top of the bar at Oz. His body's classic: a big gym-whittled chest (though hairier would be more to my taste), a small waist, a big bubble butt. Down his muscled shoulder and right arm, there's the black lightning strike of a tribal tattoo. He's college-aged, the age I teach, with a shaved head, a scruffy goatee the color of sourwood honey, and a sheepish smile atop unselfconscious gyrations.

Nothing inspires me more to write a poem than studying a hot man I know I can't have. I sip the blue fire that black light makes of my gin and tonic and begin composing lines of verse in my head, lines that veer from frustrating reality to satisfying fantasy.

> *My captive grunts against silver-gray duct tape*
> *sealing his mouth, fights his bonds as my pickup*
> *crests the ridge, achieves the mountain cabin.*

Watching him is torment. I should leave. The boy's oblivious to my desire, to my existence, and I've had more than enough gin tonight. It feels like unwelcome weakness, craving beauty I can never possess, and I'm wondering at what age I'll have to pay to make love to a boy like that.

> *I lift him*
> *bound hand and foot into my arms. Armpit musk,*
> *long eyelash flutter. He loves his helplessness, loves*
> *my strength, moans with greed beneath his gag.*

I give him another reluctant glimpse—trying to memorize his white smile and brown nipples—and then I depart. At the door, like Lot's wife, I look back. Tonight's deity has moved along the bar to the spot where I sat and now thrusts himself into the air of my absence. On Bourbon Street, among slovenly tourists, I carry my icon home.

> *Flung on the bed, pants*
> *tugged down about roped ankles, beneath me*
> *his bubble butt bucks and begs, his heartbeat's tight*
> *fist slickly grips. My messiah's prayers are tape-muffled,*
> *as are his thanks. Sweat's silver gathers between us.*
> *All night inside this lie I wake, I wake, I live again.*

III. The Angel of Royal Street

I'VE SEEN MANY men in New Orleans that I've ached to ravish; I've published poems about several of them. (In other words, those hot

men and my own immoderate lust have contributed nicely to my
résumé.) There's so much manly scenery in the city that any brief
stroll down the street will provide a randy poet with fodder for
verse. Witness the following:

> I doubt a Whitman allusion's witty use is sufficient
> to woo him—*Passing stranger! You do not know
> how longingly I look upon you*—this eminently fuckable
> boy in his mid-twenties I pass near Brennan's.
> He's sporting big shoulders and thick round mounds
> of pecs a tight T-shirt shows off, cargo shorts and
>   furry calves,
> the black curly hair and beard that always hone
> my hunger, with the obligatory blonde tramp in tow.
> As usual, good manners veil my fascination, leave me
> conjecturing what cosmic rules or karma obviate
> a sweaty, lengthy daddy/boy scene. What have I been
> or done to determine that all I most want is denied?
> In what I mutter, stopping, turning to watch him
> stroll off—*Holy Gawd!*—is wonder at least, wonder
> and passion I can remember, if not fully savor.
> What's left of him is to imagine what sort of
> sweet slavery I might arrange for a submissive angel,
> meanwhile gobbling crawfish and gratiné oysters,
> swilling sublimations of Abita Amber, toasting to the few
> creations left that stun, as I lunch overmuch
> with my heat-weary husband at Acme Oyster House.

IV. Ghost and Vampire Tour

AFTER A DRINK at Lafitte's Blacksmith Shop, we tourists follow the Haunted History tour guide about the Quarter. Here's Madame Lalaurie's, site of an infamous haunting; and the Sultan's Retreat, site of a mysterious massacre; and legendary Marie Laveau's old home; and Miriam's Voodoo Temple, with her sleepy snake, icons of the gods, and offerings of rum. Here, supposedly, is an alley where the bodies of two men were found hanging, drained of blood. And here, in this peeling red building, a criminal kept a young man gagged and bound to a chair while he nightly drank his blood.

Near Saint Louis Cemetery No. 1, the tour guide leads us into a Rampart Street bar to take a break. I order a Hurricane-to-go—decadence cheap and legal. It's deep red with grenadine, the juice of Persephone's pomegranate, the ruby seeds the dead break between their teeth. In a deep lounge chair I settle back, and I study the most desirable of my fellow tourists. He's wearing khaki shorts, a white T-shirt, and a black vest. His hair is wavy, his goatee dark, his eyes Mediterranean. The hoop of his earring's glinting, as is the black gloss of his forearm hair. I sip my Hurricane, fish the maraschino cherry out, close my eyes, eat it slowly, and slip into another sadistic fantasy.

Vampirism and BDSM are kindred, more than easy to intertwine. In this delicious alternative universe, I force the dark boy down, rope his thrashing hands and feet, lash him to a chair, and plaster duct tape over his protests. His onyx eyes are wet and wide with fear and longing. I kiss my captive's moist brow, smooth his bushy eyebrows, lick the salty beard stubble on his neck, tongue the black hair dusting his heaving chest and heart. I chew on the pink azalea buds of his nipples till he's sobbing against his gag and my mouth's flooded with the taste of rust.

V. Frodo, 2005-2009

HE'S A YOUNG writer and editor from New York City. Mutual Saints and Sinners friends have explained that he's in an open relationship and is interested in trying BDSM with a top who knows what he's doing. The first time I see him, in the courtyard of a bed and breakfast on Esplanade Avenue, he's on his cell phone with his husband. *Looks like Elijah Wood, the guy who plays Frodo in those Lord of the Rings films, I think. Cute, but too slender for me, plus no beard. Still…it'd be fun to break him in.*

That turns out to be true. A month after our casual meeting in May, he reads one of my online short stories, "Captive," and e-mails me to ask how often I live what I later write. That November, despite his husband's petulant complaints, Frodo flies to Virginia to visit John and me. I pick him up at the Roanoke Airport a little before midnight. As soon as he's in my pickup truck, I cuff his hands, blindfold him, and tape his mouth before driving us home. He spends most of the next few days naked, with a slave collar around his neck, servicing us, being hogtied, bucked and gagged, and ass-ravished. In between sex-bouts, we get him drunk on Manhattans, cook him up solid meals, and enjoy long, stimulating conversations. For several years in a row, John and I rendezvous with Frodo during Saints and Sinners. One year, I'm tying Frodo's hands behind his back and screwing him on his belly in a musty room in Olivier House. Another year, John and I are double-dicking him (a nigh-mythical position I thought only porn stars achieved) in the Faubourg Marigny.

Eventually, Frodo leaves his husband. Eventually, Frodo and I, in New Orleans for another Saints and Sinners, are sitting on a bench among blooming crepe myrtle in Jackson Square, and he's telling me that he has a new partner who wants to be monogamous, that now he and I can only be friends. I shrug my shoulders, only mildly regretful. I've lived long enough to know how quickly Eros moves on. I've learned how to savor the god's blessings as deeply and as eagerly as I can, while already preparing for the inevitable abandonment.

VI. Erik, 2010

AS SOON AS Erik enters our hotel room, he's pushing me up against the wall, kissing me hard, and biting my chin. John joins us, and pretty soon we're all three naked on the king-size bed. Erik's a glory: soft brown chest and belly hair, big soft nipples, big uncut cock. I give the hairy cleft of his curvaceous butt a long and eager rimming before he sits on John's prick.

After showering, the three of us attend the opening reception of Saints and Sinners at the Hermann Grima House. While we sip drinks in the courtyard, other festival attendees stare at us with confused envy. *Who's that stupendously handsome young man with Jeff and John?* they're no doubt thinking. *The guy's so good-looking he could be a Hollywood actor. The guy's young enough to be Jeff's son.*

True enough. I'm just as amazed by his presence. I'd met Erik, a wildlife management major, the previous spring, only a few weeks before he was due to graduate from Virginia Tech. One of the most desirable boys I've ever met—tall, gracefully built, with arrogant eyes, wavy auburn hair, and a beard-stubbled jaw—he soon made it clear that he wanted to bed me. I was delighted and astonished. There are not a lot of guys his age who are into gray-bearded daddy bears my age. Several times, before he graduated and left town, he visited John and me for big meals and vigorous threesomes.

Erik's a graduate student at Louisiana State in Baton Rouge, and he's driven down to the French Quarter to spend a few days with us. I want to impress him with my generosity and largesse, since I'm so damned grateful that he's still willing to share his beautiful body with us. Plus, in a long tradition of desperate older men bribing greedy younger men, I figure royal treatment will keep him interested. And so, he stays for several days in our super-pricey room on the concierge floor of the Royal Sonesta. We take him out for rounds of drinks and expensive meals.

During one of those fancy dinners—shared with a fourth, my wonderful publisher, Steve Berman of Lethe Press—Erik, tipsy after a few Sazeracs, manages to leave off texting on his cell phone long enough to state, "Well, I know I'm remarkably attractive, so I'm going to take advantage of that as long as I can."

He's right, of course. He *is* exceptionally handsome. Still, as a country boy brought up on traditional Southern manners, I'm shocked and repelled by Erik's blunt expression of vanity. I am, however, far too besotted by his beauty to say anything. Steve, a brash and exceedingly frank Yankee from New Jersey, has no such compunctions. "My God! Who would even *say* that?" Steve blurts. The two begin to bicker, Erik brandishing his over-inflated ego, Steve again and again deflating it. My mortification increases. I detest conflict. I'm relieved when the bill arrives and we can leave.

Despite that discomfort, for a while Erik's a welcome addition to this year's New Orleans visit. He and John share a Jacuzzi in the room while I attend sessions. The three of us sit out on the balcony beneath the dripping awning, looking out over the Quarter and watching a violent spring storm roll through town. Erik, no doubt proud of his fine physique, spends all the time in our room entirely naked. That's fine with me: it gives me the precious opportunity to admire his broad shoulders, shapely pecs dusted with chestnut fur, perfect ass, and strong, hairy thighs.

One afternoon, while John's working on his laptop on the balcony, Erik and I, laughing and grappling, start wrestling on the bed. He's the kind of boy who brings out the dominant in me. I want him to be shy and submissive and beg me to tie and gag him and suck his soft nipples till they're sore and give it to him up the ass slow and sweet and deep. But no, he's aggressive and pushy in the sack. We're literally fighting for top, thrashing and cursing, rolling around. His resistance isn't arousing, it's annoying.

When he finally lets me overpower him—the boy's easily as strong as I am, and certainly more limber—and I have him on his belly with his hand bound behind him and a ball-gag strapped between his teeth, I lose my erection. Why? This is crazy. He's so desirable it's ridiculous. Maybe that's part of the problem. I've always been insecure about my physical attractiveness. At this age—fifty—and this weight—two hundred plus pounds—it's very hard for me to believe that this perfect young stud really wants me. That deep disbelief, on top of his previous aggressiveness, won't let me get hard enough to do what I most want to do: fuck him till he's sobbing. *Pitiable old man*, I think.

Erik gets impatient and wiggles free. Now we're wrestling again. This time he forces me down. Well, okay, I've always been versatile in the top/bottom department. Pretty soon he has my hands tied before me, my knees roped to my elbows, my own ball-gag in my mouth, and my calves on his shoulders, and he's pushing his big cock up my ass. Grinning down at me triumphantly, he mutters, "I'm gonna give it to you good, Daddy." And so he does. It hurts at first, because I don't bottom all that often and his cock is really big, but now it's feeling great, and I'm thinking, *Damn, you glorious bastard, this is hot as hell. I should have just let you take top to begin with.* Right before he comes, he pulls out, spurts all over my face, and rubs his juice into my beard.

That fine pounding turns out to be the acme of our relationship. Another night, Erik goes out to the bars on his own. He returns to the room at 3 a.m. with a complete stranger, a young punk he's picked up off the street. He's eager for a four-way. "Crabs? STDs? I don't think so," I say. When Erik protests, I invite him to find other accommodations. He backs down fast, shows the trick out, then spends the next hour in the bathroom, vomiting noisily and profusely. John and I look at each other, grim-faced. *More trouble than he's worth*, we silently agree. The next morning, we all exchange hugs before Erik drives back to Baton Rouge. We're relieved to see him go. Over the next few months, our e-correspondence tapers off.

FIVE YEARS LATER, writing this essay, stalker-style I look at the few photos I have access to on Erik's Facebook page. (He long ago unfriended me.) Sporting a full beard, he's handsomer than ever. I wonder how he's doing, whether I should have been more patient with him. How could he not have been an egotist? Hell, I'm a minor egotist too; what kind of monster would I have been, would I have become, if I'd been that beautiful at that age? I should forgive his bad behavior, his entitlement, and his vanity. If I'd met him when I was young and single, I have no doubt I would have fallen for him hard and he would have broken my heart. As it is, I'm still thankful that such a hot boy once shared my bed.[1] Erik was another of Eros' gifts that moved on too soon, but what a splendid gift he was.

VII. Tripp, 2010-2011

TALK ABOUT EROTIC overlap. Tripp starts flirting with me only hours after Erik's tied me up and fucked me. I've just read from "Demon Seed," a kinky short story of mine, at a Saints and Sinners event at the Bourbon Pub, and afterward Tripp comes up to tell me that he's a fan of my work, especially the BDSM-themed fiction.

One thing leads to another, and now we're indulging in a make-out session on the bar's balcony, kissing passionately, my fingers inside his shirt, caressing his chest hair and chunky pecs and tugging on his nipple ring. He's adorable: a stocky cub with thick hair, dark sideburns, and goatee. Again, I'm taken aback and profoundly thankful that a tasty young guy is into me.

"I'm in an open relationship," he says, fondling my crotch.

"That's good," I say, squeezing his ass.

"On Sunday, I'm going to be bartending here at the closing reception, so maybe I can come up to your hotel room after I get off work?" he asks, stroking my beard.

"Hell, yes," I reply, nuzzling his neck.

The next night, Saturday, Erik's departed, and I'm one of the readers at an event celebrating the release of *Bears in the Wild: Hot and Hairy Fiction*. It's held at a local bed and breakfast, Auld Sweet Olive. Tripp's in the audience with his partner, Will. When it's my turn, I read a few paragraphs from "Scruff-Cub," a short story

---

[1] Steve Berman often reminds me that all Narcissus ended up with was a wet hand.

about an adulterous relationship between two partnered gay men. They agree on a kidnapping scene, and soon the titular scruff-cub, a hirsute young redneck bottom, handcuffed and tape-gagged, is being led into the top's house for several days of bondage, rough treatment, and passionate adoration. At the reception following the reading, as I'm signing books, a grinning Tripp strolls up to me and whispers, "I wanna be Scruff-Cub." I cock an eyebrow. "That can be arranged," I say, imagining him bound and moaning beneath me.

At the closing reception, I get buzzed on a series of very strong Cape Codders that Tripp keeps mixing for me. John and I have a fancy dinner at Galatoire's, then return to the hotel, eager to greet our guest. As promised, Tripp shows up as soon as his shift is over. We all get naked fast. God, he's so luscious, his chest and belly so hairy and beefy, his butt so firm and sweet. I eat his ass and lengthily finger-fuck him. We share kissing and tit-sucking and cock-sucking for a good hour before achieving sticky finales.

Tripp sleeps between us all night, cuddling hungrily. In the morning, we wake early and start up again. As soon as we're done, Tripp discovers twelve peevish messages from his partner on his phone and decides that heading home immediately is a wise idea. We see him off and then begin packing for our flight home. This has been the most sex-soaked SAS ever, and I'm damned grateful. I'll be turning fifty-one in a couple of months. I know well that erotic outlets are likely to dwindle precipitously as I age further.

The very next month, Tripp, traveling for business, meets John and me in a motel room in Hendersonville, North Carolina. This time I get to pull out the leather gear, since Tripp has made clear via e-mail that he wants to try a bondage scene. We all drink a little German wine before getting into it. I tie Tripp's hands behind him, rope up his chest and biceps, and strap a Wiffle-ball gag in his mouth while John takes photo after photo on his iPhone. Just as I expected, the cub looks downright glorious trussed up. John and I take turns fucking him, then cuddle with him a while before pounding his eager butt yet again. Tripp leaves, flushed, sore, and satisfied.

The next May, John and I have just entered the lobby of the Hotel Monteleone for a drink at the Carousel Bar when we hear Tripp shouting our names. He's looking better than ever, with a full black beard and a black button-down shirt. Instead of drinking at the Carousel, which is insanely crowded, we grab gin and tonics from a Bourbon Street bar and carry them up to our room in the Royal Sonesta, the very room where the three of us made love a year ago.

We sit out on the balcony, enjoying the spring breezes, listening to a carillon, sipping drinks and catching up. When John steps into the room to take a business call, I join Tripp on the couch. I open his shirt, play with the hair on his chest, and fool with his nipple ring. We kiss and snuggle a little, but when I start working his hard-on through his shorts, he pulls back and says, "Hey, uh, Will's made me promise not to mess around with y'all unless he's there. I hope you understand."

I do. I'm disappointed, but I'm not surprised. Husbands of hot men are bound to get anxious. Tripp's not the first partnered man I've played with, and hopefully he won't be the last. I'm a poacher, I know. I have no rights in this context. After another bout of necking and fondling, afraid he'll do something he'll regret, Tripp heads home.

The next night, John and I have a polite, slightly awkward dinner with Tripp and Will at Feelings, stop by their cozy apartment so they can change into their leathers, then have a few beers at the Phoenix, the leather/bear bar in the Marigny. One of the other SAS authors expresses interest in a three-way, so we hug Will and Tripp goodbye and take a taxi back to our room with said author. As often occurs in New Orleans, where I tend to down Sazeracs, gin and tonics, mint juleps, Hurricanes, absinthe, and red wine in swilling abundance, I have had far too much alcohol to do more than watch. One of the greatest inconveniences of aging: the dreaded "whiskey dick." (Cf. *Pitiable old man*, as stated above.)

Less than a month later, mid-June of 2011, back home in Virginia, I'm cussing impatiently while trying to peel the shells off hard-boiled eggs and John's mixing martinis for our daily cocktail hour-or-two when his open laptop hiccups on the counter. John reads the message and gasps. "It's from Will. A note on Facebook. Tripp's dead!"

Neither of us can believe it. A sudden heart attack, only thirty years old. We carry our drinks into the living room, take a few sips, and stare out the windows into the late spring green. The windows are streaked with rain, and in the flowerbeds before the house, frowsy spirea and hydrangea are blooming. In Pulaski, Virginia, a hummingbird hovers over a clump of blood-red bee balm, sipping thirstily. In New Orleans, Louisiana, a beautiful body I once made love to is lying stiff and cold on a slab.

John starts to cry. I hold him, dry-eyed. I'm far too numb to cry. This is too great a shock, too unbelievable. Weeping is something I rarely allow myself in front of witnesses. I have attended several deathbeds—my grandmother's in 1987 and my mother's in 1998—fighting back tears as would any man brought up as I was on the stern, scruffy mythos of mountain masculinity. If I shatter, who will comfort kin? Who will hold the world steady and whole?

Later that summer, I'm driving my rusty pickup truck down a rural back road in southwest Virginia, enjoying the green on the mountains and the local country music station, when Justin Moore starts singing "If Heaven Wasn't So Far Away," a song I've never heard before. Out of the blue, I think of Tripp. The deaths of elderly family members, I realize, were more about losing the persons loved within than losing the bodies loved without. Their bodies, for me, were simply vehicles for the selves inside. Tripp's death is different. I prized his sweet body as much as his sweet soul. His flesh was part of what I cherished, and so the loss seems doubled. I miss more than his humor or kindness. I miss his kisses, his brown eyes, his sweaty hugs, his furry submission. And if I'm feeling this much loss, the pain that his partner Will's enduring is incomprehensible.

"Losing them wouldn't be so hard to take, / If heaven wasn't so far away," Justin Moore sings. I pull over to the side of the road, beside a bank of burgeoning kudzu, cock my baseball cap over my face, and cry. When the song ends, I dry my eyes, take a long breath, and head on down the road toward home.

Today, mid-May of 2015, writing this essay, I face that sadness head on. I click on the folder of e-photos John took during our three-way bondage fest in North Carolina, images I haven't been able to bring myself to look at since Tripp died. I study his face and the details of his body. The images still arouse me. I still can't believe such a sweet, sexy young man is gone. I regret my mannerly restraint on that Royal Sonesta balcony four years ago. I wish I'd ignored Tripp's request that we restrict ourselves to cuddling. I wish I'd remembered Robert Herrick's advice, "Gather ye rosebuds while ye may." I wish I'd made Tripp suck my cock. I wish I'd tied his hands behind his back and strapped a ball-gag in his mouth—the way we both liked it—bent him over the parapet, and fucked him hard from behind while his drool dripped like rain on the flagstones below. Finished, I wish we'd cuddled and kissed in that big bed for hours, stroking each other's nipples and cocks and beards. That's a day I wish I'd seized.

VIII. Galatoire's, 2015

IT'S BECOME A tradition, having a fine meal at Galatoire's on Sunday night after Saints and Sinners has come to an end. The blazer I'm wearing is a few sizes bigger than the one I wore here during my first visit to this city in 1996, and I still resent dressing up, much preferring camo shorts and a muscle shirt, and John has had to remind me yet again how to tie a tie, but the good food is worth the discomfort. We start with a couple rounds of Sazeracs, then move on to our favorite appetizer, oysters en brochette, then some expensive red wine, crabmeat Sardou, seafood-stuffed eggplant, broccoli with Hollandaise, soufflé potatoes, and finally bread pudding with banana sauce. New Orleans is supposed to be about sensual pleasures—food, drink, and sex—and we bears are consummate hedonists.

Stuffed and ready to shed our dress clothes, we return to our room at the Hotel Monteleone. We have a plane to catch in the morning, so we hit the sack early. I wake around 3 am to use the bathroom, then lie back in bed, stare up into the darkness, and think about the many sojourns I've spent in this city. This year was without erotic extramarital incident, and I'm fine with that. At fifty-five, my beard's almost entirely gray, and the muscles I keep up in my home gym are more than matched by the gourmand's gut I bear. I really don't expect men to want me any longer. A regrettable but inevitable truth. Everyone's time is running out, and I'm pretty sure my heyday's behind me.

Still, I'm remembering Frodo, and Erik, and Tripp, the hot men whose favors I've savored here. I'm remembering all the famous authors I've met at SAS: Dorothy Allison, Patricia Nell Warren, Felice Picano, Andrew Holleran, Jewelle Gomez, and more. I'm remembering regular festival attendees I'm so pleased to see every spring. Paul J. Willis, who created the entire festival and miraculously manages to organize it every year with the aid of Amie M. Evans, the exquisitely dressed New England femme I have such a crush on. Savagely witty Greg Herren, a force to be reckoned with on literary panels. Jameson Currier, publisher of Chelsea Station Editions, thoughtful and funny and generous, who's published several of my essays and poems in his handsome magazine. 'Nathan Burgoine, adorable otter and fine writer from Ottawa. Sweet men from Maine, Sven and Nate Davisson. The Terrible Triad—Dale Chase, Bill Holden, and Jerry L. Wheeler—who've been so supportive of my writing. Michele Karlsberg, that handsome butch publicist from Staten Island. Kathleen Bradean and D. L. King, erotica vixens extraordinaire. Fay Jacobs, priceless Rehoboth Beach humorist.

I'm also remembering two specific SAS events. One was a panel I spoke on in 2014, "Writing Alone, Growing Together, Creating Your Own Writing Community." An audience member asked the panelists what sort of support systems we as queer writers had found. "This is it," I replied. "Back home in the mountains of Appalachia, I feel very isolated, ignored, and unappreciated as a queer writer, even at a university the size of Virginia Tech. Saints and Sinners is really the only place I feel accepted and welcomed, albeit for only four days a year."

Admitting that painful truth seemed to highlight or underscore it for me. *Only four days a year? Shit, that's rough!* I thought, only seconds after saying it. Since I spoke on that panel, a year of intense work conflicts and disappointments has left me feeling more alienated than ever. Retirement can't come soon enough.

The other SAS event I'm pondering was a walking tour of the French Quarter. Led by Frank Perez, it focused on queer history in New Orleans, including gay carnival, Southern Decadence, and the notorious UpStairs Lounge fire. I was especially pleased when Perez pointed out buildings in which Tennessee Williams had lived. During my senior year in college, I read nearly every Williams play I could find, including his autobiographical *Vieux Carré*, set in the Quarter. Long before Williams was born, Perez pointed out, poet Walt Whitman had also found refuge here, perhaps even achieving a gay awakening. Whitman wrote "Once I Pass'd Through a Populous City" about New Orleans, saying, "Yet now of all that city I remember only a man I casually met there who detain'd me for love of me," though he eventually censored himself, changing the man to a woman.

Perez's tour provided evidence of a poignant fact: generations of queer people, of queer authors, have found haven and community in this city. Walt Whitman and Tennessee Williams were two of them. I am, luckily, another. Today I spent with wonderful writers from the U.S.A., Europe, Canada, and Australia, talking about creating and publishing queer literature, and now I'm lying beside my husband in the very hotel in which Tennessee Williams used to stay. Thanks to Saints and Sinners, I've become part of that long heritage of authors past and present, authors that the city of New Orleans has nurtured and nourished. It's a privilege to be part of such a tradition.

fellow country boys giving themselves over to me in dream, in the beds of pickup trucks and in the haylofts and horse stalls of barns and in the thick of summer woods.

country boy

AT AGE FIFTY-NINE, I STILL CALL myself a country boy. Why is that? What does that mean?

I'm country because I grew up in Summers County, West Virginia, where my father grew up before me. I spent my youth walking the meadows and woods beside him and helping him plant, tend, and harvest his vegetable gardens.

I'm country because I learned as a child important lessons about avoiding outdoor dangers: how to recognize poison ivy from yards away; how to step carefully over a fallen log, checking first to see if a snake might be curled on the other side; how to recognize the differences between poisonous and nonpoisonous snakes. When I was a boy, my father killed a copperhead by the Greenbrier River in Caldwell, West Virginia, and pried its mouth open with a stick to show me its hypodermic fangs. When I was a boy, he caught a black snake beneath my great-aunt's porch, and she demanded that he kill it, and I cried and begged him not to, and he let me touch it—not slimy at all—before he carried it out to a wild strawberry patch in the woods and let it go.

I'm country because my father

taught me to recognize the call of the red-winged blackbird, nesting in cattails around our farm pond. He taught me how to identify nuthatches and pileated woodpeckers, chickadees and snowbirds and the flute-like call of the wood thrush, closest cousin to the nightingale we have.

I'm country because I learned how to split cross-sections of oak and red maple with maul and wedge, how to split smaller sections into stove-lengths with an axe. I learned how to start a hearth-fire with kindling and feed it with carefully placed, seasoned wood. I learned how to tap maple trees, make spiles out of elderberry twigs, collect the sugar water in zinc buckets, gather those buckets, simmer sugar water down to maple syrup, rich and sweet on buckwheat cakes. I learned how to hoist bale after bale of July hay and how to stack them in the barn loft, so they would air out, not mold, fester, rot hot, and burn.

I'm country because of all the strawberries I've picked, the lamb's quarters and raceweed I've pulled from garden earth, the tomatoes I've suckered and corn I've hoed and potato beetles I've crushed. I'm country because of the peas I've shelled and green beans I've strung and potatoes I've dug and corn I've husked. I'm country because of the many down-home Southern Appalachian meals I've made for friends and kin: brown beans with chowchow and cornbread, wilted lettuce, creecy greens, half-runners and collards with ham hock, biscuits with sausage gravy, country ham with redeye gravy, blackberry cobblers, apple crisps, custard and buttermilk and sweet potato pies.

I'm country because of the Nature Interpretation classes I took during my undergrad days at West Virginia University: dendrology and ornithology, aquatic seed plants, mammalogy, geology, and forest zoology. I know the bark of the river birch and sycamore, the bud scars of the black walnut, the samaras of the box elder, the buds of the pawpaw and the cucumber tree, the flowers of the witch hazel and the chicory, the flight of the flicker, the calls of the vireo and screech owl, the colors of the golden orb-weaver and the ring-necked snake, the flickers of mica in mountain streams and the dull gleam of coal along interstate roadside cuts.

I'm country because of the men I've yearned for and the men I've loved, musky men with hairy bodies and full beards, men in flannel shirts and camo pants, cowboy boots and work boots, cowboy hats and baseball caps, men with big arms and hard chests, soft skin and tattoos, fellow country boys giving themselves over to me in dream, in the beds of pickup trucks and in the haylofts and horse stalls of barns and in the thick of summer woods, all our shared sweat and saliva and semen offered up to the land we love, to the Goddess of the Garden and the God of the Greenwood.

true defeat, complete defeat,

is to be silenced.

offensive hillbilly queer

Recently, I was invited to speak to a local book club here in Pulaski County, Virginia. All of the ladies in attendance appeared interested; several responded enthusiastically; many said they would buy the book, for themselves or for relatives.

It was a pleasant experience—we authors do love an audience—though one aspect of the afternoon had me mildly off balance. I'd been asked to discuss not my own publications but my father's. I doubt that any of my books would have appealed to that audience of polite, well-dressed, elderly ladies living in the mountains of southwest Virginia. Daddy's book did appeal, as I knew it would.

Perry Mann's *Mann and Nature: A Collection of Essays* contains thirty personal essays that focus on topics close to my own heart: country living, farming, Appalachian self-reliance, environmentalism, mountain landscapes, and the shifting beauties of the seasons. The collection has found favor with a wide range of folks. Daddy, as of this writing, is ninety-one years old, has always wanted to publish a book, and since its release, has proudly reported to me a slew of fan letters, hard-copy and e-mailed, and many an invitation to read at bookstores in our region. He has, in other words, achieved a modicum of what I never have: a mainstream audience.

I am honestly pleased at the positive reception of his book, at the same time that I'm admittedly envious. I'm as voracious as any writer for critical attention and ego-food, yet I have gotten little of both. (Or not enough: to a narcissist, no amount of affirmation is ever sufficient.) My work has been, to a great extent, neglected, passed over, and ignored, or so it feels to me. As a result, my bitterness is considerable, my envy of more successful authors acidic and intense.

Only the good Southern manners my mother bred in me allow me to hide these unattractive resentments on a day-to-day basis. That, and a few cautionary examples: other writers I've met who have expressed the same snarling envy. I've seen how ugly such behavior is, and so I refuse to reveal my bile in public. I admit to such feelings in this essay only because, for me, writing is about honesty, no matter how uncomfortable or unseemly.

It is that very honesty that has limited my audience. I am aware of that. Hoist with my own petard, that irresistible Shakespearean phrase. This awareness does not reduce my bitterness a whit.

My husband, understandably weary of my incessant complaints, often points to the controversial nature of what I publish and politely suggests that I've chosen my path and so should gracefully accept the consequences. Well, no! At the same time that I wouldn't do anything differently, given the chance, I also reserve the right to snarl. Simply put, articulating my welling acrimony makes me feel better. I'd rather spit acid than swallow it.

WHAT'S CONSIDERED CONTROVERSIAL and what's considered acceptable depend on context. Had I been born somewhere other than Southern Appalachia, or if I had left my native region and made a life in some far-off liberal city, things might have been different. As it is, I was born in Clifton Forge, Virginia, and grew up in Covington, Virginia, and Hinton, West Virginia, both small mountain towns. I attended West Virginia University for undergraduate and graduate degrees, then taught there briefly. For the last twenty-three years, I've taught at Virginia Tech, living in both Blacksburg, a liberal university town, and Pulaski, Virginia, another small mountain town. I have stubbornly remained in a region in which I feel alternately anomalous and pretty much at home.

Today, as I contemplate my publications, it seems as if I've written nothing *but* the controversial. True, there are a few innocuous poems about Appalachian food and family ties, which should be palatable to mainstream folks. Other than that, almost everything I write is likely to offend someone somewhere. My preferred topics are those that my people—Southerners and Appalachians—would surely regard as inappropriate, even "vulgar," a word my genteel mother used with matchless acerbity. The more devout would call my books perverse and satanic; at least one Amazon reviewer has used the word "vile."

And what are those topics? Like most writers, I am drawn to the problematic, to sources of tension and conflict. The first in the list is homosexuality.

With the help of lesbian friends, I realized I was gay when I was sixteen. Being gay in America is still difficult. Being gay in a small town in southern West Virginia in the 1970s was especially challenging. I've dealt with confusion, fear, anger, shame, desire, and hope of varying intensities ever since. During my WVU undergrad days, I began to explore the gay community, share erotic experiences with other men, and write poetry making sense of my (frequently unreciprocated) desires. To my pleasure, gay literary journals began accepting some of these pieces for publication in the early 1980s.

During my graduate-school days in Morgantown, I wrote a collection of love poems as my creative thesis. One batch was inspired by a promiscuous bartender, and another by a charming narcissist who compulsively bounced checks, neither of whom was particularly interested in me after the first few nights together. That didn't matter. I was young, ardent, and hungry as hell for sex and romance. Their indifference and their good looks enflamed me, inspiring me to write a plethora of lovesick poems.

As if mere homosexuality weren't sufficiently taboo for whatever ornery muse goads me to write what I do, when I moved to Blacksburg to start a new job at Virginia Tech in 1989, it wasn't long before I was groin-deep in other controversial and forbidden topics: BDSM and adultery. Bondage had fascinated me since childhood—so many roped-up superheroes in comic books and hog-tied cowboys in Westerns. I'd begun to identify with the leather community as early as my sophomore year in college, when I read Patricia Nell Warren's novel *The Beauty Queen* and related powerfully to a butch gay couple that shared loving but sadomasochistic sex. I managed some dabbling with a few willing partners, serving as top for Steve, bottom for Jim.

Then I met The Mythical Thomas at Virginia Tech and fell passionately and catastrophically in love. I've already written about him elsewhere: our kinky sex-play, our secretive meetings behind his partner's back. He was the submissive muscle-cub of my dreams, and the aftermath of our affair left me in agony. I've never gotten over it. That's good, I guess. Wounds can be an inexhaustible source of creative energy. My first book of poetry, *Bones Washed with Wine*, was entirely inspired by my feelings for him, and much of my second collection, *On the Tongue*, was as well. Both volumes are quite frank about the emotional turmoil and ambivalence of adultery and the deliciously kinky sex we shared. Such verse has a long tradition: the European troubadours often wrote of their longings for other men's wives.

No, the elegant book-club ladies—or the mainstream audience I'm using them to represent—would not find such poetry appealing, I fear. Nor would they relish my other works, most of which explore gay sexuality and fetish to some extent. There are my many erotic short stories in assorted anthologies, several of them collected in *A History of Barbed Wire*, and my vampire-themed volume, *Desire and Devour: Stories of Blood and Sweat;* my intense kidnapping thriller, *Fog: A Novel of Desire and Reprisal;* my violent, homoerotic Civil War novels, *Purgatory* and *Salvation;* and my novella, *Camp Allegheny,* included in *History's Passion: Stories of Sex Before Stonewall*. There's surely enough candid queer material in *Edge: Travels of an Appalachian Leather Bear* and *Binding the God: Ursine Essays from the Mountain South,* my two essay collections, to put them off. *Loving Mountains, Loving Men* is tamer, fairly free of explicit Eros, if readers can tolerate discussions of the conflicts between my gay and Appalachian identities. But even *Ash: Poems from Norse Mythology* has a few gay love poems, as well as "Valhalla Revised," which details enthusiastic man-on-man fucking in a queered version of the Norse afterlife.

My more recent poems, only a handful of which have appeared in literary magazines, tend toward two topics, neither of which is likely to garner me many mainstream fans: (1) frustrated middle-aged lust for men much younger than myself, and (2) the Confederate experience in the Civil War.

"There's no fool like an old fool," my mother used to sigh, referring to my father's wandering eye. I say that to myself sometimes, as I quietly admire assorted young men half my age. Yes, I know: how banal, what a cliché, a middle-aged man yearning after much younger flesh. No one would guess what vigorous fantasies I entertain behind my polite professional façade, my smiling equipoise. Being a university teacher doesn't help: virile scenery everywhere. Neither does living in Pulaski, with its plentiful array of hot country boys/scruffy mountain men: younger versions of myself, exactly the type I'm most attracted to.

Of course, I would never approach a student with seduction in mind. The power inequality makes that unethical, and the potential consequences to my professional life might be disastrous. (These concerns, needless to say, have not always deterred other middle-aged men in my position, most of them straight.) At least one of my essays in *Edge,* "Drambuie," deals with this kind of socially forbidden desire—a deep erotic appreciation I felt for a student on Study Abroad over twenty years ago. Almost all of my new poems in this vein are about lust and Eros in suspension, frustrated, never acted upon. "The Old Lecher Does Not Seduce an Overnight Guest" is an illustrative title. I have enough of these poems for a meaty volume. I'd like to title the book *Boys I Can't Fuck,* but I suspect I'll go with the milder *Boys I Can't Keep.* If I can't ravish them, I can, by God, write poems about them. That volcanic lust has to have some outlet.

Then there are the few poems about successful encounters with younger men who, thank all the god/desses of concupiscence, appreciate older men, a daddy bear in my case. These poems not only fly in the face of those who insist on monogamy—as I do not—but are likely to disgust people who find the concept of sex over thirty repulsive. More verboten and unsavory verse!

Most of the poetry I've produced over the last four years has been based on the same research that spawned the Civil War fiction mentioned above. I'm not African American and I'm not a Yankee, so I don't write about the black or northern experience of that war. My paternal grandmother's maternal grandfather was Isaac Green Carden, a Confederate soldier. I myself grew up around Confederate monuments, in both Covington and Hinton. Therefore, I write with clear Southern sympathies, though often from a gay perspective. My work "queers" the war, so to speak.

Though the ladies' club members, most of them Southern-born, might appreciate some of these poems, as would many denizens of Covington, Hinton, and Pulaski, I can assure you that the faculty and students at Virginia Tech do not. (The staff is another matter: most of them are locals.) The majority of people living in Blacksburg and connected with the university are not native Southerners. To them, my fondness for the Stars and Bars and "Dixie," my admiration for Robert E. Lee, Stonewall Jackson, Turner Ashby, and Jeb Stuart, are downright incomprehensible. During my tenure bid, at least one colleague—or so it was furtively reported to me—was disturbed by "Unreconstructed Queer," my essay about the Confederate flag. Those in my department who might know of my work—and very few do, from what I can tell—probably assume that I'm a redneck, a hillbilly, poor white trash who's managed to infiltrate the ivory tower. If they don't know I have black in-laws and a biracial nephew, they might also assume that I'm a raving racist. My bushy beard, faded denims, cowboy boots, tattoos, rusty pickup truck, and enthusiasm for country music don't help.

So, THE OPENLY queer and often erotic elements in my work are likely to offend lots of Southerners/Appalachians/conservative country folk, and my sympathy for white Southern citizens and Rebel soldiers in the destructive War between the States is likely to offend city folks/liberals. What audience is left?

Not a lot. I've managed to develop a small literary reputation in both Appalachian literature and queer publishing, and I'm thankful for that. Lethe Press has been particularly supportive: they've reprinted two of my books and published several more. But I have a strong suspicion that I'd have a far larger audience if I weren't compulsively drawn to such contentious topics. Once in a while, an enthusiastic reader e-mails me, and that means a great deal. I cherish those messages as evidence that my work does indeed reach the like-minded. Still, I get few invitations to give readings, and my books receive few reviews.

Edge, my first book of prose, received a handful of reviews. In one published in *Journal of Appalachian Studies*, the writer described me as "contrarian." I like that word. He was right. When I was younger, I used to rejoice in my openly expressed difference: it made me feel special, unique, courageous. Lately, though, I'm tired of always being in a minority, tired of being the one to talk honestly about forbidden topics that most people don't want to hear about. It's demoralizing and isolating. It makes for regular conflict, both internal and external, and, after several decades, that can be exhausting.

The outright attacks have been the most unpleasant. During my first semester as an untenured professor, an anonymous homophobe e-mailed all the presidents of Virginia Tech's alumni chapters railing about my publications. After *Loving Mountains, Loving Men* appeared, another anonymous e-mail told me to "Get medical help!" One editor, when his literary journal published an essay of mine detailing my semi-tongue-in-cheek lust for country music singer Tim McGraw, spent a full paragraph in his introduction to the issue explaining why he would not have accepted the piece, had he been the nonfiction editor. I was mortified, then furious, then sneeringly amused.

MY FATHER ALWAYS encouraged me to be a nonconformist, to ignore that suffocating small-town constriction, "What will people *think*?!" My mother was just the opposite: she was very concerned about reputation and others' opinions. That difference made their marriage difficult, and I contain their conflicting voices inside my head. When I write about provocative topics, my frank defiance of convention is always mixed with self-doubt and uncertainty; I vacillate between extremes of pride and shame. At the same time that I think my writing should be as honest as it possibly can (my father's influence), I dislike giving offense (my mother's influence). My self seems split, like a fallen oak trunk's axe-cleft heartwood. This painful ambivalence will, I fear, never be resolved.

Today, I'm weary and sad. Writing this essay has been clarifying but disheartening. Tomorrow, most likely, my brain chemistry will shift, and I'll feel better. One thing's certain: I'll keep writing what I feel driven to write, however unsavory, offensive, and forbidden the topics might be. Not to do so would be cowardice.

We Civil War buffs are always thinking in terms of victory and defeat. Often, I feel defeated, especially when I remember the high hopes of literary fame and prestige I once entertained and compare them to my present career. In order to continue, however, I must remind myself that true defeat, complete defeat, is to be silenced, to fall silent. I feel confident, despite my despairs, doubts, and dissatisfactions, that I will not be silenced by anything short of incapacitating illness or death. When I think of truth-tellers of the past—men and women who suffered and died in terrible ways—I contemplate my comfortable existence as a professor, feel thankful to have a home amid the beauty of my native mountains, and remind myself that there are far worse fates than literary obscurity.

she's one of those women who, despite my devotion to male beauty, male deities, and male energies, remind me of how splendid and multifaceted female power and female caring can be.

amy

"You're a poet. Who are your muses?" a friend asked me recently.

My muses have always been male. For me, the word "muse," thanks to my early readings of Robert Graves' *The White Goddess*, means a human being inhabited by a spiritual presence that inspires in an artist longing, love, and the creative impulse. Graves had in mind a goddess inhabiting a female muse who inspires a heterosexual man—he consigns male muses and homosexuality to the realm of "morbid pathology"—but I've blithely ignored that heterosexist bias. Other books I savored in college—Ian Young's anthologies *The Male Muse* (1973) and *The Son of the Male Muse* (1983), and May Sarton's lesbian novel *Mrs. Stephens Hears the Mermaids Singing* (1965)—all allowed me to "queer" the concept of the muse.

My spiritual path, Wicca, encourages me to see the divine as immanent, god and goddess inherent in all human beings, while homosexual desire encourages me to see the bewitching presence of the god flickering inside the erotic power of mortal men. Thus, my own set of muses have been men who, for me, for a time, embodied

Eros, Pan, Apollo, and the Horned God. I wanted them, pursued them, briefly possessed them, revered the beauty and divinity they distilled, then, losing them, wrote lovelorn poems as a way of coping with their loss.

My heroes have been as male as my muses. Most of the historical figures I venerate are men. A few notables would be Confederate soldiers like Robert E. Lee, Stonewall Jackson, Jeb Stuart, and Turner Ashby. (Only the ignorant would equate this regional pride with racism, I feel compelled to add.) More contemporary would be the many celebrities who serve as erotic icons for me, actors and country-music singers I'd love to spend a BDSM-drenched weekend with. Think Gerard Butler, Colin Farrell, Tim McGraw, Jason Aldean, Jason Momoa, et al.

I've never understood the fascination with "divas" that so many gay men share. Joni Mitchell and Sylvia Plath would be as close as I get: creative women whose work I admire, who've been role models of sorts. Female celebrities like Cher, Reba McIntire, Dolly Parton? All fine ladies whose music I enjoy, but nothing to wax obsessive about. Men have my full attention (except for the few women who stoke up my inner bisexual with their beauty: Jessica Lange, Jane Seymour, Lucy Lawless, and Nigella Lawson).

"You're a dyed-in-the-wool Southerner. Surely you have a favorite *female* icon from the South?" the same friend asked me. Again, I'm at a bit of a loss. Belle Boyd, Confederate spy? I don't have time for the research. Paula Deen, butter-loving cook? She's already overexposed.

One woman comes to mind. My sister Amy is an excellent embodiment of that mix of contemporary and traditional that makes the New South. She's as close to a Southern heroine as I can get. Few folks outside of Summers County, West Virginia, know her, but she's one of those women who, despite my devotion to male beauty, male deities, and male energies, remind me of how splendid and multifaceted female power and female caring can be.

I DIDN'T ALWAYS find her such a gift to the world. Though I was thrilled to receive a baby sister—the family story goes that I danced around the room, a four-year-old dervish, when my father called from the hospital with the news—soon enough the sibling rivalry began, first in Covington, Virginia, my mother's hometown, then in the environs of Hinton, West Virginia, my father's native ground, where we moved when I was around eight. My family is like many: grandmothers and mothers dote on sons, and grandfathers and fathers dote on daughters. I reveled in female attentions—my mother cherished me, and my paternal grandmother, Nanny, adored me more than anyone has before or since. Still, my father was the great power in our family. Everything revolved around him, his interests, needs, and enthusiasms. I suppose I might have been the apple of his eye till he brought Amy home (it's hard to remember much about my first four years), but once she arrived, his attentions shifted to her almost entirely. Or at least that's how it felt.

No amount of female loving could make up for the removal of my father's focus. Amy was his "little doll-baby." He punished me for minor infractions. She, on the other hand, could get away with anything. She put sugar in his lawnmower's gas tank; she poured water in his boots. Sometimes I was blamed for such wickedness and punished with a doubled-over belt. Sometimes, if she were found guilty, she had only to cry, and Daddy would hug and console her.

This inequity maddened me. In fact, I vaguely recall keeping a journal of such unfair events—budding writer that I was—so that I might report them to my ever-sympathetic grandmother. My father seemed infinitely more interested in my sister and in himself than in anything I might do. To this day, I think my hunger for male attention is rooted as much in this emotional history as in my homosexuality. I am fairly sure that my literary ambitions and lust for recognition have very much to do with trying to prove to my father and, by extension, to the world, that I am remarkable, magnificently talented, worth making a fuss over, etc. No attention, no acclaim is ever enough. Only my mother's coaching in good

Southern manners keeps my narcissism from being more ravingly apparent than it is.

Such family tensions and resentments are rarely clear in photographs. A few years back, Amy and I discovered an old cache of black and white photos my parents took of us as children at Touchstone. (Touchstone was the solid structure of knotty pine my father built by hand and ran as a popular roadside diner before transforming it into a residence in which my family lived for our first five years in West Virginia.) In one photo, Amy and I are sitting on a fallen elm by the Greenbrier River. Since my father was always trying to save money, he often dressed us in hand-me-downs and cut our hair at home. Thus, we have on baggy, mismatched (well, honestly? Hideous!) clothes—plaids, paisley, polyester— and are wearing bowl-cuts. Amy's tow-headed and, despite the aforementioned fashion handicaps, adorable; I'm awkward, long-limbed, with black nerd glasses. Our heads seem oblong, like aliens'. We look like urchins. I don't think any orphanage would have had us. "The Children from Mars," we dubbed our past selves, flipping through the pictures and laughing till our sides ached.

Those children in the photos were country kids, though we didn't know it at the time, since Appalachian rural and small-town life was all we knew. We helped my father with his innumerable chores around the farm, weeding gardens, digging potatoes, picking green beans, gathering firewood, carrying zinc buckets of "sugar water" to the great vat where it was boiled down to make maple syrup, feeding the pigs, and herding cattle (a task Amy found frightening, small as she was). We played on the shale pile—a rocky road-cut topped by exposed tree roots, a fine place to "pretend like" we were Tarzan or assorted comic-book superheroes. Once Amy fell and bloodied her knee on the sharp shale. I carried her up the road to Nanny's—perhaps my first expression of a protective instinct for friends and kin that I've since developed in spades.

One spring, we picked and sold so many damned strawberries that Amy and I were able to ride the Greyhound with Nanny to

Daytona Beach, where my father's sister Doris lived. It was our first big journey into the outside world and our first sight of the ocean. The trip stimulated me but made Amy anxious. As I recall, whenever the bus stopped for a meal break, all Amy would order was stewed prunes, since they could be eaten fast. She was terrified that the bus would leave without us.

This anxiety highlighted a difference between us that was to grow more obvious, one that paralleled a glaring and inconvenient disparity between our parents. My father—an intellectual, nonconformist, and iconoclast—has always had a vigorous detestation of cities and has had next to no use for the world beyond the borders of West Virginia in general and Summers County in particular. Since his preferences were all-important, we almost never traveled. (The concept of "family vacation" seems oddly foreign to me even now.) My mother, on the other hand—much more "normal," much more eager to fit in—always had a hunger, usually unconsummated, for the larger world. One of the many regrets of my life is that she died before I became financially comfortable enough to treat her to the travel she dreamed of.

My father's suspicion of—even contempt for—the outside world is common to small-town and rural folks, I think. I have a strong streak of it myself; travel is very stressful for me. The presence of strangers and noise and, most especially, everything I can't control makes me wary, irascible, and, well, fearful. Nevertheless, I've taken after my mother when it comes to "Out There" far more than Amy has. Though I don't want to remain in any city long, I enjoy brief visits, and travel is one of the few things I'll spend money on. I've seen most of the American cities that interest me, and I've been to Europe many times. But we Appalachians are known for our devotion to the home-place, and Amy illustrates this better than anyone I've known. Other than her college years and infrequent vacations, she's almost never left Summers County. She seems entirely content there, and sometimes I envy that. My sister's always seemed more easily satisfied and far less in need of variety than her perpetually restless, tormented, and discontented brother.

Amy's heterosexuality made Summers County far more palatable to her and made her far more palatable to Summers County. Another major difference between us cropped up when I was sixteen, when I made close lesbian friends and discovered what my confused interest in certain boys meant. Amy was the first family member I came out to. She was, I think, nonplussed for only about twenty-four hours before we started comparing notes on the "hunks" we craved: Billy B., Billy G., Robbie, etc. This shared secret and the co-conspiracy it engendered brought us closer. Both of us were convinced that knowledge of my homosexuality would horrify my father and downright kill my mother.

Our high-school years couldn't have been different. I was a shy, socially awkward bookworm, with a pudgy body, bouts of acne, shaggy dark hair, stilted manners, and thick glasses. Other than the aforementioned lesbian friends, I was a loner. Amy was shapely, gregarious, and attractive (even briefly a cheerleader), with a slew of friends, parties, and other social activities to keep track of. I envied her. She seemed golden, blithe, and free of the fears, despairs, insecurities, and neuroses that plagued me.

She had her own streak of protectiveness, however. Once, after nerdiness and regular association with a butch/femme lesbian couple had garnered me a reputation as queer, a little bully, in Amy's presence, inadvisably called me a faggot. She started screaming "Fuck you!" at the kid till he fled, then followed him down the hall of the high school, continuing to assault his ears with obscenities. I'm still grateful.

One irony of our shared youth was her frequent success at courting the aforementioned Hinton "hunks" I frustratedly hankered after. In high school, she briefly dated Robbie, Keith, Steve, Billy B., and Randy. Once, in the Summers County Library, we encountered Randy together. She and he flirted, while I rounded a shelf so I could ogle him through a gap in the books. At one point, as he scratched his torso, a shirt button came undone, giving me an ample glimpse of his smooth brown chest. Amy confessed to me later that she was half-tempted to say, "You'd better button up fast. My brother gets excited easily." As blasé as she was about the erotic, we often joked that I'd gotten my sex drive and hers too. This fact was to make my life often complex and miserable, hers uncomplicated and relatively content. I envy her that, as well as her dates with all those small-town studs.

As popular as she was with boys, she took no disrespect from them. Her size helped; she was five foot nine and solidly built. Not fat or even plump, mind you; just not a "celery-eater," as we both contemptuously referred to fashionably emaciated girls. Once a potty-mouthed brat, passing Amy in the high-school halls, said, with unbelievable effrontery, "You look like you have a nice juicy cavity. Let me enter." She seized him by the shirt collar, threw him up against the lockers with a bang, and shook him till his teeth rattled. That take-no-shit warrior spirit that I've seen in so many of my lesbian friends is something I mightily admire in my sister. Often my inveterate politeness hampers that impulse in myself, but Amy has always been less tentative on such occasions.

I was so lonely, so starved for a meaningful relationship or even simpatico sex for so much of my youth, while she enjoyed flirtations and dates that, remembering those years, I tend to simplify, to exaggerate my own suffering and to forget her sorrows. There was a boy in high school she was very fond of, even involved with to some extent. One foggy night, a car accident occurred along the Bluestone Reservoir. The boy was permanently paralyzed from the neck down. My guess is he still haunts her. She lost several friends—to car accidents and overdoses. Small-town kids are hard-pressed to find entertainment. Sometimes the entertainments found prove fatal.

Despite her losses, she and I continued to embody extremes: she seemed happy, fun-loving, and optimistic, with many a male admirer, while I was over-sexed and perpetually single, struggling with depression and anger. I had yet to make peace with my identities as a country boy, a mountaineer, and a Southerner. Instead, I was hungry as hell to get out of Hinton, to find some kind of gay life at West Virginia University, three and a half hours away, and then move on to a queer-friendly city.

Our college years only emphasized our differences. I took to university life and Morgantown's urban diversity with enthusiasm. Amy, like many other Hinton kids, found WVU too big, too intimidating. Homesick, she returned to Hinton every chance she got. While I studied, she and her friends partied, encouraging me to scold her with the Tennessee Williams line, "You're not young at thirty when you've been on a goddamn party since you were fifteen." At one point, she developed a strange rash and had it examined at WVU's Student Health Center. The doctor proclaimed, "This is either Rocky Mountain spotted fever or the tertiary stage of syphilis." Imagine that! It took her a few days to discern that she'd borrowed a friend's medication and developed a violent allergic reaction to the ampicillin. That scare was the last straw, I suppose. She transferred to Concord College in Athens, West Virginia, much closer to home, only a forty-five-minute drive across the county line from Hinton.

It was during her time in Athens that I began seeing the traditions of our family emerge in her. One year, she shared an apartment with a lesbian friend of ours who was a less than apt cook. (Once Amy woke from a nap to discover that Leigh had taped paper bags above and around the stovetop to protect the walls from spaghetti sauce spatter; the recipe, Leigh explained, had said not to cover the sauce.) Amy and I were accustomed to very good and very plentiful Appalachian food at home, so she responded to this less than ideal roommate situation by learning how to cook. I remember visiting her in Athens and being amazed: the dinners she prepared were always delicious. The insouciant, popular partier was following in the steps of my father and Nanny by becoming a top-notch country cook. My little sister, I realized with a start, was an independent adult, one who was taking care of me as my elders had all my life, by providing me with a remarkably flavorful home-cooked meal.

She was becoming a traditional Southern woman in this respect, much to my gourmandish delight. At about the same time, she did something less traditional: she became involved with a black man.

Michael was from Talcott, a little community at the other end of Summers County, home to the legendary folk hero John Henry. His mother, Joyce, was a grand matriarch; he had eleven siblings. My mother, Clara, was horrified. She'd discovered my homosexuality while I was in college and had taken it hard. (Every time I went home, I regaled Mommy with outrageous tales of drag queens and other extreme queers just to remind her that my leather/Levi's look was tame in comparison and that she'd better count her blessings.) But Amy's sin was infinitely worse to a woman who'd been raised in Virginia in the 1920s and 30s. "Nigger lovers and queers, that's what our parents raised," Amy and I used to joke. Our co-conspirator status deepened. Now we both were outside the pale. "Chicks what loves niggers is pigs," we used to chant together, borrowing an illiterate slogan she'd seen on a bathroom wall somewhere.

I liked Michael just fine. He was quiet, polite, and possessed of a dry sense of humor. His family was welcoming and lively, and they provided spreads of food mouthwatering in their quality: homemade rolls, fried chicken, potato salad, deviled eggs, rum cake, and cream pies. Once again I envied Amy—she had the solid relationship I'd yet to find—but I was glad she was content. One evening I got into a horrible shouting match with my mother when she objected to Michael's race. "Do you know how goddamn lonely I am? Be thankful at least one of your children is happy!" I screamed. From our mother, my sister and I might have learned a deep appreciation of Southern manners, but from our father we'd inherited a profound disinterest in what other people might think.

That individualistic defiance was to serve us well. Amy and Michael got next to no public disrespect in Summers County, since my father had been the prosecuting attorney for years and later a prominent lawyer. But when Amy and Michael traveled together outside of Summers County, she'd return with tales of the scornful, hate-filled looks they got, at gas stations, in restaurants. I had no problem equating that hostility with the homophobic jeers my friends and I sometimes heard as we exited gay bars. Some miserable old racists glaring at my little sister? I wanted to kill them, to feed their uncoiled guts to dogs.

    I had a brief sojourn in the big city, decided it was definitely not for me, and came back to the mountains. Amy graduated from Concord, worked as a substitute teacher in Summers County, grew tired of the unmannerly brats, and ran a little restaurant in Hinton, The Upper Crust, which served lunches to local community groups like the Kiwanis and Rotarians. Then one night, despite my father's position of power in the county, Michael ended up in a scuffle with some local cops. Clear racist motivation. That was a turning point, I believe: Amy decided that she needed to be in a better position to protect herself and her own. After a stint as my father's legal secretary, she married Michael and then returned to Morgantown, tolerating the absurd traffic and mall-sprawl long enough to receive a law degree from WVU in May 2002. By then, I'd met my partner John, and one day he and I found ourselves, for the first and probably the last time, in the odd position of shopping for pearls. We bought Amy a strand for her graduation present.

    For years, Daddy, Michael, and I have had to some extent vied for Amy's attentions, but on December 24, 2004, someone new entered the scene who put us all to rout, her son, Michael Ferrell McCormick Mann. As John and I drove to Lewisburg, West Virginia, after the delivery to see Amy and my new nephew, we passed the John Henry statue on the mountain above Talcott. Someone had spray-painted "Nigger" across the statue's chest. My first reaction was fear for my new kin's future, but then I thought of Amy: her protectiveness, her position in Hinton. I gave a grim chuckle. "Well, one thing's for sure," I drawled, "long as that boy stays in Summers County, no one's gonna fuck with him."

    I'm not much on children. To use the Misfit's line from Flannery O'Connor's "A Good Man is Hard to Find," "[c]hildren make me nervous." Especially noisy ones and badly behaved ones, of which there's a plethora these days, which only encourages my tendency toward agoraphobia. (Cf. my previous comments about travel: what I cannot control makes me anxious.) But Ferrell, as we call him, is a pretty cool little monster. He possesses the same enthusiasms I did at his age—superheroes and dinosaurs—so much so that, when John and I want to buy him Christmas presents, John drags me to Wal-Mart long enough to lead me through the toy aisles and ask me what I like, knowing that what I choose Ferrell will also relish. My nephew is, apparently, so much like me—his smarts, his willfulness—that Amy has even said to me, "You didn't need to have a child. I had a little Jeff for you." I wonder sometimes what my mother—who died in 1998, six years before he was born—would think of him. Despite her lingering objections to interracial relationships, I know she would have been irresistibly charmed.

How can I not approve of a kid who's like me in myriad ways? He has his mother's genial nature, which helps me hope that he'll be spared my darker moods. He has her good looks too. The line I use to describe him is, "He makes Obama look homely." The boy will be a mocha-colored heartbreaker. I just hope he's kinder to his admirers than the men I've admired were to me. And I'm hoping that a nation that had the sense to elect Obama for president will prove to be a kinder place for him to live than it might have been in the past. On his father's side, he's the descendant of Southern black folks. On his mother's side, he's the descendant of a Confederate soldier. Talk about a living embodiment of reconciliation, a melding of the South's multitudinous pasts.

Amy has since followed in my father's footsteps and become the prosecuting attorney of Summers County, the first woman to hold the position. What with work and raising Ferrell (who recently got "Most Polite" in his class; my mother would have been proud), Amy's incredibly busy, so, despite the fact that we live only an hour and a half apart, we see one another no more than four or five times a year.

Sometimes, in summer, my sister comes over to Pulaski,

Virginia, where John and I live. We take Ferrell to the nearby water park; afterwards, we grill hamburgers out on the back deck. Sometimes John and I drive over to Forest Hill, where Amy and Michael live, out in the West Virginia countryside, near the site of my father's gardens. She always makes huge, fattening, and thoroughly delicious meals that make me feel as happy and cared for as any food can: pork roast, country ham, biscuits, deviled eggs, hash-brown casserole, broccoli casserole, all the comfort foods that Southerners have lavished on their loved ones for generations. Over dinner and stiff drinks, we trade gossip and amusing stories, our shared sense of humor a mix of our mother's supercilious, scathing wit and our father's bawdy vulgarity. "Lord, there she was, in a halter top! Poor thing, she really should have covered up. And that girl's big butt was eating her shorts, I tell you. It was just nasty!"

There is a delicious sense of camaraderie in mocking the same things. While Ferrell displays his new Spider-Man pajamas or T-Rex toy, or runs out to see how his pet bull is doing, Amy and I are excoriating the Christian Right and the latest moronic Republican politician. After such a visit, she always sends John and me home with fresh vegetables in summer, or canned goods she and Daddy have put up: hot peppers, green beans, lime pickles, corn relish, or chowchow.

Mythology helps me see depth and divinity in the daily. Just as I've glimpsed gods in the men I've loved, so I clearly perceive in my sister Hestia, goddess of the hearth; Cerridwen, goddess of the cauldron; and Athena, goddess of wisdom and war. As with many of my lesbian friends, in Amy there's that combination of Mother Goddess and warrior I so appreciate. As with many of my bear friends, there is in her a wonderful amalgam of strength, nurturing, and protectiveness. Amy's as close to the ideal woman as any I've ever known. She's one of a handful of folks in my life I have absolutely no desire to outlive.

I tend to give backhanded compliments. In Ferrell's case, I'm always telling Amy that he's a freak, because he's so good-looking, smart, and thoughtful for a kid his age. Once, she called to tell me about his latest amazing statement. Home from kindergarten, he'd hugged her and said, "Mom, I wish you were my sister instead of my mother. Then I'd have more time with you." She assured him that she'd be around for a long time yet.

I must admit I choked up. What I thought was, "Well, kid, you beat me out. You've got most of her attention now. But, in this respect at least, I win. She's *my* sister. *I* got all those years with her that you didn't, and they've been a privilege and a delight." What I said was, "My *god*! He's a *monster*! Enough about him. If I come home next month, will you make me a bunch of fried apple pies or a batch of those delectable buttermilk biscuits?"

I never dreamed that same-sex marriage would be possible in my lifetime. It's a marvel both strange and unexpected. It feels downright miraculous.

two mountain weddings

I.

A SELF-DESCRIBED HILLBILLY, I claim the Appalachian Mountains of Virginia and West Virginia as home. When marriage equality came to those states in 2014, I arranged to be married in both of them.

The wedding in my hometown of Hinton, West Virginia, wasn't official. An ornery rebel from way back, I desperately wanted to march into the Summers County Courthouse, where my sister works as the prosecuting attorney, and scandalize the local folks—many of them, I assure you, devout, conservative Christians—by demanding a marriage license. My partner John, however, thought the cautious thing to do was to be legally married in Virginia, the state in which we reside, so as to reduce the likelihood that our marriage might be invalidated if future political events turned against us. We were, to use the colloquial, covering our asses.

Without a marriage license, the West Virginia wedding wasn't one sanctioned by law, but it was the one that carried, for me, the most emotional weight. On Saturday, December 6, 2014, we held it in my family home, a solid wooden house built in 1920 in which I'd spent many of my formative years and which I'd bought from my father earlier that year. The event was full of a delicious diversity that combined many of the disparate elements of my life.

There were, first of all, the grooms, two bears (that's gayspeak for beefy, bearded gay men). John wore his Harris Tweed jacket, dress pants, shirt, and tie; I wore my Prince Charlie coatee, tuxedo shirt, and kilt—the Maclaine of Lochbuie tartan, since my mother was a McCormick, one of the families connected with that clan. Having bought the kilt in summer 1994, when I was much thinner, I was damned grateful for the presence of that amazing invention, the kilt-strap extender.

An Appalachian drag queen officiated, albeit not in drag. West Virginia sociologist Okey Napier—who sometimes performs as the infamous Miss Ilene Over—is a pagan, as am I, so the ceremony he'd composed included such Wiccan elements as honoring the quarters, the four elements, and gods and goddesses.

Three lesbians attended. Hinton resident Laurie Bugg, the ultimate West Virginia Mountaineers fan, has been my friend since high school, when we used to walk across the New River Bridge at night and talk about the forbidden and futile same-sex infatuations we were suffering from. I'd met Cindy Burack in the fall of 1979, the first semester of my junior year at West Virginia University (WVU), and we've been sharing triumphs and travails ever since. She's now an author and political theorist in the Women's, Gender and Sexuality Studies Department at Ohio State University. Her wife, Laree Martin, an attorney for the United States Postal Service, I've been wildly fond of ever since I tasted the homemade Napoleons she made back in 1995, when she and Cindy were first dating.

Two Jews attended. The wonderful owner of Lethe Press, author Steve Berman, who's been kind enough to edit and publish many of my books, had driven down from southern New Jersey to attend the ceremony, accompanied by his mother, Sandy Berman, a woman whose priceless wit matches her son's. As sharp as is their banter, the two of them could form a comedy team.

The remaining members of my family were there—mountain folks who, from the beginning, have been supportive of my gay identity. My sister, Amy Mann, is an attorney, a fine country cook, and an exemplar of small-town values. My father, Perry Mann, in his mid-nineties and a retired attorney, has been publishing op-eds in West Virginia newspapers for decades—essays that lambast the NRA, conservative Christians, homophobes, and environmental destruction, and laud the virtues of nature, liberalism, and rural living.

Amy's son, Ferrell, served as the ring bearer. My mother Clara was present too, in a manner of speaking. She'd died in 1998, a little over six months after I'd met John, but she died knowing that, after so many years of loneliness, I was with a man who was good for me and good to me. Her ashes, contained in a blue pottery urn, stood in the corner of the room in which John and I were married.

After the ceremony, John put on an iPhone playlist of songs by Joni Mitchell, my favorite musician, while I mixed cocktails, poured champagne and wine, and served up the many delicacies that John and I had prepared. (Yes, we catered our own wedding. It was cheaper, and we're both experienced cooks, so the quality was infinitely better than store-bought or stranger-made.) We had sausage balls, spinach/bacon/artichoke dip, a bacon and jalapeno cheese ball, strata, and buttermilk pie, plus my sister contributed her Swedish meatballs, and Sandy had brought all the way from New Jersey a tasty homemade chocolate-chip cake. If there's one thing both mountain folks and bears know how to do, it's eat and drink with gusto.

The second wedding—the legal one—occurred in our house in Pulaski, Virginia, on December 21, 2014, beside our newly decorated holiday tree, a Canaan fir cut at a tree farm in an adjoining county. The date was significant for me, since it was the pagan holiday of Yule, the winter solstice. A handful of our favorite neighbors attended, and a Methodist deacon who lives right across the street performed the wedding. So as to honor my spiritual path, he based the ceremony on the pagan ritual that Okey had used in Hinton a few weeks before. To add to the pagan flavor, everyone passed a flame from candle to candle to mark the solstice and the returning sun.

After the ceremony, John and I served up another passel of treats we'd prepared: a Roquefort and pecan cheese log, a crabmeat and artichoke casserole, lemon chicken skewers, Cajun glazed mushrooms, and spinach poppers, along with the chile con queso our artistic neighbors Ken and Leslie had contributed. After our guests headed home, John and I ended the evening on a Big Queer Note by playing our favorite song from *Wicked*, "For Good," and watching the DVD of *Victor/Victoria*, our number-one feel-good film.

What I find most remarkable about our legal wedding is not the event itself but two events that bookended it. Spending nearly all my life in Appalachian towns, around Southern religious conservatives, has made me cautious, vaguely paranoid, and always on my guard. As I've mentioned in other publications, I may look, dress, and sometimes act like a mountain redneck—actually, that's one of many identities I proudly claim—but I'm honest about who I am. Anyone interacting with me for very long is going to learn that I'm gay. In such interactions, I hope for the best but expect the worst. Some would call this stance pessimistic. I would call it realistic. I want to be prepared if someone responds negatively to my homosexuality.

So, when John and I entered the Pulaski County Courthouse on the gray morning of December 5, 2014, to apply for a marriage license, I was steeled for possible hostility and ready to return it in spades. I wore my usual country-boy garb—cowboy boots and hat, sweatshirt and camo pants, and a raggedy Western drover—in that context a deliberate combination of "Don't Fuck With Me" signifiers. Kim Davis—the county clerk in Kentucky who refused to issue same-sex marriage licenses—had yet to hit the news, but I already knew her kind very well. I was ready to lay on my usual polite Southern charm, but if that was met with pious sneers and the contemptuous wrinkling of noses, I planned to get nasty. After all, on this issue, the law of Virginia—as of October 6, 2014—was newly, amazingly, on my side.

The ladies behind the counter in the Circuit Court's office didn't bat an eye, though John and I were surely one of the very first same-sex couples ever to apply for a marriage license there. Rather than being rude, they were friendly and congratulatory. After a few minutes of paperwork, John and I were out the door, relieved that no unpleasant scene had been necessary.

I was almost as pleased a few weeks later, when John and I took the documents certifying our marriage to the Human Resources office at Virginia Tech. The folks at the HR office were just as friendly and nonchalant as the ladies at the Pulaski County Courthouse. This was less of a surprise, since university employees and university towns tend toward the liberal, but still, you never know where you might encounter a purse-lipped, disapproving homophobe.

A few months after our wedding, John's kin recognized our new status as a married couple. John's a member of a large family: his two parents, both originally from Massachusetts; four brothers, Andy, Robert, Joe, and Roger; four sisters-in-law, Linda, Thana, Amy, and Nancy; plus one niece and five nephews. John's brothers are scattered about the globe, in California, Florida, Minnesota, and the Netherlands, but every now and then they manage a big reunion. In March 2015—during Virginia Tech's spring break, a week that John's family had deliberately chosen so that I might attend—almost everyone convened in Daytona Beach, Florida, where John's parents live.

For five days, John and I shared a spacious seventeenth-floor condo on the beach with his brother Robert and sister-in-law Thana and spent every evening with his family. During the days, there were oceanside walks and time to relax and read. It was Bike Week in Daytona, meaning that the entire town sounded like a hive of riled-up bees, so one afternoon a bunch of us strolled downtown to see the bikers and motorcycles. With my bushy beard, shaved head, myriad tattoos, and sleeveless V-Twin shirt, I felt right at home. Thana even joked that my presence gave our little group "street cred". . . this, despite the fact that John has never let me buy a motorcycle.

During the nights, there were communal feasts. John's kin are as appreciative of good food and drink as mine are, and several of them are enthusiastic cooks, so there were many strong cocktails and succulent meals: Robert's Hendrick's gin martinis, Sangrita, and Sazeracs; grilled steaks and baked potatoes; locally caught steamed shrimp; Linda's coconut cream pie and Key lime pie; and one of my specialties, barbequed country-style pork ribs, accompanied by cole slaw and Thana's Durgin Park cornbread.

It was just before one of those great meals that John's brothers and sisters-in-law gave us a card, signed by everyone, congratulating us on our marriage, and a surprise wedding gift, in recognition of the fact that, despite having been a couple since 1997, it was the first family gathering in which he and I were officially married. The gift was a cylindrical case made of black leather, perhaps as a nod to my status as a leather bear—an erotic penchant I don't discuss around John's family but which is made abundantly clear by many of my publications and is thus a kind of public knowledge. Inside the case nestled three sleek chrome flasks, a tiny funnel, and two metal cups. It was, they explained, a martini travel case, apropos for two bears who travel fairly often and fairly often consume strong drink.

Both gift and gesture touched me greatly. That black leather case was the solid embodiment of our relationship's legal legitimacy, of our equality. I sat back during the dinner that followed, sipped my wine, and was thankful for many things: the presence of a smart, solid, considerate spouse like John in my life; the company of so many warm, multifaceted, and caring in-laws, who'd redefined and expanded my concept of kin; and the astounding national changes that had allowed same-sex marriages finally to be recognized.

II.

DURING A PANEL discussion I attended in April 2016 at the Saints and Sinners Literary Festival, an androgynous young person in the audience, who must have thought herself the Cutting Edge of Radical, scoffed at same-sex marriage as a "homonormative" bourgeois institution, a form of assimilation not worth the respect of "progressive" queers. Achieving the legality of same-sex marriage, she implied, was a triumph not worth celebrating.

Profoundly annoyed, I raised my hand, shifted in my chair to give her only the slightest sliver of my attention, and used the indirection of Southern manners to indicate, in that passive-aggressive mode of which we children of Dixie are masters, that she was a fool.

What I thought but was too polite and politic to say was, "You're no doubt one of those fragile members of Generation Z, who—given the improved world that my generation's courage and activism helped to create—is wasting your time expatiating about frightfully important issues like 'preferred gender pronouns,' how intolerant the 'cisgendered' can be, how very dreadful 'microaggressions' are, how oppressive 'binaries' can be, how much one needs a 'trigger warning' to 'feel safe,' and whether someone is sufficiently enlightened to use the asterisk after 'trans.'"

What I did say was something like this: "I'm fifty-six years old. I never wanted to be married because it never occurred to me that I ever could be. But now, due to the surprising and sudden change in the law, I can be married, and so I am. I never dreamed that same-sex marriage would be possible in my lifetime. It's a marvel both strange and unexpected. It feels downright miraculous. This sort of legal equality is important. Very important. In fact, it's huge."

Of course, full legal equality for queer folks has yet to come, and I'm only referring to the rights of U.S. citizens. (My friend Cindy Burack has published a new book about the U.S. State Department's international interventions on behalf of LGBT rights overseas. Needless to say, in many countries, the situation is dire and deadly.) We may be able to marry, but now there are religious liberty laws to wrangle with. In many states, employees can still be fired if they come out as gay or lesbian. Obviously, there are many more battles to be fought.

As one of those pessimists/realists mentioned earlier, I'm not convinced that such conflicts and controversies will ever end. I cannot believe that a Utopia of "Equality for All" will ever materialize. The evidence of human history argues against the possibility of such a paradise. (In fact, global warming leads me to expect just the opposite: a fraught and horrible dystopia.) As social scientists have pointed out, a suspicion of the different is deeply engrained in the human psyche, thanks to our tribal origins. Even if queers one day achieve full legal equality, I cannot imagine that other sorts of equality—social equality?—will entirely be ours.

We're members of a very small minority. "One in ten" is apparently not accurate. When I track down Internet information about the percentage of Americans who identify as LGBT, the numbers I see are all under 5%. In other words, if you're queer, unless you live in a gay ghetto, you're going to be surrounded and outnumbered by heterosexuals most or all of your life. Their straight concerns will always be profoundly different from your queer concerns.

This is inevitable. This is human nature. As much as I like to bitch about how small my audience is as an Appalachian gay author, that regrettable fact makes perfect sense. I write about gay men, about bears, about rednecks and hillbillies, about leather sex, about small-town and rural life. Why should most straight people or urbanites be interested in such material? It must feel irrelevant to them at best, revolting to them at worst. I'm certainly not interested in the literature they're likely to enjoy, books about the struggles of heterosexuals, parents, or city-dwellers.

So, will we queers always be a tiny minority and thus at a disadvantage? I think so. I accept that. Besides, assimilation and social acceptance have their downsides. I blame both for the disappearance of gay and lesbian bookstores and the adulteration of all-queer spaces, as cool young straight liberals and bachelorette parties invade gay bars and gay neighborhoods by the droves. Despite what that impudent child at Saints and Sinners might think, same-sex marriage does not necessarily equate with bourgeois assimilation. One can be married and still be rebellious, transgressive, and radical in a plethora of ways. I certainly plan to be.

Yes, the fight for legal equality is crucial and must continue. As for myself, rather than assimilating, rather than unrealistically expecting eventual equality on all fronts, I prefer to relish the benefits of my odd/outcast status as a member of a sexual minority. I prefer to savor the warm and supportive camaraderie of my fellow queers, my defiant, eccentric, and peculiar clan. Let us be the exceptions. Let us be exceptional.

his ink-etched torso wrapped

naked and sweaty in my

ink-etched arms.

comparing tattoos

AT LAST HE'S SHOWING ME MORE SKIN than electric-fence ethics might normally allow. Not because we're lovers, managing a rough-sex assignation in a Potomac Highlands cabin, for reality is never as generous as that. No, because, professor and pupil, customers at Hot Rod Tattoo, we've been inked by the same man. Because he's excited, that effervescent enthusiasm of the young, and wants to show off to someone simpatico his new tattoo. Because he's innocent, unable to smell yearning, or he's the most disingenuous of teases.

We're alone together in the hallway, minutes before class is due to begin. I've fantasized about him all semester, complex scenes involving bondage and penetration, dreams he doesn't begin to imagine or to share, yet here he is, grinning before me, black-bearded Dionysus close enough to embrace, thick cologne of evergreen and lime in my nose. He's tugging down the collar of his black t-shirt to show me the new tattoo etched across his shoulder blades. Gingerly, feeling like a criminal, I take the garment's collar between thumb and forefinger and pull it further away from his back to study the shaded letters. A favorite saying of his father's, a phrase from William Blake: "He who kisses the joy as it flies lives in eternity's sunrise."

Kissing, if only. I'm stunned, amazed, looking down upon exposed skin, pale black-Irish nape of his neck, ridge of his spine. Boy I could love, if circumstances were more obliging, boy who could make of me a thorough fool. Closest I've gotten to the god in a very long time.

What is there to do but take in the nearness and the sight of his body as deeply as I can, to seem unmoved, to hide the Quasimodo hump of desire, to demand from this sadistic cosmos an acting award? My new concept of heaven's a world where this urge to kiss him is not suppressed, is not unseemly or unwelcome. Far from paradise, I comment on the artist's fine shading, then let the cloth of the collar slip from my grip. He flips open his cell-phone now, punches some buttons, shows me the tiny photo: he's bare-chested, half-turned to the camera, profile of some Caravaggio Christ's dark beard and dark hair, letters like a meticulous bruise welting his white back. Every desirable thing distilled, clear as moonshine, burning blue.

Next is the not-climax, the not-touching-kissing-stripping-shoving-back-against-the-wall, the not-pleading-or-offering-to-pay. Next is the anticlimax of pulling up my own sleeve to show him the Horned God on my left shoulder, surrounded by black frozen fire, to describe the ink-expansions to come. "Awesome, dude!" is his generation's ridiculous, endearing response.

Two o'clock sharp, I usher him into class, step into automatic after thirty years of teaching, leave behind images of his ink-etched torso wrapped naked and sweaty in my ink-etched arms. This evening I'll drive home to my husband, past the gleaming cream of dogwood, the mine-fire flicker of redbud blossoms. I'll get my drink on, consuming what can be consumed. I'll lie down in sheets, not Arcadia's grass blades or pine needles, and grow drowsy to Netflix. Insomnia will run its fingers over tattooed letters and a black beard. This is beauty's curse, its siren whisper: what's unattainable makes all the rest worth nothing.

For the momentous occasion of my first hustler, I'd like to take my time.

whoremonger

I.

A COUPLE OF WEEKS BEFORE MY fifty-seventh birthday, I finally paid for sex. The boy was a slender, smooth, blond nineteen-year-old.

Anyone familiar with me or my publications will be confused by this statement. I'm notorious for lusting after dark-haired, hairy-chested men—cubs, otters, and bears, in gay parlance. I like muscular guys, stocky, burly, brawny guys, and I have little use for thin ones. (In this respect, I can sympathize with Sykes Jones in Zora Neale Hurston's short story "Sweat" when he says, "Ah sho' 'bominates uh skinny 'oman.") Most nineteen-year-olds look far too young for me. I want mature men, not boys. Rare are the exceptions to this rule.

So, to clarify: I paid for sex, but the sex was not for me. A buddy who's done me many, many favors had a long erotic dry spell. I like to provide for friends when I can, so I sent him a check, a sort of early birthday present, funds with which he might purchase time with a rent boy he'd met online. He was pleased with the outcome, and I was glad to repay his kindnesses with such a priapic gift.

"But paying for sex is illegal!" gasp the priests of Propriety. "Yeah, so?" would be my response. I'm the son of a lawyer and the brother of a lawyer. As far as I'm concerned, law is a human construct as flawed as any other, one for which I have no particular innate respect, being a rule-breaker from way back, one I'm more than willing to flout as long as I can avoid peskily inconvenient legal consequences.

At what age is it appropriate/will it be necessary to pay for sex? I've been asking myself that question since I was in my twenties. I've had a ferociously burgeoning sex drive since I first discovered the pleasures of onanism in the seventh grade, prompted by a series of comic-book images depicting the DC superhero Flash extensively rope-bound. Growing up gay in a small southern West Virginia town, I was devoid of erotic opportunities. While my heterosexual counterparts went out on dates and attended the prom, I stayed home, studied, and ran through loads of Kleenex, while I fantasized about binding and gagging my hairy-chested, black-bearded pussyhound hunting buddy, Mike, and kidnapping assorted television and film stars. Only the companionship of a few lesbian friends helped keep me sane.

If the downside of this isolated queer adolescence was a state of painful and perpetual sexual frustration, the upside was a very high grade-point average in high school, which led to a scholarship that covered my college tuition. At West Virginia University, I wasted no time in losing my virginity—luck and the right contacts introduced me to my erotic initiator, a thickly built, hairy RA who bedded me between my first and second days of class—but my undergraduate years in Morgantown, from August 1977 to May 1981, proved to be nearly as frustrating as my high-school years had been. Well, more frustrating, since I'd had a taste of man-on-man sex and, that appetite whetted, wanted more as often as possible.

There were the very rare one-night stands, nearly every one of them a one-off. Men seemed to have no interest in bedding me a second time. Perhaps they could sense the clinging romantic in me; perhaps they thought a second romp would mean that we were dating, an emotional commitment that they didn't want. Perhaps I was simply unappealing, though I look at photos of myself at that age and see a fairly attractive, shaggy-headed, black-bearded boy—slight compared to my present heft—whom, odd to say, I'd bed if I could. For the most part, my visits to the local gay bar didn't lead to erotic frolic. Instead, I danced with lesbian friends and yearned pathetically after good-looking men I was far too shy to approach. Being a BDSM enthusiast only limited my options more.

Porn became my friend: first vanilla *Blueboy*, then kinky magazines like *Honcho* and *Drummer*, where I got to feast my eyes on muscular, bearded men roped up or posing in leather. Once in a rare while, I even got to enjoy pornographic films, the most memorable being *Wanted*, in which penitentiary prisoner Al Parker is seized by fellow inmates, gagged with a washcloth, and gang-raped in a shower. That scene will always get me "het up" (that's Appalachian for "heated up").

At the time, I felt like my small-town insecurity and shyness, my average looks, and my distance from bustling urban gay neighborhoods had consigned me to an exceptional fate, a unique and agonized celibacy in which I was cursed, like Tantalus, always to look but never to touch, always to lust after what could not be had. Now, at age 59, I suspect in retrospect that many folks, male and female, queer or straight, suffer from some version of carnal dissatisfaction. Who gets enough sex? Who doesn't have to rely on masturbation as a major sexual relief?

Well, I'm sure there are some—the young, the beautiful, the charismatic, and the lucky—but I've never been in that blessed group, and I've never known many of its members. As you age, you compare stories with more and more people—stories full of what Thoreau calls "quiet desperation"—and your perspective widens, and your illusions die, and so do many of your hopes, dismissed as being improbable, impossible, or, at the very least, wildly unrealistic. Not for nothing that the Irish poet W. B. Yeats once said, "I shall be a sinful man to the end, and think upon my death bed of all the nights I wasted in my youth." Many if not most of us can relate.

My capacity for passion is deep, and my capacity for passion is wasted. That was true during my days at WVU, and it's true today. But back then I still had grand dreams of meeting The Right One, someone fascinating who would be equally fascinated with me, someone who would match me passion for passion. Like most young people, I thought my life would be special, extraordinary in some way. I had no idea of the bitter compromises, tacit resentments, and quotidian routines of long-term relationships and marriage. I had no idea what "bed death" meant. I had no concept of how slowly and ruthlessly, in any life, Eros recedes, how the god's visitations grow less and less.

So, with no boyfriends in sight and with very few one-night stands to enjoy, I jacked off to porn, dreamed of a better future, took advantage of bodily pleasures requiring no one's consent, i.e., food and drink, and commiserated with friends. One lesbian pal in particular I envied. Cin was a charming, popular sort, running through a string of girlfriends, trading in one for another. She was also a practical person with great hopes of financial wealth to come. Unlike me, she'd come from the upper-middle-class suburbs of Washington D.C., and she intended to improve her lot even further. Here, among all my gay and lesbian friends, was one likely to become well-off. Her professed motto was, "He who has the most toys when he dies wins."

Cin knew of my erotic frustration, for I whined constantly about my celibacy. She also knew about my poverty. During my undergraduate years, my father sent me $250 a month for living expenses. This meant that, like many penurious West Virginians, I ate a lot of brown beans, cornbread, and low-budget casseroles based on canned soups. My economic status wasn't likely to change significantly, because I've never possessed interests, enthusiasms, or skills that make me particularly marketable. One day, when I announced that the only way I'd ever enjoy sex again would be to pay for it, which wasn't likely to happen since I certainly didn't have the funds to afford such a concupiscent splurge, Cin, supremely confident of her future earning potential, announced, "When you turn thirty, I'll buy you a hustler for your birthday!"

She was serious, I think, even though that declaration became, over the years, a sort of joke. I would most probably have taken her up on the offer, but we fell out after graduation. By August 1989, when I turned thirty, we were completely out of touch. I was leaving a poorly-paid teaching position at WVU for a poorly-paid teaching position at Virginia Tech and was soon to find that Blacksburg, Virginia, was as devoid of erotic outlets for gay men as Morgantown had been. From various sources, I heard that Cin had returned to Northern Virginia and was indeed making the huge income that she'd always dreamed of. Then the ongoing jokes about prostitutes became bitter: "If only I'd stayed friends with Cin, I'd be rolling in hot hustlers by now!" At age thirty, without Cin or a decent salary to bankroll my whoremongering aspirations, I proudly proclaimed to friends, "I refuse to pay for sex until I hit fifty!"

II.

IT WAS A double-haggis birthday at Pennygate Lodge, an elegant Georgian guest house in the village of Craignure on the Isle of Mull. The traditional Scottish breakfast included scones, bacon, sausages, grilled tomatoes and mushrooms, a fried egg, and a patty of haggis, and the dinner entrée was a chicken breast stuffed with haggis and covered with a whisky sauce. Great eating for a Scotland enthusiast like me. Not only did August 8, 2009, contain much Gaelic gustatory pleasure, parenthesed, as it were, by haggis, but it also contained an unusual surprise.

Approaching that landmark birthday, I'd known that turning fifty would kick my grim, depressive, and surly side into overdrive, so I'd arranged a series of pleasures to distract me from my gray-bearded, less-than-buff, half-a-fucking-century status-to-come.

Over several months, I got a tattoo sleeve on my left arm, images to join the face of the Celtic Horned God already there—a thistle, a shamrock, a Lambda, a Mars symbol, a Scottish targe and spears, a flaming sword, a bear paw, the Norse rune for "warrior," *Tyr*, plus the letters CSA in flames, to honor the Confederate soldier who was my great-great-grandfather. When acquaintances queried me about the sudden addition of all that ink, I'd drawl, "Well, I'm turning fifty this year. I considering having an affair, buying a new truck, or getting a tattoo sleeve, then decided that the latter would be the cheapest option."

My partner John and I had also planned a big two-week summer vacation to countries where two of my bloodlines originated, Ireland and Scotland. In Ireland, we hit the Burren, Galway, Inishmore, Clifden, Connemara, Kylemore Abbey, and Westport. In Scotland, we visited Blair Castle, Culloden, Ullapool, the Isle of Lewis and Harris, and the Isle of Skye, reaching the Isle of Mull the day before my birthday. My mother's family, the McCormicks, hailed from that Hebridean island, a beautiful place that John and I had visited before, so I figured being there might give me a little historical perspective and take some of the sting out of hitting fifty.

After that breakfast haggis at Pennygate Lodge, John and I played tourist. First, we drove out to Fionnphort to catch the ferry to Iona, the tiny island from which St. Columba had spread Celtic Christianity throughout Scotland. My face was set in half-snarl as I toured the historic abbey, as it is in most Christian sites. As a pagan, I would have much preferred that Christianity with all its proselytizing—a species of thought invasive as kudzu—had stayed in the Middle East and left the indigenous religions across the globe alone, most especially the Celtic and Norse gods and goddesses I owe my allegiance to.

After that, back on the Ross of Mull, we took the tiny road to Lochbuie, seat of the Maclaines of Lochbuie, the clan that includes the McCormicks as a sept. There, by the loch's gray shingle, stood elegant Lochbuie House, home of the clan chief. There loomed the stone keep of Moy Castle, covered in scaffolding, being restored. In a boggy pasture nearby, we wandered around a wonderful circle of standing stones, which meant more to me as a pagan than Columba's abbey on Iona ever could. Standing inside such a Neolithic circle is as close to a sense of the sacred as I get.

When John and I got back to Craignure, we decided to have a few drinks in the local pub before heading up the hill to Pennygate Lodge for that haggis-graced birthday dinner. It was over pints of Belhaven ale that John revealed his big surprise.

"So, I'm trying to line up a special treat for you on our last day in Glasgow, the afternoon before we fly home."

I'm a Leo. I crave ego-food; I revel in gifts and treats. I'm always echoing Daisy Miller, in Henry James' novella of the same name: "That's all I want—a little fuss!" Grinning, I imagined Glaswegian options. "A treat? What would that be? A formal apotheosis? A horde of handsome groupies? A wheelbarrow full of pastries? A Pulitzer Prize?"

Used to my hyperbolic tendencies, John rolled his eyes. "What I have in mind's better than all that, or at least I hope you'll think so. I'm trying to hire you a hustler."

My mouth gaped open before curling up into an even larger grin. I probably showed a little fang (being a vampire aficionado with appropriately large canines). "Fuck me. Really? You've got to be kidding. What put you in mind of that?"

A few months earlier, John reminded me, a good friend's wife had treated her to an evening with a high-class courtesan in Seattle. (Hopelessly unconventional myself, I've attracted over the years delightfully unconventional friends.) That example had inspired him. He waved his iPhone at me. "I've been chatting with this Glasgow guy for days, trying to arrange a similar experience for you."

"Well, damn, what's he look like?" I blurted, a looksist from way, way back.

"I don't want to get your hopes up. How about I show you his photo after it seems pretty certain that he'll be free that day?"

"Shit, okay. Well, here's to Eros," I said, swilling the last of my Scottish ale. Hope, excitement, embarrassment, and uncertainty all washed over me like a choppy series of North Atlantic waves. John and I had met in the summer of 1997; by summer 2009, we were long past the initial passion that most couples share at the start of their relationships. He knew all too well, after twelve years together, my restless need for erotic variety, most especially BDSM, an interest he'd never shared. Like many gay male couples, we'd moved from monogamy to an open relationship after the first three or four years together. Each of us infrequently had had our "treatie-bits," as I called them, on the side, most often when he traveled for business and I was home alone. This was the first time, however, that he'd played my Pandarus. I was both surprised and grateful.

"LOOKS LIKE OUR Glasgow friend will be available," John said over breakfast the next morning, as I scarfed up buttery mushrooms and yet more spicy haggis. He was discreet, waiting for the servers who were pouring us more tea to leave the room before pulling out his iPhone. "Here you go. His name's Robbie. I think you'll like his looks."

I snatched the device from John's hands. "Uuuurrrrrrr," I growled, staring at the image on the phone's little screen. I've hated cell phones for years; not only do they erode good manners, they've exponentially increased the amount of banal chatter I have to listen to every time I leave the house—blah blah blah blah in the grocery store, in the airport, in the restaurant. In that moment, however, I was very thankful for such technology. It was a miracle of modernity, like mail-ordering a fuck-buddy, as simple as ordering haggis patties for breakfast.

"He was the only one on this site who was your type. All the others were very young—hairless, blond, thin boys."

"Screw that. Who wants a boy? Give me a man. A man like this." I stared at the photo: a good-looking guy with a clover-honey-hued goatee grinned back at me. Looking to be in his early to mid-thirties, dressed in a tight sky-blue T-shirt, he flexed his left arm, displaying a nice biceps bulge. I read the stats out loud: "'Six foot two, two hundred and twenty pounds, very hairy, seven-inch dick.' Hell, yes!"

"I thought he'd tick all your boxes," John said, sipping his tea. "Beard, body hair, muscles. Butch."

"Yep, just the sort of stud I like. Good job!" I stroked my beard and tongued a canine. "He looks like some of the working-class guys I grew up with back in West Virginia."

John nodded. "He is. He's an auto mechanic."

"Nice. Is he a top or a bottom?"

"Both. He's versatile."

"Good!" I said, fork-spearing a chunk of haggis. "Does he do kink?"

"I asked. Not usually, but he says he might be convinced."

"Yum. A man that handsome really should be tied up. How much does he charge?"

John shrugged. "He's a birthday gift. It doesn't matter what he costs."

I come from a long line of self-sufficient, frugal country farmers, and that family frugality was exacerbated by my father's experiences growing up in the Depression. To this day, I wash plastic storage bags and aluminum foil so as to use them over and over again.

"I don't want you to spend a lot of money."

"How often do you think we'll do this? It's your only fiftieth birthday. Don't worry about it."

"How much?"

John sighed, long accustomed to my stubborn parsimony. "One hundred pounds an hour."

"Argh. Are you sure you want to—"

"*Yes*. How many hours would you like?"

"What will you be doing while—"

"I've already chatted with a gay masseur not far from our

Glasgow B&B. His name's Cameron, and he's very cute. I'm going to get a massage while you spend time with Robbie."

I smirked. "A massage? With a happy ending?"

"Not sure. We'll see," John said, expressionless.

"That'll work." Nodding, I thought of Robbie's honey-colored goatee, that confident butch grin, those hard biceps. "Two. I want two hours. For the momentous occasion of my first hustler, I'd like to take my time."

CRARAE GARDENS, a little south of Inveraray Castle, was more of a lush arboretum than a garden. Strolling through it, John and I admired the many varieties of rhododendrons and magnolias, wild rhubarbs, huge firs, rushing cascades, and, of all things, an array of Himalayan plants, including blue poppies. Most memorable, however, was a phone conversation John had with Robbie in our rental car, in the gardens' parking lot. The gist of the conversation was that the whoremongering afternoon in Glasgow was definitely on, which was a relief, but what grabbed me was Robbie's accent, which I could clearly hear emanating from John's iPhone.

"My God," I gasped, after John had ended the call. "What a hot accent! He sounds like the actor I'd most like to bed."

"Gerard Butler, right? Well, they should sound similar. Butler's from around Glasgow too."

As John drove us along Loch Fyne to our accommodations in Inveraray, The George Hotel, I watched the landscape tumble by and contemplated the deliciousness to come. *For two hundred pounds, surely I can convince Robbie to let me tie his hands behind his back and gag him with a sock. I'll be just as rough or tender as he likes. I wonder if he'll let me fuck him? Hmmm, now one hundred pounds an hour takes on delectable double meaning. I'll pound him all right. Ummm, to hear that sweet, thick Glaswegian accent moan, "Take me hard, Daddy" through his gag, his hairy legs propped on my shoulders as I plow him and feast on his tits. Or, hell, he can tie me down and pound me. Whatever works. Anything to get hold of a guy so hot.*

That was the voice of my inveterate lust, one of myriad conflicting selves inside. Other selves, more anxious ones, had different things to say. *Will you feel pathetic, humiliated, knowing the only reason he's having sex with you is because of money? Will he let you kiss him? Be affectionate? Cuddle afterwards? Or will it simply be cold, mechanical sex? He's thirty-five at the oldest; you're fifty. Surely he won't find you at all attractive. Who knows what might be going through his head when he sees you naked?* "Poor old pervert. Look at those love-handles, that flat ass. Look at all the gray in that beard. No wonder the old poof has to pay for it." *Will you see palpable contempt in his eyes, or, worse, mockery? What happens if he can't get hard? What happens if you can't get hard? Will it all just be an egregious waste of money?*

ON OUR SECOND day in Glasgow, the last day of our trip, my date-of-sorts with Robbie was scheduled for 4 p.m. The weather was classically Scottish—low clouds, chilly air, steady rain. It was a good day to stay inside, snuggle, fuck, snuggle more, then fuck again. John and I rose late, had tea in our room at the Georgian House, went out for lunch, and then explored the nearby botanical gardens. The tree ferns were amazing, as were the anthuriums, whose penis-like spadices I felt compelled to stroke, but I fixated most, superannuated predator that I am, on the carnivorous plants: the Venus flytraps, pitcher plants, cobra lilies, and sundews. *By nightfall, with any luck, I will have devoured a beautiful man,* I thought. *Meanwhile, I wish these savage plants would snap up all these obnoxious goddamn shrieking children.*

Back in our room, John set two hundred-pound bills on the bedside table. While we waited for Robbie's arrival, John read a novel and I caught up in my travel journal, recording our trip to Inveraray Castle, plus our walks around Glasgow the previous day: George Square with all its statues, St. Mungo's Cathedral, the Victorian Necropolis, a South Indian dinner at Dakhin, and several rounds of single-malt in a gay bar with great stonework, Delmonicas.

The appointed time of 4 p.m. passed, then 4:15, 4:30, 4:45. "Stood up by Robbie? It's 4:55," I noted in my journal.

"Where *is* he?" Frowning, John punched Robbie's number into his iPhone. No answer. John waited five minutes and tried again. No answer. By 5:30 and several more failed attempts to contact my would-be First Hustler Ever, things were clear enough.

"Damn it," John sighed. "He's bailed on us. I can't believe it. After all those careful arrangements."

And after all my sharp anticipation and anxiety, I thought. *Talk about an anticlimax, in all senses of that word.*

"Look," I said, patting John's knee, "it means a lot to me that you went to all that trouble and that you were willing to set up such a thing. I guess he doesn't need or want our money." "I guess not. To hell with him. It took me days to plan. What a waste of time and energy." John seemed more upset than I was, so I did my best to distract him with silly humor. "The No-Show Ho of Glasgow! Ought to be the title of a poem! The subtitle could be 'Ah cain't even *pay* a man to sleep with me!'" I wailed. "Lawd knows Ah *tried* to be a whoremonger!" then, paraphrasing Robert Frost, "Well, one day, I know I'll be telling this with a laugh somewhere ages and ages hence. The Scottish Stud Not Taken. Sob!"

What was I really feeling? My lust felt disappointment, my anxiety felt relief, and my boundless insecurity asked uncomfortable questions: *Did he bail on you because he decided he wasn't willing to try kink? Or did John send him a photo of you and he was so turned off he couldn't conceive of bedding you? Was he afraid you might tie him up and hurt him?*

For the most part, I felt indifference. Placidly, I sipped my tea, shrugged my shoulders, and thought, *Oh, well. Too bad. It might have been fun.* Perhaps that was my birthday present courtesy of the aging process and the cosmos: the insulation from deep hurt that comes from not caring. *Shit, I really am middle-aged*, I thought, surprised at my own unexpected serenity. I suppose a vulgar statement I've since savored online is true: the "give-a-shit factor" plummets as you age.

(Indulge me in two asides here. Internet-surfing, I just stumbled upon a book I need to read, *The Life-Changing Magic of Not Giving a Fuck* by Sarah Knight. With a title like that, who can resist? Plus I'm reminded of an illustration in *The Liberal Redneck Manifesto*, by Trae Crowder, Corey Ryan Forrester, and Drew Morgan: the redneck's eyes are "devoid of fucks to give." In the same book, "the single most defining characteristic of a redneck" is "a redneck don't give a damn." I aspire to such perfect equipoise. I've come a long way, but I still have a ways to go.)

III.

IT DIDN'T OCCUR to me that day in Glasgow, but it does now: such a sedate response to erotic letdown was drastically different from the distressing times I'd been disappointed by men in my youth. Several of those disappointments loom large in my memory.

In my undergrad days, there'd been lithe and handsome Mark, part of the first three-way I'd ever had (in my sophomore year, on the closet floor of a dorm room in Stalnaker Hall, along with that beefy RA who'd first bedded me). *What a hot, hot guy*, I thought, running my hands over his body and taking him into my mouth. *I want more of him. I'd love to get to know him better.* A few weeks after that initial daisy chain, we agreed to meet for a restaurant date. He didn't show, which tore me up, unreasonably hopeful, immoderately hungry, and emotionally fragile as I was.

In 1980, there had been Jack, the closest I ever got to a relationship in my early twenties. He was twice my age, with a gray beard, a mop of silvery hair, and a Yankee accent. I met him that spring at a Metropolitan Community Church service and was instantly captivated. We slept together several times, and I grew besotted by his lean, well-muscled build and big carpetbagger cock. I managed to see him a few times during Summer Break, despite my job in recreation at Pipestem State Park, at the other end of the state, and even traveled hours on a train and then a goddamned Greyhound to spend a handful more days with him. (God knows I was too broke to afford my own car.) I was ecstatic finally to have a boyfriend, my first. That wild beard, those hard pecs, that fat dick brought out obsessive reverence in me.

That fall, after a dinner date, he abruptly dumped me. "You're too intense for me. Every time you open your mouth, some kind of anger jumps out," he announced, leaving me sitting in front of the Mountainlair in the dark with my head in my hands. A few weeks later, he took up with a garrulous, rabbit-toothed, emaciated queen. I wanted to die. Every morning, when I woke and consciousness of that loss returned, I'd lie in my bed and thrash around, digging my thumbs against my eyelids and temples, as if trying to keep reality's needles out of my brain. Only when I attended Bette Midler's film *Divine Madness* did the despair lift a little. Listening to her sing that classic combination of "You Can't Always Get What You Want" and "I Shall Be Released" gave me a rushing catharsis that I'm still grateful for. (In other words, "Thank you, Divine Miss M!")

In the summer of 1982, just before I started grad school at WVU, I spent weeks hanging around the Double Decker, Morgantown's local gay bar, and admiring the bartender, Steve, with his big biceps and his red moustache. One evening, he took a shine to me and took me home, an event which felt downright miraculous. He looked like some sort of pale-muscled Arcadian deity, bound and gagged in candlelight. We slept together on and off for nearly a month before he took up with a bigger, older, better-looking man and left town. I pined over him compulsively all autumn.

Then there'd been charming Paul, with his broad shoulders and charismatic smile, to whom I'd been introduced by mutual friends. One cold night, January 1983, we ran across one another at the Double Decker. He'd just broken up with his boyfriend, he explained. I saw my chance. We danced, we got drunk, and I took him back to my shitty, one-room efficiency apartment beneath a garage. He was as desirable naked as I'd imagined.

I had great hopes, as usual, but the next Friday night he didn't appear as promised at my place. I was planning to take him out to dinner on a graduate student's salary: I made $4,000 a year. My generosity was clearly a sign of my desperation. I stayed up past midnight, sick with despair, craning for the sound of his car, too poor to afford phone service and so unable to call him to ask where the hell he was.

The depth of the pain I felt that night is hard for my present self to comprehend. Everything erotic or romantic Meant So Much. I wrote pained poetry about first Steve and then Paul for years.

What changed so radically? How had that trusting, hopeful, heartsick, horny cub in Morgantown, West Virginia, become a blasé, gray-bearded daddy bear sitting on the edge of a bed in Glasgow, Scotland? How had that tender, oversensitive boy become a man who dismissed the disappointment of the No-Show Ho as minor and forgettable? (Forgettable, except perhaps as the subject of an essay or poem. We writers are always on the lookout for fuel.)

I don't know the answers off the top of my head. I've never actually cogitated on these questions. But that's what writing an essay can be for: parsing out one's heart-history. So here we go.

Let's move from less important to more important reasons. By age fifty, sex was no longer a fascinating novelty, and the sex drive that had raged in my youth had subsided somewhat. I'd been to bed with many, many, many men since I was that yearning, lovelorn boy. Well, not just beds, I must boast. Also, offices, forests, a desert ravine, several basements-cum-dungeons, the back room of a barber shop, a gay bar restroom, a woodland cabin's loft, a car, a pasture, a barn, a garage, the bed of a pickup truck, and the seat of a motorcycle. I've always been obsessed with mortality and a big fan of carpe diem, and even though, to a man like me, no amount of sex is ever enough, I've managed fairly well in this incarnation, despite being no beauty and despite spending most of my life in not-particularly-queer Appalachia.

Another significant difference? As I've earlier made clear, I was, like many, a romantic idealist in my youth. I had grandiose expectations that this planet and this reality simply couldn't live up to. It was hard for me to separate sex from love. Like the lesbian in the joke who brings a U-Haul on her second date, I became emotionally involved fast. I expected sex to be transcendent, transformative, a ritual act in which pagan gods embodied in mortal men would intertwine with deep, mutual feeling. Inspired by Plato's *Symposium*, Emily Brontë's *Wuthering Heights*, and poetry by Shakespeare, Keats, and Yeats, I was full of Sturm und Drang and thought in spiritual and literary terms: the Beloved, the Muse, theophany, beautiful men as embodiments of Eros. In fact, in my M.A. thesis, *The German Darkness*, a book of lovelorn poems I'd written about Steve and Paul—men I'd fallen in love with for the simple reasons that they were handsome, nicely built, and had slept with me—the introduction's titled "The Muse with the Moustache."

Now I would change that to "Beard" or "Goatee." These days, moustaches look ridiculously dated to me. In 1991, however, in Blacksburg, Virginia, a muse with a moustache lived up to all my amorous expectations: the aforementioned Mythical Thomas. The equation that romantic literature had led me to expect was complete: profound attraction (even, in this case, profound mutual attraction) + wracking ardor + time for the ardor and the attachment to build + inevitable separation = lovesick anguish + lingering nostalgia and regret + a plethora of creative inspiration.

In the painful aftermath of that affair, I found my interior landscape transforming, the way violent volcanic or tectonic activity rearranges the surface of our planet, changes that provided me with a surprising benefit. As internally wrecked as I was, I became not at all interested in cultivating another emotional connection, and that disinterest, ironically, seemed to make me more attractive to other men. When it came to love, well, I'd felt that, and it had mutilated me. Sex without love? I could take it or leave it.

And so, I became the sort of gay man I'd once found so mystifying in my youth: one in it for the erotic experience, for the adventure, the pleasure, the fun, one not searching for romance. That youthful yoking of love and sex finally broke. Sex was something to savor in the moment, not something momentous that might lead to spiritual experience, emotional transformation, the Muse and/or The One Great Love. It shrank in importance to join food and drink as just another bodily pleasure.

As soon as I became indifferent to sexual encounters, my erotic luck changed. After a serendipitous meeting in a gay bar, I became the occasional BDSM boy-toy for two older men, a well-off top and bottom living in Richmond. Still later, after yet another Eros-blessed meeting at a Pride event, I got adopted by a pair of bears in Roanoke, Virginia. With both couples, I enjoyed long weekends of drinking, eating, and carnal amusement. Then came online flirtations on leather and bear sites, which led to infrequent play with a series of hot men: a very skilled Roanoke sadist, a masochistic bodybuilder covered with tattoos, a "straight" boy I "kidnapped" in a Walmart parking lot, a gun-toting mountain boy much like me who was adept with a flogger and who fucked like a jackhammer.

Note above a critical word, "play." Age and experience eventually reduced my youthful neo-Platonic quest for beauty and soul-shaking romance to a casual search for erotic recreation and libidinal entertainment. Among all my salacious adventures, there was no romantic entanglement, no need or desire for one. I discovered, belatedly, a concept I've since come to relish: the "fuck buddy," what folks on cruising apps call "friends with benefits," or NSA, no strings attached.

By the time I met my present husband John, I'd become as much of a rounder/Don Juan/slut/stud as my age, looks, and geographical region would allow. Between Thomas's exit in 1991 and John's entrance in 1997, my romantic illusions had eroded away like a clear-cut West Virginia hillside. Monogamy and domesticity—both things that I thought came naturally to me—were no longer of real interest. The only domestic things about me, I've discovered, are my love of cooking, a trait inherited from a long line of rural forebears, and my tendency to be a homebody, which is born of my misanthropy. Human beings piss me off more often than not, so avoiding them by staying home as much as possible seems wise.

Did I change from romantic youth to blithe satyr due to life's traumas and men's betrayals, or did I slough off false expectations, social mores, and illusions I'd absorbed from literature and popular culture and become more truly myself? Has it been a process of maiming and amputation, or a process of metamorphosis and flowering, or, somehow, paradoxically, both? Anyone of a certain age can ask the same questions and probably never come up with certainties. I do suspect that my youthful eagerness for romance and emotional connection probably came across as NEEDY, which explains why the men I pursued so often fled. It was only when my belief in romance crumbled that that appearance of pathetic neediness vanished, which led to more frequent sensual harvests.

The last and more salient reason that the Glasgow Ho's No Show was of little consequence? It's the most obvious, of course. I had a partner, now my legally married husband. The letdown was erotic, not romantic, physical rather than emotional. I was powerfully attracted to Robbie, or at least to the little photo on John's iPhone, but I didn't know him. John and I have never had a particularly strong carnal connection, but after so many years together, well, history counts for a lot. It carries great weight, true gravitas. My loins may not be loyal, but my heart is. I have heart-strong connections to John and a few family members and friends. At this age, I don't have the energy for or the interest in any more.

The Soul selects her own Society? That's for damn sure. Truer and truer as the years go by.

IV.

THERE ON THE bedside table lay the two hundred-pound bills. I slurped up the last of my tea, snatched up the bills, and waved them at John.

"How about you call that masseur and spend some time with him? I want *someone* to have a hot time."

John shook his head. "I'm not in the mood. Not worth the money."

"You're sure?"

"Yes."

I rubbed my beard. "Well, we're flying out tomorrow morning," I said. "Let's see what kind of feast we can purchase in place of a hot and hairy Glaswegian escort, shall we?"

Here's the answer to that question. At City Merchant Restaurant, we had several pints of Tennant's lager. As usual, we split a few starters: battered prawns, plus fried oysters with peppercorn Szechuan mayonnaise. For entrées, John got halibut with tapenade and pesto, and I gobbled delicious collops of beef with whisky sauce and haggis. We had slews of roast vegetables on the side: new potatoes, cauliflower, carrots, and snow peas. Then we split a bottle of champagne, and we finished with a cheese plate: four Scottish cheeses with oatcakes, celery, grapes, and quince paste. The bill came to 96.20 pounds.

"One hundred pounds left after all that food and drink," John pointed out. "We can keep it for future U.K. trips."

Oh, hell, I thought, *I wonder if Robbie's ass is hairy. I wonder if he likes his nips worked, if he kisses strong and deep.* "You bet," I said, sinking my teeth into the last grape. "It's all for the best. Who knows? The bastard could have given me crabs. Maybe we can try again in ten years."

Sated, we ambled off to a bear bar for Scotch and one last toast to my fiftieth birthday. On the way, brooding gifted me with a small epiphany. Were I single, were I young, I knew I'd be racked by handsome absence, by blue-ball regret. As it was, I offered up a prayer of thanks to all my pagan gods: *Here's to indulgent husbands and rich victuals' pleasures, all that can be counted on. Here's to age, how it dismisses what's trifling, leaches ache from appetite, and drains consequence from what cannot be kept.*

a great irony occurs to me: that hostile, homophobic town I was so desperate to escape forty years ago so that I might live my life as an openly gay man has become the very place where I most enjoy gay and lesbian camaraderie.

big queer convocations

I.

IN APRIL 1978, THE SPRING semester of my freshman year at West Virginia University, my lesbian friend Laura drove me home to attend my paternal grandmother's 75th birthday celebration. I was penniless and without a vehicle, but Laura and I rode in style in "Prince," her 1963 Plymouth Valiant convertible, down I-81 and Route 19 and on along the wood-lined back roads that led to my hometown of Hinton, West Virginia. The redbuds, I remember, were in full bloom: explosions of pink champagne amid spring's green-gold hills.

We descended Sandstone Mountain—a tortuous kiss-your-own-rear-bumper road that must be nerve-wracking to flatlanders—then the road leveled off, following the railroad tracks. Soon Hinton came into view, sprawled along the New River. We were only three or four blocks into town when Laura looked over at me, grinned, and said, "So... where are the gay bars?"

We both howled at the absurdity of the question. That plural noun, "bars," was the funniest part. As if a small, isolated, conservative town like Hinton (population around 3,000) would have one gay bar, much less more than one. For decades now, I've been telling this little story to folks curious about where I come from. It's a way to emphasize how very much *not* queer-friendly Hinton is, how very far it's situated from any public places where gays and lesbians might safely congregate.

In this respect, Hinton is like innumerable rural towns all over the nation: because of religious fundamentalism and the homophobia that inspires, it's a difficult, even a dangerous, place to be queer. When, in 1976—thanks to Jo Davison, a lesbian biology teacher, and Bill and Brenda, two lesbian friends—I realized at age sixteen that I was sexually attracted to men, Hinton immediately became a place to escape. There was no way to be openly gay there. Homosexuals, if they were mentioned at all, were objects of scorn and contempt, to be avoided, driven away, or bludgeoned senseless. And so, my friends and I stayed in the closet as best we could, read lesbian and gay novels, and dreamed of fleeing to college and, after that, to some exciting city where we might live in more welcoming circumstances.

When I got to West Virginia University, I hurled myself into the queer life there. My freshman year, the bar to go to was the Fox, where gays and straights mingled uncomfortably, and at least once I ended up backing my butch lesbian buddy Bill in a brawl with two huge queer-haters. My sophomore year, it was the Rendezvous, where intimidating drag queens like Miss Corley and Miss Leroy held court. Later, there was Angie's Den of Sin, as we called it, situated well beyond the outskirts of town, where patrons' tires were occasionally slit. Still later, during my WVU graduate-school days, there was the Double Decker, where I fell madly in love with Steve, a red-mustached, promiscuous bartender, and Paul, a charismatic user who resembled the young Ernest Hemingway. After I'd graduated and become an instructor at WVU, there was the Class Act, a basement bar entered from an alley—"an underground shame-hole," to borrow a phrase from *Absolutely Fabulous*. It's still there, I gather, under the new name Vice Versa.

Meanwhile, my attitude toward my hometown was gradually shifting. With queer friends and social spaces in Morgantown to help me make sense of my gay identity, it became time to come to terms with my Appalachian identity. I began to appreciate my kin more. I began to see things about Hinton and rural West Virginia that I missed and found increasingly valuable: the dialect, the traditional values, the good manners, the landscape, the food, the folk culture...and the country boys, the sort of men I'd first learned to desire and after whom I'd fashioned my own personal style (the boots-and-baseball-cap look I've jokingly come to call "redneck chic"). For years, I spent summers with my family in Hinton—partly for financial reasons and partly because I felt increasingly at ease there. Still, even then, there were queer-starved, summer-night jaunts with friends to the Shamrock in Bluefield, where Miss Helen, despite her wheelchair-bound status, guarded the door with a baseball bat, and the Grand Palace in Charleston, where statuesque drag queens shimmied and pranced.

I was never in my element in gay bars, despite my hunger for queer companionship. Though I enjoyed dancing with friends—songs by the Village People, Donna Summer, and the Pointer Sisters come to mind—I was far too shy and introverted to pursue men I found desirable, and only rarely did mutual attraction shared with a stranger lead to something more. And, as accustomed as I was to small-town life, the loud music and crowds in bars became, as I aged, less something to enjoy and more something to tolerate in order to spend time with other queer folks.

In August 1989, when I moved to Blacksburg, Virginia, to teach at Virginia Tech, my bar days pretty much ended. The nearest gay bar, the Park, was in Roanoke, a forty-five-minute drive away, and I had no interest in taking the risk of drinking and then driving home. I do have one amusing memory of the Park, though. In the mid-1990s, I shared occasional frolicsome fuck-buddy weekends with burly and bearded Keith and Tony, a Roanoke couple who savored erotic variety, and one Burns Night the three of us went dancing at the Park. I wore my kilt, hoping to catch the eyes of handsome strangers who might take it upon themselves to discover whether or not it's true that nothing's worn beneath the kilt. But no! The men all seemed chagrined by my tartan garment, though all the women seemed fascinated. Luckily, I still had Keith and Tony to entertain me at evening's end.

When I met John, my present husband, in 1997, my interest in spending time in gay bars dwindled further. For a few years, we had a house in Charleston, West Virginia, and would, ever so rarely, have drinks at the Tap Room, another "underground shame-hole" where members of the leather and bear communities hung out. (For you heterosexual mainstream innocents, leather men are practitioners of BDSM (bondage/discipline/dominance/submission/sadism/masochism) and bears are burly, hairy, masculine, bearded gay men.) One evening there, in a contest hosted by drag queens, we got to see our buddy Everett win Mr. Mountain State Daddy, complete with studded black-leather sash. Another evening, an acquaintance infamous for stripping naked and dancing after he'd had too much to drink provided everyone with a sweaty floppy-genital show, one punctuated by many a horny patron's appreciative hoop and holler.

During our travels together, John and I have often visited the local gay bars (all tracked down beforehand via the Internet): in Key West, in Provincetown, in Vienna, Amsterdam, Copenhagen, and Bruges. We've frequented the Green Lantern in D.C., where, on Thursday nights, shirtless men drink free. During trips to New Orleans for Saints and Sinners, the queer literary festival, we've admired go-go dancers gyrating atop the bar in Oz and leather-clad daddies glowering in the dark corners of the Phoenix. In San Francisco, we've checked out the original bear bar, the Lone Star Saloon ("All these guys look like they're from West Virginia," John whispered to me), and the Eagle, where a handsomely goateed and shirtless youth licked and spit-shined my black harness-strap boots.

On June 13, 2016, the many gay bars I've frequented were very much on my mind. The day before, an armed madman murdered forty-nine people, most of them Latino, at Pulse, a gay nightclub in Orlando, Florida. In the aftermath of the massacre, queer friends on Facebook reminisced about their favorite gay bars, and articles appeared here and there—in print journals and online—about the importance of gay bars as safe spaces and community centers.

So many people seemed shocked and surprised at what had happened in Orlando. I was not. I've been steeling myself for violence ever since I walked into my first gay bar in 1977. Then, I'd envisioned frat boys with baseball bats, not semi-automatics, but still, I'm always intensely aware when in a public queer space of a grim possibility: that space might be disrupted by violent, homophobic outsiders. This caution/paranoia exists partly because I grew up in a place hostile to homosexuals, and partly because Jo Davison, the lesbian biology teacher who helped me come out, told me horror stories about gay bars in her hometown—Columbus, Ohio—being busted by policemen who beat and intimidated the patrons. "They used rubber hoses, because those cause a lot of pain but don't leave marks. When you step inside a gay bar you've never been to before, look for the rear exit, so you can escape if the place gets raided," she'd advised.

I've been preparing for the worst ever since, at the same time that I haven't let fear curtail my freedoms, dictate my behavior, or hamper the sometimes ferocious frankness of my very gay and often erotic publications. Still, having drinks with John in late June 2016 at the Tavern on Camac in Philadelphia's "Gayborhood," or, in mid-July, at the London Pub in Oslo, Norway, I was more aware than ever that anything could happen at any time, that John and I might be ended at any moment.

II.

THE PULSE SHOOTER can rot in hell, as far as I'm concerned. For four decades, I've done my best to be brave in the face of homophobia, and no terrorist attack like that which occurred in Orlando is keeping this almost pathologically ornery and defiant West Virginia redneck/leather man/daddy bear out of a gay bar if I feel like lumbering into one for a martini or two. What is far more likely to keep me out is geographical distance and the strong preferences that have developed as I've aged. In other words, these days not only do I prefer to drink at home, I prefer to enjoy my queer spaces at home as well.

John and I have become inveterate homebodies. During the day, I'm either teaching at Virginia Tech, preparing for classes, or trying to write, and he's either working at his desk or traveling on business—to Texas, Tennessee, Oregon, South Carolina, California, and any number of other states. In the evenings we're weary, and we prize our quiet time together, which usually involves a couple of stiff drinks, home cooking, profound relaxation, and Netflix or DVDs. Sometimes we watch queer series like *Where the Bears Are* and *RuPaul's Drag Race*, or campy film classics like *Addams Family Values*, *The Birdcage*, *Victor/Victoria*, or *Hairspray*. Other times, we might watch the superhero/action films I relish. The *Captain America* and *Avengers* movies and anything from the *X-Men* franchise are my most recent favorites, though *300* and the *Lord of the Rings* trilogy are always to-be-seen-again options. (Yes, fundamentalist Christians, these are the details of Our Sinister Gay Agenda. Scared yet?)

Every now and then, though, we're in the mood for queer companionship. When that happens, we don't drive an hour to Roanoke to gyrate at the gay bar (the Park is, amazingly, still there). We're both in our fifties: the bass thumping and jostling crowds of such an establishment are not in the least appealing, plus the much-younger regulars would no doubt regard us sad old bastards with palpable contempt. (And, honestly, I've had enough of Generation Z's electronic-gadget addiction, bad manners, political correctness, and sense of entitlement. The more I avoid them—the generation that makes retirement look sweet—the better, though certain venomous colleagues and Virginia Tech administrators make retirement look even sweeter.)

"The Soul selects her own Society," wrote Emily Dickinson. It's a line I've often thought would serve as a fine T-shirt slogan for introverts like me. Spending time alone, with my spouse, or with small groups of close friends has always been more enjoyable than noisy public spaces with crowds of strangers. So, when John and I start hankering after the simpatico company of other queers, instead of going out, we encourage a select few gay and lesbian friends to join us for a weekend. Luckily, we possess the resources to make such private gatherings possible...which is to say that we own two comfortable and roomy residences and possess the salaries sufficient to purchase loads of liquor and groceries.

Sometimes we invite said few to our house in Pulaski, "Tabbywood," a brick Georgian-style house where guests can shower attention on our cats, relish the meals produced by our plethora of cookbooks, or admire my collection of daggers and swords, prints of Confederate generals, or pagan altar. (I am, admittedly, an odd amalgam of elements.)

More often, though, we invite them to spend the weekend in "Fabled Hintonia," as I've been grandly dubbing my hometown since my undergraduate days. These are the hedonistic gatherings I've dubbed "Big Queer Convocations," aka BQCs. I like to think of them as the Southern Appalachian version of Gertrude Stein and Alice B. Toklas's salons in Paris.

Our Hinton house was built around 1920. It's a solid wooden two-story structure not far from the Summers County Courthouse. Set beside a little park and near the edge of a cliff that drops down to railroad tracks and the New River, the house looks out over whitewater rapids and the mountains beyond. My family moved there in the mid-70s, and I considered it home from the ninth grade on through high school and college and long after. Several years after my mother died, my father sold the house, to my deep disapproval and displeasure. In 2014, the folks to whom he'd sold it decided to move to Florida, so John and I bought the place. Now it's the site for BQCs, during which much quaffing and feasting occur.

Creating a feast is something I'm skilled at now, but that hasn't always been the case. When I was an undergraduate, I hardly knew how to fry an egg. Though descended from a long line of fine country cooks, I had not yet inherited their skills. I was too busy growing a beard, studying Romantic poetry and dendrology, lifting weights, browsing through gay porn magazines like *Drummer* and *Honcho*, and trying to become tough and butch so that I wouldn't get my ass kicked by queer haters.

Luckily for me, several of my college friends knew their way around a kitchen and made sure my poverty-stricken self didn't starve. Allen fried me pancakes and cooked up big pots of brown beans. Brenda made beef stew and spaghetti and big Sunday-morning breakfast "glops": fried potatoes, onions, and peppers mixed with eggs. Laura created vegetarian stir-fries, tabbouleh, hummus, and tofu dishes, all quite exotic to a small-town West Virginian like me.

Eventually, my enthusiasm for eating translated into a passion for cooking. During graduate school in the 1980s and later as an instructor at WVU, I worked up a handful of specialties with which to feed my queer friends: eggplant Parmesan, broccoli and bacon quiche, tuna casserole, omelets, and chicken soup with Bisquick dumplings. During visits home, I had my grandmother teach me Southern staples like piecrust and biscuits from scratch. In the 1990s, lonely and horny in Blacksburg, I began to go to Europe once a year over my summer break, and there I became fascinated with international fare. My collection of cookbooks waxed, and soon I was driving home to Hinton on weekends (since I had next to no friends in Blacksburg) and making my family British, Greek, German, French, Belgian, Mexican, and Italian specialties.

When I met John in 1997, two accomplished cooks came together. We've been preparing solid meals of great variety ever since, for ourselves and for the rare set of guests. Culinary skill is to be expected of us members of the gay bear community: we're big men who prize comfort and love to eat.

So, the BQCs in Fabled Hintonia center upon food and fellowship. John and I arrive on a Friday, lugging boxes of groceries. We turn the hot water back on and adjust the thermostat. In cold weather, we bring in firewood from the wood box on the porch. We make sure that the guest beds are all made and towels are set out. Then I open up the cookbooks and start work on a menu I've been planning for weeks.

Around 4 p.m., my sociologist friend Okey (the fabulous and ferocious drag queen, Miss Ilene Over, who's the focus of a later essay in this book) arrives from Huntington, West Virginia, bearing huge bottles of wine, loaves of bread, and assorted cheeses. Around 5 or so, my political theorist friend Cindy appears, bringing desserts from Just Pies, a chain of bakeries around Columbus, Ohio. Promptly at 5 p.m., John sets out the requisite appetizers—cheeses, breads or crackers—and I prepare drinks: wine for Okey, Bud Light for Cindy, and martinis for John and me.

Sometimes Cindy's partner Laree arrives from D.C., bringing a plethora of gourmet treaties from upscale grocery stores. Occasionally, Mizz Patty—a queer-friendly straight woman from a small Nebraska town who's traveled the world and speaks German like a native—accompanies Cindy, bearing the ingredients required to prepare her specialty, baked grape leaves stuffed with goat cheese and sun-dried tomatoes. Other times, Cindy brings along her Ohio housemate Lee, a radical lesbian feminist, cat lover, and union worker.

One of the advantages of creating queer space in my home, rather than finding it in gay bars, is the much greater control I have over that space, and, like most American men, I'm a big fan of being in control. I choose the participants—folks I know well, care about deeply, and trust—and I choose the music. No thumping disco tunes or any frenetic drivel that passes for popular music today. Instead, our iPods shuffle through old favorites: John's Barbra Streisand and Bette Midler, my Joni Mitchell, Carly Simon, and Judy Collins. (I'm a big country-music fan, but none of my guests is, so I save that genre for solitary drives to work in my pickup.)

The menus? My guests often request those. I always ask them beforehand what they most hanker for. For dinner, favorites include Hungarian cabbage rolls, stuffed peppers, haluski (fried cabbage and noodles), pinto beans and cornbread, and homemade pizza. Sunday breakfasts are nearly always buttermilk biscuits and sausage gravy, though North Carolina liver mush, ramps and scrambled eggs, and Tex-Mex *migas* are tasty alternatives.

Before, during, and after eating, the conversation flows. Sometimes we've read one another snippets from our latest works-in-progress: Cindy's book about the U.S. State Department's intervention on behalf of LGBT rights overseas; Okey's drag queen romance, *Make Me Pretty, Sissy*; or my gay vampire novel, *Insatiable*, in which my fanged alter ego takes on mountaintop removal mining. Sometimes we share funny stories, as in Okey's latest outrageous gem: "That restaurant server was so rude, obviously a homophobe, glaring at us, so when he gave me attitude, I looked up at him and said, 'Honey, would you like to butt-fuck an old showgirl?' He turned red as fire and never came back to the table! They had to assign us another server!"

Quite often, the conversation runs toward a gratifying bitch-fest/cussing session, long bouts of savage grousing that John quietly avoids. There are few pleasures more delicious than comparing notes with like-minded people who detest the same things you do. During the BQCs we enjoy said pleasure in spades, aiming our contempt at both the far left and the far right.

We excoriate Republicans, conservatives, and religious fundamentalists; we joke about "nasty women" and "grabbing pussies." We deride Generation Z, among them spoiled, well-off students who feel "unsafe," fear "microaggressions," and demand "trigger warnings," or young politically correct queers. "Bless their hearts," I drawl, rolling my eyes and curling my lip. "After all the struggle and suffering that our generation endured, after all we accomplished, these brats are arguing about 'preferred gender pronouns?'"

With a second martini, my ire waxes hotter. I snarl about colleagues I loathe, the latest disrespect I've suffered at Virginia Tech, the editor who said he was tired of how I "fetishize rednecks." Cindy describes the latest bullshit that the transgender language police are pushing: "It isn't called a vagina any longer. They insist that we call it a 'front hole.' No F-to-M person wants to be reminded that he still has a vagina." Okey tells us about the latest homophobe he put in his place, the latest fundamentalist he told to kiss his queer ass. "Honey, when I first did drag, I carried a brick in my purse, and, the way the country's a'goin', I have half a mind to carry one again!"

After purging ourselves of bile, we move on to dessert and hysterical television entertainment—Brother Boy in *Sordid Lives* ("Do you see my pussy now?" and "Shoot her, Wardell! Shoot her in the head!") or Bubbles Devere in *Little Britain* ("Is she as... beautiful as they say?"). Sometimes, I play the guitar or the piano, or, more rarely, the Appalachian dulcimer. Three times out of four, Okey and I stay up late, talking about his difficulties as a gypsy instructor, my frustrated literary ambitions, and the neopaganism we share.

Then the short weekend is over, and we must leave our safe queer sanctuary and go back into an overwhelmingly heterosexist world where we feel little at home. Before we disperse, we compare schedules, already planning the next Big Queer Convocation in Fabled Hintonia. After our guests have left, John and I turn down the heat, turn off the hot water, and pack up leftovers and recyclables to take back to Pulaski. As we leave Hinton, a great irony occurs to me: that hostile, homophobic town I was so desperate to escape forty years ago so that I might live my life as an openly gay man has become the very place where I most enjoy gay and lesbian camaraderie. I will, I feel fairly sure, go back to that house and that town as long as I live, and I'll continue to create a haven there for my queer kin.

III.

I'M WRITING THE final section of this essay on November 10, 2016, two days after Donald Trump has won the Presidency of the United States. As a gay man, I'm devastated, numb, nauseated, frightened, and furious. Trump and his running mate Pence have made clear their hostility toward queer people and their rights. They have mentioned their desire to repeal same-sex marriage by stacking the Supreme Court with conservatives.

Like comedian Trae Crowder, I identify as a "liberal redneck." To my disappointment, though not to my surprise, one set of those I consider to be My People—small-town and rural folks, those who live near me in Pulaski and Hinton and in similar places all over the nation—is to a great extent responsible for Trump's triumph. That triumph spells dark days for another set of My People, gays and lesbians.

I'm trying to make sense of this situation. I'm trying to decide how to go on, how to grapple with a future turned very grim, how to continue without being devoured by my own rage and dread. Yesterday, I had only enough energy to lift weights in my basement gym, read a few pages from a new translation of the Norse *Poetic Edda*, and, in my husband's absence, drink heavily all evening and post as my new Facebook cover photo an image John sent me from Oregon, a hand-lettered sign that says "FUCK DONALD TRUMP."

Today, browsing more of *The Poetic Edda*, I'm thinking about what the past teaches us about coping with the future. For decades, I've been interested in my Celtic and Teutonic roots in Scotland, Ireland, and Germany, and I've been reading Norse mythology and Icelandic sagas. I've also been collecting swords and thinking about what it means to be a warrior and what I—a middle-aged author of the twenty-first century—can learn from long-dead Highland chiefs and medieval Vikings.

The concept of the clan is dear to me, and, as an Appalachian, the clan mindset comes to me naturally. My family and my (mostly queer) friends *are* my clan. If I'm to resemble a warrior in any way, then my job is to provide for my clan and protect them, as much as is possible. My writing must be a kind of warfare: speaking as a gay man and a liberal Appalachian, no matter how frankly queer, angry, defiant, and erotic my words might be, no matter how offensive and unacceptable to conservatives and the mainstream.

Today, as I imagine America under Trump, I realize that not much has changed in my relation to and attitude toward the outside world. Things have just intensified. As I've said, I'm always expecting the worst and preparing myself to deal with it. As a queer and as a hillbilly, I've always regarded the larger world as hostile to me and those I love, and I've always fiercely cherished my clan and passionately hated my enemies. (I'm a heathen: I feel no Christian obligation to love or forgive my foes.) Now, after Trump's victory, the world simply feels more hostile and the things I love more fragile, more in need of defense. For the first time in my life, I'm seriously contemplating the purchase of a gun.

That deepening sense of the world's enmity will give me the drive to continue doing what's necessary, despite the sick despair I'm feeling today. I'll celebrate the natural world—the sugar maple's fiery orange, the tabby cat snoozing on the bed, the chickadee chattering in the spruce. I'll continue to publish in-your-face gay poetry, fiction, and creative nonfiction, small literary rebellions in the spirit of my Rebel ancestors. I'll arrange Big Queer Convocations as often as I can, in quiet, conservative Hinton, in Republican-poisoned West Virginia. I'll arrange for my people the small pleasures—music, talk, food, and drink—that have always helped beleaguered human beings endure hard times.

Next month—December 2016—some of us will gather again. I'll honor Hestia by making a grand meal and preparing a fire. I'll clean ashes from the hearth, lay on newspaper, kindling, and dry logs, and strike the match. My husband, friends, and I will drink and laugh and feast. I'll do what vigilant men have always done to keep their people safe: check the perimeter, secure the doors, pull drapes against the cold. I'll watch the flames and think of my forbears, scruffy Scots and burly Vikings gathering in long-ago crofts, castles, and halls. They're drinking ale and mead, adding wood to the fire, savoring bread, cheese, and roast meat. Some among them—the grizzled and the wary ones—are keeping their senses alert, weapons at the ready, acutely aware of the surrounding dark.

> *I respect other folks' heritage. I'd hope to receive the same respect in return, but these days that hope seems vain.*

confederate

"Demur—you're straightway dangerous..."
—Emily Dickinson, "Much Madness is divinest Sense"

"A foolish consistency is the hobgoblin of little minds."
—Ralph Waldo Emerson, "Self-Reliance"

1.

THE CONFEDERATE MONUMENT IN my hometown of Hinton, West Virginia, was erected in 1914. I have no doubt that my great-great-grandfather, Isaac Green Carden, a Civil War veteran, was among those who funded the monument's construction and witnessed its unveiling on May 23 of that year. A Rebel soldier in uniform stands on the base, with moustache, sideburns, canteen, and hat, his "weight balanced on one leg, rifle butt on the ground, both hands holding the barrel, gazing toward the horizon," says Cheryl Kula, whose essay about the monument, "To Remotest Ages," appeared a century after its unveiling in the Summer 2014 issue of *Now and Then: The Appalachian Magazine*.

The inscription on the front of the base, beneath an image of Robert E. Lee, says, "This monument erected in honor of American valor as displayed by the Confederate Soldiers from 1861 to 1865 and to perpetuate to remotest ages the patriotism and fidelity to principles of the heroes who fought and died for a lost cause." The inscription on the left side of the base reads, "This monument is dedicated to the Confederate Soldiers of Greenbrier and New River Valleys who followed Lee and Jackson." The inscription on the right side says, "Sacred to the Memory of the noble Women of the Confederacy who suffered more and lost as much with less glory, than the Confederate Soldier." On the back of the base, the inscription reads, "Erected in the year 1914 by Camp Allen Woodrum, Confederate Veterans and Camp Bob Christians, Sons of Confederate Veterans and their friends" (Kula 36).

2.

How would you feel if you visited a memorial honoring one of your ancestors only to find that monument defaced? Pocked with bullet holes, perhaps, or shattered with a sledge hammer, or broken in half? Or removed entirely? If you're like me, you'd feel shock, and then sadness, and then rage, and then the urge for retribution.

3.

I was in London, leading a month-long Study Abroad program with two wonderful Virginia Tech colleagues, "Jane the Good" and "Jane the Wicked," as they call themselves, when that insane little shit did what he did in Charleston, South Carolina on June 17, 2015. White supremacist Dylann Roof was part of an hour-long Bible study discussion at the Emanuel African Methodist Episcopal Church before he pulled his Glock, the same brand of gun I own, and shot nine members of the church, all black.

It's vile and vicious enough to shoot strangers without good reason. (The only good reasons I can think of are these: you're a soldier and they're enemy soldiers; they're trying to take your life; they're threatening the ones you love.) It's even more contemptible to pretend to be friendly and join in their conversation before attacking them. You are, in effect, turning on those who gave you welcome, the same sort of betrayal that occurred in Glencoe in 1692, when the Campbells massacred their hosts, the McDonalds. Not for nothing that Dante positions the betrayers at the very bottom of hell, stuck in the ice around Satan.

The car that Dylann Roof was driving when he was captured on the day after the attack had a three-flag Confederate States of America bumper sticker on it, a design similar to that of a baseball cap I own. Of the many photos of Roof found after his arrest, one shows him posing with a handgun and the Confederate battle flag, a flag my forebear fought for.

Just about everyone knows what followed. In July 2015, thanks to Nikki Haley, then the governor of South Carolina, workers removed the Rebel battle flag flying over the Confederate monument on the State House grounds. Then various retailers across the country stopped selling merchandise that displayed the flag, even, absurdly, the toy replica of the "General Lee," the car driven by Bo and Luke Duke on *The Dukes of Hazzard*. I'm trying to imagine some delicate child being "traumatized" by the sight of that flag, painted atop the tiny plastic vehicle that some benighted, politically incorrect playmate brought out to zoom around.

That flag's been displayed by white supremacists and racist pigs like Dylann Roof for decades, so I understand why so many Americans would hate it and want to remove it from public display. What those people don't understand, or refuse to think about, is that the American soldiers who fought for that flag and for the Confederate States Army have innumerable descendants like me living today. If you attack that flag, if you ignore the statement,

"Heritage, Not Hate," if you assume that hate is all it means for anyone who displays it or respects it, you're not only engaging in thoughtless generalization, you're attacking the memory of those Southern soldiers and also their descendants. If we respond with angry alienation, you shouldn't be surprised.

I'm a gay man who's grown up in the South, and the homophobia of fundamentalist Christianity has made my life here sometimes dangerous and always difficult. Yet I'm not demanding the dismantling of local churches, no matter how virulent I might find the local species of Christianity, and I don't necessarily assume that those wearing crosses around their necks or sporting icthys stickers on their vehicles are folks who'd want to stone me to death or rob me of my civil rights, were they to know of my sexual orientation. They might be, they might not. Until they prove hostile, I'm going to give them the benefit of the doubt. But then I was raised with manners and a live-and-let-live attitude, unlike those prescriptive sorts who deign to explain what my symbols mean to me.

4.

EVEN BEFORE THE Roof shooting, the faddish frenzy of removing Confederate flags from public spaces was waxing apace. One especially absurd example occurred in 2014, on the campus of Washington and Lee University in Lexington, Virginia.

My mother's ancestor, Cyrus McCormick, inventor of the reaper, donated so much money to W&L that there's a statue of him on campus. My father, weary of public-school teaching, returned to college in his fifties, earning a law degree from W&L before beginning his legal career. I was a child when he graduated, and I still have vague memories of driving through the beautiful mountainous landscape between Covington, Virginia, where we lived then, and Lexington for the on-campus ceremony. I don't remember much about the graduation, but I do remember one vignette from that trip.

Daddy showed me the President's house, in which Robert E. Lee had died in 1870. Beside the house was a garage.

"That used to be a stable," Daddy said. "That's where Lee kept his famous horse, Traveller. You remember that picture of Lee hung in the front parlor of the Old Homeplace? That's a photo of him riding Traveller." Yes, there was reverence in his tone. Yes, there was deep respect.

In October 2010, I went back to W&L for research. I'd started to write the first of my two Civil War novels, *Purgatory*, and I was composing *Rebels*, a collection of poems "queering" the War. I visited Stonewall Jackson's grave, leaving a lemon, his favorite battlefield snack, there. I visited Traveller's stable-turned-garage and Lee Chapel. For those of you who don't know, Lee Chapel contains a wonderful marble statue, "The Recumbent Lee," by Edward Valentine, depicting Lee asleep on the battlefield. In the basement are the family crypt, where Lee and members of his family are entombed, as well as Lee's office, kept as he left it, and a small museum. Right outside the side door to the crypt, Traveller is buried. On his grave plaque, previous visitors had left coins and an apple in remembrance.

In 2014, a bunch of W&L law students got a case of the ass, to use the hillbilly vernacular I'm fond of, called themselves "The Committee," and demanded that the Confederate battle flag, a symbol they apparently found as frightful as a swastika, be removed from Lee Chapel. To the disgust and dismay of many, including myself, the President of the university agreed to do so (Rife).

I try to imagine myself entering a chapel and demanding that all crosses be pulled down, because, as a pagan and a gay man—two groups historically persecuted by Christianity—the sight of them makes me uncomfortable. Perhaps, the next time I visit a friend's home, I'll demand that certain paintings or pieces of furniture be trashed because I have aesthetic objections to them. Or perhaps strangers should approach me in the parking lot of Food City and insist that I remove the Obama bumper stickers from my pickup truck. Or perhaps I should do the same when I see detestable Trump stickers on strangers' vehicles.

What gall, what disrespect. This is the sort of solipsism, hypersensitivity, and, most of all, entitlement, I've come to expect from Generation Z. "I demand that everything in my environment accommodate me because I'm a very important person," seems to be the attitude.

What have you achieved in your lives, members of "The Committee," compared to what Robert E. Lee achieved? Why should anyone kowtow to you? Read a few books about Lee, his amazing military strategies, and all that the South suffered during the Civil War. Surely you knew the history of that university before you applied for admission there. If you don't like the presence of Lee at W&L, or the demonstrations of honor he deserves, or replicas of the flag he fought for, go home. Attend another university.

5.

IN *CONFEDERATES IN the Attic: Dispatches from the Unfinished Civil War*, author and journalist Tony Horwitz asks Shelby Foote, the prominent Civil War historian, "Why did the South in particular cling to remembrance of the War?" Foote replied, "It was fought in our own backyard...and you're not apt to forget something that happened on your own property" (146).

Thanks to my family history, I myself have a very strong sense of how not-that-long-ago the Civil War occurred and thus how much it's likely to linger in Southern minds. My father, Perry Mann, Jr., knew our Confederate ancestor, Isaac Green Carden, during Daddy's childhood and during the last years of the Civil War veteran's life.

Isaac grew up on the Carden farm near Forest Hill, West Virginia, in what my family calls the Old Homeplace. He was the father of Arminta Carden, who married Erastus Ferrell, a landed sort who'd spent his childhood on a big bottomland farm along the Greenbrier River. When Erastus married Arminta, he sold his half of the Ferrell property to his brother, and the newlyweds settled into the Carden farm to start a family. One child of that union was my father's mother, Pauline Ferrell, who was raised in that same house. Isaac Carden's buried on a hilltop right behind the Old Homeplace, in our family graveyard. According to his grave marker, he was born August 10, 1841; he was a private in Lowry's Battery, Light Artillery, in the Confederate States Army; and he died February 28, 1932.

In 2012, I found a regimental history online and special-ordered it: *Lowry's, Bryan's, and Chapman's Batteries of Virginia Artillery*, by J. L. Scott. The very first page of the book says: "This series is dedicated to the men who served in Virginia Units during the War Between the States. It is the purpose of this series to preserve, as a part of our heritage, the deeds and sacrifices of these men." There my forebear was, listed in the roster of Lowry's Battery: "Carden, Isaac Green: enlisted June 8, 1861, at Indian Creek. Present through final roll. Paroled in Charleston, June 12, 1865. Age 24, 5'11" tall, dark eyes, dark hair. He was living in Hinton, W. Va. in 1916" (25). Isaac apparently enlisted along with his brothers, Allen and John, and all three of them survived the war.

I found out quite a bit as I read the three chapters dedicated to Lowry's battery. Isaac first saw battle, it seems likely, at the Battle of Scary Creek, outside St. Albans, West Virginia.

What an ironic juxtaposition between his life and mine. I have lesbian friends in St. Albans I occasionally visit, and I've often stopped for hot dogs at the Red Line Diner there and admired assorted well-built, goateed mountain boys about whom I've entertained many a kidnapping fantasy. A historical marker stands on the edge of the diner's parking lot, and just beyond that marker flows Scary Creek. The marker's inscription reads:

BATTLE OF SCARY
First Confederate victory in Kanawha Valley fought here July 17, 1861. Charge of the Rangers under Captain (later General) Jenkins won the day. Whitelaw Reid described the event as a war correspondent with Gen. Cox's Union forces.

After that initial battle beside the future site of one of my favorite hot-dog joints, the battery saw action in 1862 in Pearisburg and Narrows in Virginia, and Princeton, Lewisburg, Fayetteville, and Charleston in present-day West Virginia, all towns I've spent time in ("my backyard," to use Foote's expression). Isaac's battery wintered at Thorn Springs, near Dublin, Virginia, a place I pass every time I make the drive from Pulaski, Virginia, where I live, to Blacksburg, Virginia, where I teach at Virginia Tech. In 1863, his battery spent time in Saltville, Virginia, an important source of salt for the Confederacy, and then East Tennessee. In 1864, they saw action at the Battle of Lynchburg and invaded Maryland under Jubal Early, then fought at Second Kernstown, Third Winchester, and the disastrous Battle of Cedar Creek. They spent the last winter of the war in Narrows, a scenic little town I drive past whenever I head back to Hinton for a visit (Scott 1-20).

In the 1970s, my father was the prosecuting attorney of Summers County, and years later my sister followed him in that position. When I visited them in the prosecutor's office, set in one of the huge red-brick turrets of the Summers County Courthouse, I'd often visit Isaac, which is to say I'd stop in the central hallway of the courthouse to study a black-and-white photograph hung on the wall. The photo, taken October 15, 1907, is that of a reunion of Confederate States Army veterans at Forest Hill's Primitive Baptist Church. Now called the Fairview Church, it's right up the hill from where I spent weekends with my paternal grandmother, Pauline (aka "Nanny"), when I was a child and young man. The church is only a little farther than a good hard stone's throw from the house where my sister lives and the fifty-some acres of pastureland and woodland on which I used to range about as a boy. Again, let me emphasize, my backyard.

That October 1907, the veterans gathered to celebrate the erection of a grave monument, a white granite obelisk, honoring a local Confederate hero, sharpshooter Mike Foster, who "was personally decorated as the bravest man" in the Stonewall Brigade, according to a nearby West Virginia historical marker. Foster, says the inscription on his obelisk, had been "desperately wounded near Petersburg, VA, in 1865 and died of his wounds May 22 1875," at age thirty-six. My ancestor Isaac, according to *The History of Summers County* by James Henry Miller, was a member of the Mike Foster Monument Association, a group that raised funds to make the obelisk possible ("Mike Foster/Confederate Sharpshooter"). I've since read about Foster's heroism in a Rebel soldier's memoir, *My Reminiscences of the Civil War with the Stonewall Brigade and the Immortal 600*, by a Ronceverte, West Virginia, native, Captain Alfred Mallory Edgar (68, 100). When I last visited Foster's grave, someone had stuck a tiny Confederate battle flag in the grass beside the monument, so I guess local folks still honor and remember him.

Back to that C.S.A. reunion photo. In it, about one hundred middle-aged and elderly men, most of them sporting long gray beards, pose in formal wear against a woodland background, along with a handful of women dressed in white. Isaac Carden's smack-dab in the middle, right beside that sinister Confederate battle flag that has so many fragile souls terrified these days. In October 1907, he would have been sixty-six, seven years older than I am as I write this. The hair on his head is short, still fairly dark, and his long beard is darker than most of his compatriots'. His eyes are piercing and his eyebrows are black.

In the last years of his life, my father hired a genealogist to conduct research on our family. In the process, Daddy sent me JPEGs of old photographs of Isaac that the researcher had found. In one, he's the sheriff of Summers County, posing atop a black horse, looking serious, his salt-and-pepper beard long, his eyes deep-set and dark. In another, he's a very old man, his beard even longer, entirely white, and he's posing with a woman I assume is his third wife. (He survived the first two, a not unusual circumstance in those days, when so many women died in childbirth.) In another, apparently a wedding photo, that beard is black, halfway down his chest, his eyes as intense as usual. Beside him is…his first wife? His second? In another, he's posing with his younger brother John, both of them in formal wear—white shirts, vests, and suit jackets—and both of them sporting those long, bushy beards, John's gray, Isaac's gray as well, though his moustache remains dark.

The photo that interests my narcissism the most, though, is one of Isaac taken most likely in his twenties, around the time he served in the Confederate States Army. He's got short, black hair parted on the left, black eyebrows, dark eyes, full cheeks, and a thick black moustache and beard. He looks very much like I did at that age, though my beard wasn't that bushy, my hair was already beginning to fall out, and nearsightedness required that I wear glasses. "Isaac diluted," I suppose I could call myself. Still, after spending so many years of my life wondering about my Rebel forebear, it was a real surprise to discover that he and I once looked so much alike that we could have been brothers. It's made my sense of connection to him all that more vivid.

6.

FOR FIFTEEN YEARS, I've visited New Orleans annually to attend Saints and Sinners, the biggest queer literary festival in the nation. In 2017, I attended SAS with reluctance, and in 2018 that reluctance was mixed with roiling resentment. In fact, I nearly didn't go.

When people anger or offend me, I'm adept at removing them, swiftly and surgically, from my life. The same goes for cities. I'd boycott New Orleans entirely, if it weren't for the fact that SAS has been so important to my career and has introduced me to so many great writers, editors, and publishers, folks I've grown very fond of and never see outside the festival.

In the aftermath of Dylann Roof's crimes, the Confederate flag wasn't the only Rebel symbol under assault. Thanks to political correctness and the hysterical hatred of all things Confederate, in December 2015, the mayor of New Orleans, Mitch Landrieu, and the City Council declared the Confederate statues in New Orleans "nuisances."

Landrieu and crew didn't know about, care about, or chose to ignore certain significant facts about New Orleans' Civil War history. Thanks to David Farragut, the Yankee army invaded the city in 1862, and bejowled Benjamin Butler became military governor for several months. During his tenure, he implemented martial law, sending off to hard labor anyone cheering for President Jefferson Davis or Confederate General Pierre-Gustave Toutant de Beauregard. When the ladies of New Orleans showed their contempt for their occupiers by spitting on them or insulting them—actions entirely appropriate, given the circumstances—"Beast" Butler passed General Order No. 28: "hereafter, when any female shall, by word, gesture or movement, insult or show contempt for any officer or soldier of the United States, she shall be regarded and held liable to be treated as a woman of the town, plying her avocation" ("General Order"). In other words, he was equating defiant Southern ladies with whores. It's no surprise that many Southerners still hate the Beast and that his image adorns the bottom of antique chamber pots made at that time. I'd like to own one of those myself.

In the spring of 2017, four New Orleans Confederate statues were removed: one commemorating the Battle of Liberty Place on April 24, the statue of Jefferson Davis on May 11, and the statue of Beauregard, a native of New Orleans, on May 16-17. On May 19, workers removed the statue of Robert E. Lee from his sixty-foot fluted pedestal in Lee Circle. The statue had stood there since 1884 (Litten; "Robert E. Lee").

Many angry people gathered in the streets, protesting the removal of those statues. If I'd been in town, I would have been one of them. I'm glad I wasn't. I live with enough ire as it is. I would have wanted to hurt someone: the workers doing the removal, the people celebrating by playing music and dancing in the streets. Doing research for this essay, reading about the statues' removal, makes me simmer with impotent fury. Call it redneck rage, if you will. I don't apologize for it. All my life, I've had to suppress my wrath, for my own sake and for the sake of those around me.

If there were a shooting range within easy driving distance, I'd go there now, to purge some of this bile. Who would be left after an imaginary massacre of my political enemies, on both the left and the right? Not too many. Immoderate passion does tend to isolate. Still, for god's sake, allow a man his salutary fantasies. Let me emphasize the word "fantasies," since the legal consequences of real carnage would be too extreme to make such delicious actions worth it. Make-believe slaughters are like masturbation: a private diffusion of energies that might otherwise transmogrify into public aggression. Not for nothing I write fiction full of sex and violence.

7.

FOR YEARS, I'VE put off writing this essay. First of all, as the above makes abundantly clear, the removal of Confederate statues is a topic that infuriates me. It makes me roil with hatred and ineffectual rage. These emotions are difficult to live with, as you might imagine. Also difficult to live with is the likelihood that this essay will horrify most of my fellow liberals and many of my readers, who otherwise might appreciate my honesty on everything from kinky eroticism to gay Appalachian identity.

I've expressed my impassioned opinion on Confederate symbols before, in "Unreconstructed Queer," an essay about the Confederate battle flag, published in a special 2001 issue of *Callaloo* and included in my second essay collection, *Binding the God: Ursine Essays from the Mountain South*. Certain members of the Virginia Tech English Department's Personnel Committee, it was rumored, were "very concerned" when they read that piece as part of my 2006-2007 tenure bid, after which I was successfully promoted to Associate Professor. Yes, please envision my contemptuous eye roll inside those ironic quotation marks. Academia is a place I feel comfortable in one day and another day find over-refined, oversensitive, and ridiculous. The members of that committee managed to overlook, tolerate, or ignore all the gay BDSM erotica I'd published but were brought up short by my "Heritage, Not Hate" attitude toward the Confederate flag.

In 2017, Paul C. Graham published *Confederaphobia! An American Epidemic*, a defiant and amusing book I'll refer to later. Here, let me adapt his word "Confederaphobia" in order to put my own "Confederaphilia" in further context.

Politically, I'm a liberal Democrat and always have been. I remember canvassing for George McGovern when I was a kid. My guitar case is plastered with stickers, among them "Mondale/Ferraro," "Clinton/Gore," and "To Hell with the Moral Majority." My pickup truck's rear bumper has two stickers, "Obama '08" and "Obama/Biden," and I've been a huge fan of the classy and wonderful Obamas since they first made the national scene. In 2016, terrified by the thought that Donald Trump might be elected president, I sent Hillary Clinton's campaign so much money that some of it was returned, since an individual donor can by law only donate $2,700 to a political campaign. I've spent my life detesting Republicans. I hated Ronald Reagan and George W. Bush, though my animosity towards them is nothing compared to my savage detestation of Donald Trump and his vile and venal crew.

In addition, I'm an openly gay man married to another man, and

John and I have a wonderfully diverse array of in-laws, among them West Virginia African Americans, a Hawaiian of Chinese descent, and an Indian-American. My publisher's Jewish, and I've learned a lot about Jewish culture from him. I've had a series of Muslim friends who've gotten me addicted to the cooking and eating of Middle Eastern cuisine, most especially Iraqi and Persian. As a gay man, I detest and fear conservative Christians and religious fundamentalists of all kinds. As the uncle of a biracial teenager who's descended from both Southern black folks and a white Confederate soldier, I fear and detest racists in any form. Having people of different faiths and races in your extended family is both enlightening and worrying. It makes the political the personal in very pointed ways. In my case, the defacing of synagogues, the proliferation of Islamophobia, and the rise in the number of young black men being shot in public are all issues of great concern to me, because such threats directly endanger people I love. At what point, I've joked bitterly, do I advise my nephew not to wear a hoodie in public? He's not invulnerable like Luke Cage, one of my favorite Marvel heroes.

So, with such a liberal background and with such an appreciation for cultural diversity, why do I honor my Confederate heritage, when many of my fellow liberals excoriate that heritage and when many of my fellow Confederate enthusiasts are openly and shamelessly reactionary racists and Republicans?

It seems to me that turning your back on your forebears and dishonoring your family history are a special kind of lie, a special kind of betrayal, and deserve a special kind of hell (cf. the above allusion to Dante's *Inferno*: betrayers stuck with Satan in the ice at the very bottom of the pit). I refuse to be that kind of betrayer, no matter how unpopular that makes me. Unlike Cinderella's stepsisters, I won't cut off my heel or toe to fit into some polite, tamed shoe of identity someone else has made. I won't reconstruct myself. I won't, to use Anne Sexton's term in her poetic take on Cinderella in *Transformations*, subject myself to socially and politically convenient "amputations" (56). I've spent my life giving a big FUCK-YOU finger to the right. Why should I give a flying rat's ass what the left and the p.c. police think of me? Dissent has always been my way of being in the world. Blake Shelton has a great song called "Kiss My Country Ass." Well, in terms of defiant phrasing, I beat that hot boy to it. I've been saying "You can kiss my Rebel ass" since college, which means that any antagonists of mine are welcome to pucker up.

What I'm saying here needs to be said, and I'm not alone. I've met many other Southerners who feel this way, folks without a platform, as deeply alienated and resentful as I, folks who rarely or never express what I'm expressing because the social pressure is great, especially in educated and liberal circles, not to feel these conflicts or express these opinions.

Here's an example of that social pressure. When I expressed on Facebook my heated contempt for anyone wanting to remove Confederate statues in Charlottesville, people I'd known for years upbraided and scolded me and tried to "correct" me. (You can imagine from the tone of this essay how well that went over.) A few semi-strangers denounced me as a rabid racist; one was so nasty, so full of veiled threats, that I had to block the poisonous prick. When I realized that I was waking up every morning already tense, steeled for an e-confrontation, knowing that new responses to my posts might infuriate me, I decided to use Facebook only for publicity purposes and to avoid politics. The impotent rage wasn't worth it. Since I was in no position to kick the asses of offensive e-interlocuters, why subject myself to more enraging stimuli than daily life already provides?

When people clamor to take down memorials to the Confederacy, they're not just pissing off what they assume are mindless, ignorant conservatives, "rednecks" and "hillbillies." They're also insulting people like me, descendants of Rebel soldiers, folks who might bond with them as allies on many, many other political and social issues.

I vote a straight Democratic ticket every time I go to the polls, and I'm delighted that Virginia's turned blue. Because of the pride I have in my heritage, I also have a Confederate-flag sticker on my fridge and carry a Confederate-flag key fob. In our guest room hangs "The Black Knight," a huge print of Confederate General Turner Ashby by artist John Paul Strain. Another big print of Ashby, "Knight of the Valley," also by Strain, hangs in the family house that John and I own in Hinton, as well as a framed photo of "The Recumbent Lee." In my Pulaski study, along with two shelves full of books about the Civil War, I have pictures of Stonewall Jackson, J.E.B Stuart, and Robert E. Lee, including "Lee on Traveller," that image that's still displayed in the Old Homeplace. I also have the letters "CSA" tattooed into my left shoulder. The letters look like flames and are deliberately hard to make out, since I don't feel like getting into a shouting match or a fist fight with some random asshole who thinks it's his community duty to tell me what ink I should or should not be wearing.

8.

WHAT WOULD YOU do if you knew that a hostile army was headed your way, poised to invade your land? Would you bake a batch of biscuits, stir up some lemonade, and prepare to greet them? Or would you collect your weapons, congregate with your family, friends, and neighbors, and prepare to fight them off? If you're like me, you'd choose the latter. If you were like Southern white men in 1861, you would have chosen the latter, whether you owned slaves or not. If intruders successfully overrun your land and subdue you, who knows what they'll do to you, your property, and those you care for?

9.

IN "NORTH AMERICAN Time," from her collection *Your Native Land, Your Life*, lesbian poet Adrienne Rich says:

When my dreams showed signs
of becoming
politically correct
no unruly images
escaping beyond borders...
then I began to wonder. (33)

In *Because We Are Human: Contesting US Support for Gender and Sexuality Human Rights Abroad*, lesbian scholar Cynthia Burack, attempting to account "for much of the difference in reactions to official US support for SOGI [sexual orientation and gender identity] human rights abroad," refers first to what "Christian conservatives call 'worldview' and academics often understand as 'ideology.'" She then mentions "a less judgmental perspective... offered by scientist and philosopher of science Ludwik Fleck, who would conceptualize groups such as Christian conservatives and academic humanists as 'thought collectives,'" which in turn produces a "'thought style'.... Fleck describes the experience of a thought style as one in which the interpretation of the thought collective 'appears imperative' to those within the collective while other, 'alien' interpretations seem 'like a free flight of fancy'" (91).

10.

THESE DAYS, ANYONE with the audacity to say something sympathetic about the soldiers and civilians of the Confederacy offends the current "thought style" on the left. We're immediately accused of spreading "revisionist history." History is complicated, and "revisionist history" is often history that majority opinion doesn't want to hear. Certain truths can become unfashionable. When it comes to understanding the past, a right-or-wrong mentality is simplistic and unhelpful, as is an inability to deal with contradiction. So-called political correctness can be good when it encourages inclusion, and inclusion is part of what Southern manners ideally are all about. But p.c. thinking can also turn into a mindless, uneducated, lockstep conformity. It makes certain thoughts, certain language impermissible, verboten, even illegal. (E.g. the sanctimonious, outraged indignation that so often pervades the transgender community.)

Unlike many who rail unthinkingly at Confederate symbols, I've closely studied a lot of history books, toured many a Civil War battle site and graveyard, and contemplated that war from myriad perspectives. My attempts to understand the past have illuminated a big question, a relevant question: "Why did Southern soldiers go to war?"

In *The Life of Johnny Reb: The Common Soldier of the Confederacy*, historian Bell Irvin Wiley says of the Southern people that they were "thoroughly convinced of the rightness of their cause—the defense of their homes against tyrannous and godless invaders" (123).

In *Soldiers Blue and Gray*, historian James R. Robertson, Jr. says, "Certainly 'the flower of Southern manhood' went to war in order to protect home and everything dear from Northern hordes overrunning their lands to bring them forcibly back into the Union." He adds that "[c]ontrary to popular Northern belief, the average Southerner was not fighting for slavery. Owning slaves, and profiting from their labor, were attributes only of the upper classes who constituted a very small percentage of the South's population. Most Confederate soldiers were farmers or laborers who took musket in hand to defend their homeland" (9). This was certainly the case with my ancestor.

In an interview with noted historian Shelby Foote in *The Civil War*, by Geoffrey Ward with Ric Burns and Ken Burns, Foote's asked, "Did the soldiers on both sides really know what they were fighting for?" Here's how he responded: "Early on in the war, a Union squad closed in on a single ragged Confederate. He didn't own any slaves and he obviously didn't have much interest in the Constitution or anything else. And they asked him, 'What are you fighting for anyhow?' And he said, 'I'm fighting because you're down here.' Which was a pretty satisfactory answer. Lincoln had the much more difficult job of sending men out to shoot up somebody else's home" (217).

In *Confederates in the Attic*, Horwitz says of Shelby Foote, "His great-grandfather had opposed secession but fought without hesitation for the South. 'Just as I would have,' Foote said. 'I'd be with my people, right or wrong. If I was against slavery, I'd still be with the South. I'm a man, my society needs me, here I am'" (149).

In *For Cause and Comrades: Why Men Fought in the Civil War*, James M. McPherson says, "The urge to defend home and hearth that had impelled so many Southerners to enlist in 1861 took on greater urgency when large-scale invasions became a reality in 1862" (95). He says as well that "[m]en who had opposed secession were nevertheless roused to fighting pitch by Northern invasion" (96).

11.

I'M A GRADUATE of West Virginia University, so I receive their alumni magazine. Imagine with what bitter amusement I read "Defending Our Right to the Past," by Becky Lofstead, in the Summer 2017 issue. Lofstead's article begins by explaining that members of ISIS destroyed various cultural artifacts in Iraq in 2015, including an Assyrian winged bull, and the Temple of Bel in Syria. After that, the essay focuses on Rhonda Reymond, "an art history professor at the West Virginia University College of Creative Arts," who "studies and teaches about the global destruction of cultural heritage." "Most recently," Lofstead claims, "cultural heritage has been construed as a human rights issue. In other words, one cannot separate objects or manifestations of culture from people and their rights to their heritage."

No kidding. I couldn't have said it better myself.

12.

DISGUSTED BY THE events in New Orleans, I've put my money where my mouth is. When I heard rumors that Georgia activists were attempting to sand-blast the Confederate bas-relief of Lee, Jackson, and Davis at Stone Mountain, I sent money to the Georgia Sons of Confederate Veterans. I've since donated funds to the Virginia Flaggers, who've erected several huge Confederate battle flags along I-95. On their website, they describe themselves as "citizens of the Commonwealth who stand AGAINST those who would desecrate our Confederate Monuments and memorials, and FOR our Confederate Veterans." Their website further states that they are dedicated to "defending the honor of the Confederate Veteran" and "protesting Heritage violations," a phrase I'm fond of and will have to borrow. Their "enemies are those who worship ignorance, historical revisionism and Political Correctness" ("Who Are the VA Flaggers?").

I've thought about joining the Sons of Confederate Veterans for years, and in March 2016, I tried to do so, fully aware that my homo-hillbilly self might not be welcome. When I contacted a local chapter, the following correspondence ensued.

> *Dear Sir,*
>
> *I'm a Virginia Tech professor and Pulaski resident who's interested in joining the Sons of Confederate Veterans. Do you have any advice on how to proceed? My Rebel ancestor, Isaac Green Carden (my paternal grandmother's maternal grandfather) was from Monroe County, Virginia, later West Virginia, and was an artilleryman for Lowry's Battery.*
>
> *Many thanks in advance for any help you might provide.*
>
> *Jeff Mann*

*

You will need to fill out an application. One can be printed by going to SCV.org and under forms Application for membership can be found. Fill out the middle section for your ancestor and youself [sic]. You will need to list each generation from your ancestor to you. The total amount to begin is $50.00 ... $5.00 is a onetime recording fee. I am the commander of the -------- camp.

*

Hello,

Thank you very much for this information.
By the way, I'm gay. Is that going to be a problem?
JM

*

A SCV member should conduct and their actions be that of a Southern Gentleman. Our camp at this time does not think you meet this criteria.

*

Hello,

Thank you for your honest response. I certainly don't want to spend time with folks who don't want me around. I'll support my Confederate heritage in other ways, then.
Jeff Mann

To several gay and lesbian friends, I forwarded the above conversation, with the following preface:

> Dear Folks,
> Please see the response below.
> I'm floored. I'm speechless! Has anything worse *ever happened to anyone in the history of the world?!*
> Ha! Oh, well. Their reaction is hardly a surprise.
> My mother would be crushed to discover that I never managed to become a Southern gentleman...
> Wedged Between Worlds and Welcome in None,
> Ye Ole Rebel Bear

My good friend Cindy replied:

> Dear Jeff: I think you demonstrated that you're a better person by not correcting the Commander's grammar.
> C

I replied:

> Ha!!
> Well, yes, that would have been rude... Or "wude," as that floppy-eared annoyance from a few Star Wars *movies would say.*
> Yours in Immaculate Politeness,
> J

13.

AH, CHARLOTTESVILLE.

Though I spent my first nine years or so in Virginia, growing up in the little paper-mill town of Covington, I didn't make it to Charlottesville till I was in my twenties. My mother's old friend, Elsie, drove Mommy, my sister, and me there for an afternoon's visit one summer in the 1980s. We admired the Rotunda, Edgar Allan Poe's old room, and the blooming crepe myrtles. My Aunt Jane, who possessed a streak of wildness I'd always admired, once told me, "Honey, if you ever get to UVA, go sit on the steps of the Rotunda and think of me, 'cause I made out with lots of handsome boys there." And so I did. (Visit the Rotunda, that is...not, regretfully, make out with hot men of my own.)

In March 2016, despite a foul head cold, I drove to Charlottesville to participate in two panels at the Virginia Festival of the Book. One was composed of writers who'd published creative nonfiction in *Walk Till The Dogs Get Mean: Meditations on the Forbidden from Contemporary Appalachia*, edited by Adrian Blevins and Karen Salyer McElmurray. Another panel was titled "Gay and Southern: Living, Writing, and Dealing with Discrimination," which included authors who'd had work appear in *Crooked Letter i: Coming Out in the South*, edited by Connie Griffin.

After unpacking at my hotel, I sampled the Southern delights of a mint julep, a Sazerac, fried oysters, barbequed ribs, hoppin' john, and collards at an outdoor table at The Whiskey Jar, meanwhile admiring a winsome waiter with matching pectoral and gluteal curves and several ravish-worthy bearded college boys strolling about.

The next day, after the first panel, I walked past blooming forsythia and Bradford pear trees to Lee Park, to pay my respects to the statue of Robert E. Lee. The final day, before the second panel, I walked up to the courthouse to see the Confederate monument there and the statue of Stonewall Jackson amid blossoming cherry trees and more Bradford pears.

In the months after that visit, I encountered posts on Facebook and articles online that gave me some sense of the growing controversy over Charlottesville's Confederate statues. (Turns out a fifteen-year-old child began the movement to take down the Lee statue. Talk about effrontery and entitlement. Who should care about a fifteen-year-old's opinion, other than the kid's parents?) My response was—you guessed it—rage, rage that, as usual, I couldn't implement, so I began avoiding news about the conflict simply to sidestep being swamped again and again by negative emotions. I get very, very weary of reining in my two favorite deadly sins, Wrath and Lust.

Needless to say, I couldn't avoid the news on August 11-12, 2017, when the "Unite the Right" rally occurred in Charlottesville. Rarely have I felt so conflicted, even though contradictions and internal divisions are discomforts I live with pretty much daily. At first, my hatred focused on those who wanted to take the statues down, and I was pleased to see Charlottesville being punished with such chaos. Then violence broke out, people died, and my disgust focused on the white supremacists fueling the rally, carrying the flag my ancestor fought for in order to advance their racist rancor. It seemed clear to me that they weren't there to honor Lee and defend a statue erected in his memory, as I might have been. Instead, they were there to push their own slimy agendas. *Hate queers? Fuck you. Hate Jews? Fuck you. Hate Muslims? Fuck you. Hate black folks? Fuck you. Hate Latinos? Fuck you. You nasty swine aren't my people*, I thought. *Trash! Lee would have found you all vile. You aren't worth the horseshit that besmirched Lee's boots on the battlefield.*

Speaking of trash, the fulvous fool in the White House said that there were "very fine people on both sides" of that clash. I like to give people the benefit of the doubt, but not this time. I don't think he meant people like me, Southerners who take pride in their heritage. I think he meant white supremacists. What does he know about Rebel family history? He's a greedy elitist of the worst sort. Why so many of my fellow Southerners believe his bullshit is, for me, a mystery both sharp and painful.

I said earlier that immoderate passion can isolate. I hated the folks on both sides of that conflict. I still do. So what allies are left? Very few. Luckily, I'm a loner, and my small crew of family and friends understands the convoluted complexities of my personality. Otherwise, I might as well be sitting on an ice floe.

For months after that violent rally, the statues of Lee and Jackson were covered with tarps. In February 2018, a judge ruled that the city had to remove the tarps, and, to my vindictive delight, city officials complied (Held). As long as the statues stand unmolested, Charlottesville gets my business. I'm looking forward to another drink or two at The Whiskey Jar while admiring their bearded, firm-assed waiters. If the statues come down, I'll never visit Charlottesville again. Not that anyone there cares.

14.

SPEAKING OF CHARLOTTESVILLE, if folks want to get rid of the statues of Lee and Jackson because they fought for the Confederacy, why shouldn't we tear down the Rotunda and Monticello, since Jefferson was a slave-owner? How about Mount Vernon too? Nothing like a sanctimonious judging of the past by the standards of the present. While we're at it, should we burn all the copies of Ernest Hemingway's novels because he was a homophobe?

15.

I DOUBT THAT the author and I have much in common on other political topics, but I very much enjoyed reading Paul C. Graham's *Confederaphobia! An American Epidemic.* I laughed out loud at his sarcastic treatment of various cases across the country in which people responded with fear and hysteria to Confederate symbols. My favorite's the time a student at Framingham State University in Massachusetts "was 'traumatized' when a Confederate flag sticker was seen on another student's laptop computer. This 'bias incident' was quickly reported", and a mass e-mail was sent out to all the institution's students, suggesting "that those impacted by the incident seek counselling." A campus official insisted that the university was working to "'resolve incidents that impede progress towards a welcoming and inclusive campus community.'" How welcome was the student with the laptop? Graham snarkily comments on this pretty much as I would have: "Some students, it is fair to say, are to be more 'welcomed' and worthy of 'inclusion' than others" (12-13).

For some reason, when I think of that offending student, I picture myself as an undergraduate: a scruffy-bearded, shaggy-headed country boy, out of his element, insecure, afraid, off balance, with that comfortably familiar emblem of family and regional pride on his person. (In the late 70s, it would have been a sticker on a notebook or a patch on a denim jacket, not a laptop, obviously.) If I'd received such a response from first a fellow student and then university officials, I would've been humiliated, angry, and mortified. I would've wanted to flee, to drop out and go home. I certainly would not have felt welcomed.

Graham makes some important points in *Confederaphobia*, along with all the amusing snark aimed at the overdelicate. When Southerners speak of their Confederate ancestors, he says, "[t]hese are not textbook stories, these are family stories. To strike at the symbols of the South is to strike at those things which are still held sacred and evoke the most tender responses. These are not symbols of ideas, these are reminders of people. Family members. People who we love despite the fact that we have never met" (53). Elsewhere, Graham says, "The question is not whether the same symbol can mean different things to different people—experience clearly shows that it both can and does—but whether one group should be able to <u>dictate the meaning</u> of the symbol to another group of people" (39). Finally, "Southern symbols mean to the Southerner *exactly what they say that they do*" (41), which means, if you show me a photo of a Ku Klux Klan member holding a Confederate battle flag and say to me, "That flag stands for white-supremacist racism," I'll say, "That flag might mean that to you. It might even mean that to him. But it doesn't mean that to me."

16.

WHAT WOULD YOU do if an army came through your area, your town or farm, torched the mills, factories, and civic buildings, burnt up your property, stole your food, and killed or carried away your animals? What would you do if, years later, the leaders of that army were glorified in the nation's capital by having grand statues built in their honor? Would you attend the celebration and cheer? Would you lay flowers at the foot of those statues? Would you gaze up at them in admiration? Or, like me, would you never forget what happened, carry a grudge, and dream of razing those statues to the ground?

17.

I'VE CONFESSED MY penchant for violent fantasies. Here are a couple more, which I expect you won't enjoy half as much as I will.

William Tecumseh Sherman's the man who famously said, "War is hell." There's a magnificent equestrian statue of him near the White House in Washington, D.C. It towers against the sky. One of the bas-relief panels adorning it is called "The March Through Georgia."

Surely you know what our war hero Sherman did? In October 1864, he promised General Grant that he would "make Georgia howl" (Ward 274). And so he did. When he invaded Atlanta, "he ordered all noncombatants to leave—one of the harsh acts for which Georgians never forgave him," as historian Bruce Catton says in

The Civil War (233). Later, "as the Union army left most of Atlanta went up in smoke" (235). Sherman introduced the concept of total war, taking the conflict to Southern civilians. It was, as Catton says, "the nineteenth-century equivalent of the modern bombing raid, a blow at the civilian underpinning of the military machine" (239).

After burning Atlanta, he and his army marched through Georgia, accompanied by lawless trash called "bummers," who "robbed and burned and pillaged all the way from Atlanta to the sea" (Catton 236). Catton continues with this detailed description of Sherman's march:

> Bridges, railroads, machine shops, warehouses—anything of this nature that lay in Sherman's path was burned or dismantled. Barns were burned, with their contents; food to feed the army and its animals was taken, and three or four times as much as the army needed was simply spoiled...and partly because of all this, Lee's soldiers would be on starvation rations, and the whole Confederate war effort would become progressively weaker. Wholesale destruction was one of the points of the movement. The process through which that destruction was brought about was not pretty to watch, nor is it pleasant to read about today. (239)

Not pleasant to read about today? Most certainly not.

After Savannah surrendered, Sherman cut through South Carolina, indulging in the same destruction he'd inflicted on Georgia. The capital city, Columbia, was burned. Some blame the Yankee army, some blame citizens who'd set fire to bales of hay. When asked later, Sherman, tellingly, had this to say, ""[i]f I had made up my mind to burn Columbia I would have burnt it with no more feeling than I would a common prairie dog village; but I did not do it..." ("William").

That's the man atop that glorious granite pedestal in Sherman Plaza in D.C. So certain folks want to insult *American* veterans and war dead by taking down monuments to the Confederacy because that nation wanted to perpetuate slavery? Okay. But while we're at it, how about y'all take up a collection and buy me a bazooka, because I'd really like to take a crack at that Sherman statue, considering what he did to my native region in 1864-65.

Lately, I've been learning to shoot a Glock handgun. Like most manual skills, it doesn't come naturally to me, so I don't know how accurate I'd be with a bazooka, but, hell, that Sherman statue is a pretty damn big target. Imagine! *Whooooosh! Bam!* There goes Sherman's head! His noble breast is shattered! His horse is riven in two! Look, there goes his horse's ass, flying toward the White House!

Sweet. Now on to Sheridan Circle, in D.C.'s Northwest. There in the center of the circle stands a fine statue of General Philip Sheridan. It depicts him astride his horse, rallying the Union troops at the Battle of Cedar Creek, a battle my Rebel ancestor apparently fought in.

Surely you know what our war hero Sheridan did? You can read all about it in *The Shenandoah Valley 1861-1865: The Destruction of the Granary of the Confederacy* by Michael G. Mahon, or you can watch *The Burning*, a DVD about Sheridan's activities in the Great Valley of Virginia in the fall of 1864. There's a particularly vivid personal account in the wonderful Rebel memoir, *I Rode with Stonewall*, by Henry Kyd Douglas, the youngest member of Stonewall Jackson's staff.

Douglas says that "General Grant told Sheridan he must make the Valley 'so bare that a crow flying over it would be compelled to carry his rations'" (302). Sheridan carried out his orders ruthlessly and efficiently. Catton explains that "barns and corncribs and gristmills and herds of cattle were military objectives now, and if thousands of civilians whose property this was had to suffer heartbreaking loss as a result, that was...incidental. A garden spot was to be turned into a desert in order that the Southern nation might be destroyed" (224, 226).

Henry Kyd Douglas rode down the Valley with his men after Sheridan and his troops left. He saw "great columns of smoke which almost shut out the sun by day," "the red glare of bonfires," "mothers and maidens tearing their hair and shrieking to Heaven in their fright and despair, and little children, voiceless and tearless in their pitiable terror" (302).

Douglas finishes his description of the Burning thus: "It is little wonder that General Grant in his Memoirs passes over this work as if he could not bear to touch it, and that no reputable historian of the North has ventured to tell the truth about it and defend it, for it is an insult to civilization and to God to pretend that the Laws of War justify such warfare" (302).

That's the man astride his bronze mount in Sheridan Circle, and I think I have more ammunition for this here bazooka. Imagine! *Whooooosh! Bam!* There goes Sheridan's arm! His patriotic torso's blown to bits! His horse's legs fly off in different directions! Look, there's Sheridan's head, arcing up toward the Embassy of Ireland! Hooray!

All right, a postscript, now that I've had my fun. These are fantasies that I'd never act out, even if, impossibly, I possessed the power to implement them. Sherman and Sheridan passionately fought for the North, and Lee, Jackson, and Isaac Green Carden fought passionately for the South. A big admirer of courage and devotion to duty, I freely admit that Union generals deserve their honors and their monuments, as do the Federal troops who served under them. The Union boys were just as brave and took as many risks for their cause as my Southerners did. Though war devastated the South, the North suffered terribly as well, as I'm reminded whenever I hear Kathy Mattea, one of my favorite country singers, perform that mournful Yankee song, "The Vacant Chair," written to commemorate the death of a Massachusetts soldier at the Battle of Ball's Bluff in 1861:

> We shall meet but we shall miss him.
> There will be one vacant chair.
> We shall linger to caress him
> While we breathe our ev'ning prayer.
> When one year ago we gathered,
> Joy was in his mild blue eye.
> Now the golden cord is severed,
> And our hopes in ruin lie.
> ("The Vacant Chair")

Valor should be honored, whatever the side, whatever the cause. I'm not fomenting any movement to tear down all those Yankee Civil War monuments in D.C. and across the North, because I respect other folks' heritage. I'd hope to receive the same respect in return, but these days that hope seems vain.

18.

WHAT WOULD YOU do if people you've never met demanded that a statue honoring the army that your ancestor fought in be removed or demolished, like a thing of shame? Would you shrug your shoulders, even give your blessing? If you're like me, you'd tell those would-be monument razers to fuck off, go celebrate their own forebears, and leave you alone to do the same.

19.

IN "LINCOLN IN Hell: Class and Confederate Symbols in the American South," W. Scott Poole says that the "Confederate battle flag...has become part of what Gareth Stedman Jones would call 'a language of exclusion,' a tool for those who see themselves marginalized by economic and social change to express that marginalization, even a weapon to deploy on behalf of their own sense of estrangement and alienation from American society" (122). Poole claims that the "icons of the Lost Cause, especially the Confederate battle flag, became symbols of the anger of the working class" (134). He expands on this idea in the following:

> Hinkle provides us with evidence that Confederate symbols have become representative of the attempts of the economically and culturally marginalized to secure an identity in the midst of a mass culture dominated, these new Confederates insist, by elites. The white working class has clearly appropriated Old South and Confederate emblems as symbols of antiauthoritarian defiance, expressing a sense of regional and rural revolt against elites or simply against the reigning paradigms of society. (139-140)

Class is hard for me to talk about, simply because my own positioning is so complex. My mother's father was a machinist; her mother was a nurse. Mommy herself worked in payroll at the Westvaco paper mill in Covington, Virginia. My father was a high-school teacher before he became a lawyer; in fact, he was fired from Covington High School in the 1960s because he publicly protested racist policies in that school.

On Daddy's side of the family, the Cardens, Ferrells, and Manns were all mountain farmers. "Hardscrabble" is the colorful adjective often used in academia and Appalachian literature. All his life, Daddy talked about his grandparents' self-reliance, how they raised or made just about everything they needed. Continuing those independent and hard-working traditions, Daddy raised me to chop wood and tend a garden, at the same time that he taught me to love reading and books. One year we raised and slaughtered pigs (playfully named after Republican politicians), and another year we collected sugar water and made maple syrup. For a time, we raised honeybees. We frequently had a herd of Hereford cattle on our Forest Hill property, and, in order to feed those cows, we baled hay and filled a barn with it. What we ate—the comfort cooking of my childhood, which I still love and regularly prepare—was country food, hillbilly food, working-class food, the food of poverty, the Southern Appalachian version of peasant cuisine.

Daddy was the first person in his family to go to college, and the only way he was able to afford to do that was because, after soldiering in World War II, he took advantage of the GI Bill to attend Washington and Lee. When, after years of teaching, he returned to W&L to earn that law degree, our class situation changed, but by then we'd moved from the papermill town of Covington to Hinton, a place even more isolated, rural, and working-class, albeit very scenic and without the ubiquitous reek of the mill.

According to one online source, *Data USA*, the average income in Hinton at present is $32,070, or "lower income," and the poverty rate is 15.7% ("Hinton"). Despite the many pieces of rural property Daddy bought as he gradually grew better off, despite his degrees, despite my degrees, creative activities, scholarly interests, and once-a-year vacations overseas, Summers County, that rural place, that working-class place, is what shaped us both, both our selves and our sympathies. Along with Daddy's enthusiasm for books and education, I have his West Virginia redneck qualities too: I have a strong work ethic; a contrarian independence of thought; a contempt for social pretension, fad, and ideological orthodoxy; a frugal streak; a down-to-earth hatred of waste; and a profane sense of humor. I dislike change, distrust "progress," detest urban areas, and mock over-refinement and conspicuous wealth. To borrow Poole's wording from above, I'm full of "antiauthoritarian defiance" and often express "a sense of regional and rural revolt against elites or simply against the reigning paradigms of society."

All this, despite earning three degrees, teaching in academia for nearly forty years, and publishing nineteen books? Like many authors and academics from rural, blue-collar, or working-class backgrounds, I am, to repeat my earlier phrase, "wedged between worlds and welcome in none," a displaced freak straddling classes and entirely comfortable just about nowhere.

This perpetual displacement was very much on my mind in October 2018. For years, Hinton has sponsored a festival, Railroad Days, on two weekends every October: "leaf-peepers" ride a special train from Huntington and Charleston, West Virginia, up the New River Gorge to Hinton for a day of music, arts and crafts, and fattening street-fair food. Hinton's like many American small towns—struggling, full of abandoned businesses and unemployment—so the annual event really benefits the local economy. This past Railroad Days, having battened on my usual hot dog and keeping my eye out for both hot, bearded mountain boys and well-made fried apple pies, I stood to one side with my old friend Cindy, who'd come to town for the weekend, and watched townsfolk mill by. I was thinking about the late Joe Bageant, a great writer I wish I'd met, whose books, *Deer Hunting with Jesus: Dispatches from America's Class War* and *Rainbow Pie: A Redneck Memoir*, examine the "working-class poor: conservative, politically misinformed or oblivious, and patriotic to their own detriment" (6).

"Ah, my fellow West Virginians," I sighed, in a tone that was, I'd imagine, a mixture of sadness, sarcasm, and exasperation. "A frenzy of Trump supporters, all voting against their own best interests."

What could Cindy do but nod and match my sigh with hers? She's known me since 1979, so she's intimately aware of the many uncomfortable ways my heritage has fragmented me. She'd understand me if I quoted Bageant: "After a lifetime of identity conflict, I have come to accept that these are my people—by blood, even if not politically or spiritually" (187).

After Trump was elected, there was a lot of talk about the white working class in Appalachia and the South, including a great deal of fuss over J. D. Vance's *Hillbilly Elegy: A Memoir of a Family and Culture in Crisis*. Why had so many working-class folks voted for Trump? How had the Democratic party lost their confidence?

Damned good question. When I was a young man, Republicans didn't stand much of a chance in West Virginia. The state was staunchly Democratic. In my lifetime, a prodigious and, in my opinion, profoundly unfortunate shift has occurred: West Virginia's changed from a strongly Democratic state to one riddled, blighted, lousy, infested, poisonous with Republicans, both voters and politicians (with some especially noxious ones deserving of a good horse-whipping in the state legislature at present). As Shelby Foote says in *Confederates in the Attic*, "Now I'm living to see another terrible thing—the South joining the party of Lincoln," which is to say the Republican party (Horwitz 147).

My Confederaphilia, I realize, has certainly sprung from my weirdly complex class background and my upbringing in Summers County, a county that, like many in southern West Virginia, was resolutely Confederate. And though my sympathies are divided, I to some extent understand white working-class marginalization, alienation, and rage. I certainly understand the fury evoked when people who are perceived by locals as liberal, politically-correct outsiders try to take down Confederate monuments. Such attempts say to us: "You're trash, your ancestors were trash, their struggles and losses meant nothing, and we don't care what you think or what you want."

So, to the would-be Rebel-monument removers, let me suggest this: if you care at all about members of the Southern working class, do not insult them (and me) by razing monuments they (and I) regard as emblems of a heritage we're proud of. Don't tell us what to think or how to feel. To borrow from *Confederaphobia*, don't tell us what our symbols mean. You're only going to rile us up, alienate us further, make dialogue impossible, and encourage shit-shows like that at Charlottesville. Of course, you might think that people like us are beneath your notice, not worthy of respect or inclusion, in which case I question both your empathy and your humanity.

20.

IN AUGUST 2018, my husband had business meetings in Memphis, Tennessee. Since his trip occurred around my birthday, I accompanied him. He made the sort of birthday-fuss we Leos crave, putting us up in the fancy Peabody Hotel, where we got to lounge in the lobby with martinis and watch the famous March of the Ducks. (Google it; it's quite a show.)

In terms of my splintered loyalties, however, the trip was jarring, full of juxtapositions I found painful. As we drove our rental car into town, we passed a park where once stood a statue of Confederate General Nathan Bedford Forrest. The historical marker was still there; the statue had been taken down in December 2017, and now Forrest Park has a less-than-mellifluous new name, "Health Sciences Park." As far as I know, the bodies of Forrest and his wife are still interred there ("Nathan").

While John was in meetings, I strolled down Beale Street, scouting out good barbeque joints, reading historical markers about the city's black community, and checking out the statue of W. C. Handy, mentioned in one of my favorite songs, Joni Mitchell's "Furry Sings the Blues." Then I visited the National Civil Rights Museum, housed in the Lorraine Motel, where Martin Luther King Jr. was assassinated. For nearly three hours, I wandered through its intense, moving, informative exhibits before buying my nephew a "Black Lives Matter" refrigerator magnet and a couple of books containing King's most famous quotations and speeches.

On my way back to the Peabody, I walked along the Mississippi, snuffling the rich blossoms of crepe myrtles and magnolias. When I got to Jefferson Davis Park, it was closed, "under construction," said the sign. The park was under *de*struction, actually: the statue of Davis had been removed in December 2017 and its base torn down only a week or so before (Courtney Anderson). The city of Memphis pulled some shamefully sneaky maneuvering to get around state laws that blocked the removal of monuments, and the Republican-dominated Tennessee legislature had punished the city by withholding funds for Memphis's bicentennial celebration (Horton). (Finally, something Republicans and I agree on.)

I can without confusion or conflict honor the heritage of African Americans and the heritage of Confederate soldiers, the two bloodlines that have converged to create my nephew. Both cultural legacies should be honored; they aren't mutually exclusive. Why others insist on a rigid either/or attitude I simply can't comprehend. Perhaps simple minds abhor complexity.

21.

IN BOTH CELTIC and Norse literature, elaborate curses called "flyting" are common. Here's a modern one, from a pissed-off mountaineer with both Celtic and Teutonic blood in his veins.

When you dishonor Confederate monuments, you are, in effect, pissing on the graves of my forebears. My curse is for you to suffer the same. May infidels you cannot control shatter your family gravestones, relieve themselves on your grandmothers' pelvic bones, your great-grandfathers' skulls. May vile mobs unearth your beloved ancestors' remains and scatter their bones to packs of wild dogs. After your death, may your grisly remnants meet the same fate. May your miseries and achievements, struggles and triumphs be utterly erased, scoured from history. May you be forgotten entirely, and any memorial marking your end obliterated, ground down to gravel and glittering dust.

22.

RAGE IS A hard, hard thing to contain, especially when circumstances dictate that it must be suppressed and not acted upon. Lately, I've been trying to figure out why the removal of all things Confederate so infuriates me and makes me entertain murderous imaginings.

It has something to do with honor: family honor and regional honor. Those seeking to destroy Rebel emblems and memorials dishonor my Rebel ancestor, my family history, and me.

Am I archaic, a nineteenth-century anachronism in taking such offense? To quote Horwitz in *Confederates in the Attic*:

> [Shelby] Foote's retroactive allegiance to the Confederacy surprised me. It was the honor-bound code of the Old South. One's people before one's principles. The straightjacket of scorn and stigma. "It's a bunch of shit really," Foote conceded. "But all Southerners subscribe to this code to some degree, at least male Southerners of my generation." In Foote's view, this same stubborn pride had sustained Southerners during the Civil War. "It's what kept them going through Appomattox, that attitude of 'I won't give up, I will not be insulted.'" (150)

Years ago, I stumbled upon a scientific study claiming that Southern men are easily offended. I laughed out loud. This was a surprise? Someone had to conduct research in order to figure that out? In a recent attempt to track down that study, I found online this abstract for "Insult, Aggression, and the Southern Culture of Honor: An 'Experimental Ethnography,'" by D. Cohen, R.E. Nisbett, B.F. Bowdle, and N. Schwarz, from *The Journal of Personality and Social Psychology*:

> Three experiments examined how norms characteristic of a "culture of honor" manifest themselves in the cognitions, emotions, behaviors, and physiological reactions of southern White males. Participants were

University of Michigan students who grew up in the North or South. In 3 experiments, they were insulted by a confederate who bumped into the participant and called him an "asshole." Compared with northerners—who were relatively unaffected by the insult—southerners were (a) more likely to think their masculine reputation was threatened, (b) more upset (as shown by a rise in cortisol levels), (c) more physiologically primed for aggression (as shown by a rise in testosterone levels), (d) more cognitively primed for aggression, and (e) more likely to engage in aggressive and dominant behavior. Findings highlight the insult-aggression cycle in cultures of honor, in which insults diminish a man's reputation and he tries to restore his status by aggressive or violent behavior. (Cohen et al.)

Quelle amusante. Anyone who knows the South knows this.

My own thoughts on honor have been molded by more than my native region. Since my junior-high-school days, I've been reading and rereading tales of valor in which heroes risk everything for those they love—and/or their country—and earn honor, fame, and an everlasting name, though sometimes paying the death-price in the process. In the seventh grade, for instance, I was reading the *Iliad*, in which Hector says, "He who among you / finds by spear thrown or spear thrust his death and destiny, / let him die. He has no dishonor when he dies defending / his country, for then his wife shall be saved and his children afterwards, / and his house and his property shall not be damaged…" (322).

Years later, in college, I encountered *Beowulf*. From Seamus Heaney's fine translation, here are a few of my favorite lines spoken by the title character, the leader of the Geats:

> It is always better
> to avenge dear ones than to indulge in
> > mourning.
> For every one of us, living in this world
> means waiting for our end. Let whoever can
> win glory before death. When a warrior is gone,
> that will be his best and only bulwark. (97)

Beowulf keeps "thinking about / his name and fame" (107) and was "keenest to win fame" (213). He assumes, dying the heroic death that he does, fighting a dragon that's been ravaging his kingdom, that that coveted fame has indeed been won.

Later still, I immersed myself in Norse literature and Icelandic sagas, where I found both a deep fatalism and a determination to live honorably and courageously in the face of grim fate and harsh necessity, with the hope of winning never-ending renown. From Jackson Crawford's translation, *The Poetic Edda: Stories of the Norse Gods and Heroes*, here are a few medieval words about honor and fame from "Havamal."

> Cows die,
> family die,
> you will die the same way.
> But a good reputation
> never dies
> for the one who earns it well.
>
> Cows die,
> family die,
> you will die the same way.
> I know only one thing
> that never dies:
> the reputation of the one who's died. (30)

In "Hamthismal," a doomed warrior says:

> ...we fought well,
> we stand over sword-torn
> Gothic corpses and
> set a table for the eagles.
> We earned honor here,
> though we are fated to die today—
> a man will not live one day longer
> than the Norns have decided. (339)

Juxtaposing these quotations with the removal of Rebel statues nauseates me. Imagine all those Southern farm boys, thousands and thousands of them, fighting and dying horribly at Sharpsburg, Gettysburg, the Wilderness, New Market, Spotsylvania, Atlanta, Franklin, Petersburg...or dying in less dramatic ways, wounded, malnourished, or diseased in field hospitals or prison camps. Stroll through Confederate cemeteries—as I have in Winchester, Fredericksburg, Franklin, Richmond, and elsewhere—read their names, and imagine their last moments.

What could have driven them to march onto those hideous battlefields despite the terror they must have felt? What could have made my ancestor leave his home to join the C.S.A.? A desire for slaves? A hatred of blacks? No. As many history books and Confederate memoirs make clear (please reread section 10), they fought what they perceived to be an invading army because honor demands courage and loyalty to what one loves. My guess is that every one of them who fell died hoping they would be remembered after their passing and honored for trying to protect their country and people. That hope's embodied, for me at least, in Pearisburg, Virginia, where the words "Our Heroes" are etched on the base of the Confederate statue by the Giles County Courthouse.

For them to risk and lose all that they did—*American* soldiers, I must repeat yet again—only for their honor and their fame to turn to dishonor and ignominy, for the memorials remembering them and their leaders to be pulled down in disgrace? It's intolerable, simply intolerable, as intolerable and unjust as the death of Cordelia in *King Lear*. It makes me want to close my eyes, shake my head, and mutter, "No, no, no, no, no, no, no, no," shutting out vile reality like some pathetic madman.

23.

THIS ESSAY HAS been some small attempt to pay my debt to the dead.

Why do we bother to honor the dead? What good are such actions? *Cui bono?* They're irretrievably gone, save for whatever bodily remains and material possessions they leave behind. For instance, Isaac Carden is nothing now. He's a skeleton buried in my family graveyard, a grave plaque, and a few salvaged photos. In my mind, since I had no direct contact with him, he's a memory of a memory, which is to say, he's whatever I still remember of what my father said of him. And what's memory, really, but cerebral chemistry?

I don't know why we honor the dead. I only know that they've been treated with respect throughout the ages, in myriad cultures and civilizations, from Neolithic chamber tombs on Mainland Orkney to the pyramids of Egypt to the stele of Greece to Viking ship burials and runestones and on to graves and statues in Richmond's Hollywood Cemetery and Richmond's Monument Avenue. No, those statues of Lee, Jackson, Stuart, and Davis aren't graves. But they're memorials to deceased war leaders and war veterans. The fact that many Confederate monuments were erected during the years of Jim Crow and segregation is irrelevant. When such monuments were built doesn't matter to me or to innumerable folks like me. What matters is what they mean to the descendants of Confederate soldiers and civilians now.

Civilized people honor the dead. Only vicious barbarians dishonor them.

24.

A FEW YEARS back, in February 2016, I drove down to Columbia, South Carolina, to speak at the Deckle Edge Literary Festival, where I appeared on a panel of authors who'd published in *Crooked Letter i: Coming Out in the South*, just as I would at the Virginia Festival of the Book in Charlottesville a few weeks later.

In between festival panels, I battened on local delicacies like shrimp and grits, fried okra, and fried green tomatoes topped with pimiento cheese. I also toured the town a bit. First, I wandered down to the University of South Carolina, where my husband had attended undergraduate school. There, I admired the elegant buildings, the blossoming camellias, and a few messy-haired college boys playing frisbee, whose agile youth and dark beards reminded me of how hoary my own whiskers have gotten. Then I visited the grave of Confederate General Wade Hampton at the Trinity Episcopal Church, as well as the graves of "States Rights" Gish, who died at the bloody battle of Franklin, Tennessee, and Henry Timrod, the "poet laureate of the Confederacy."

Finally, I visited South Carolina's State House, right across the street from Hampton's grave, and strolled the grounds. I studied the Confederate monument, its battle flags removed. I admired the equestrian statue of Wade Hampton, erected in 1906, and then the African-American History Monument, erected in 2001. *See?* I thought. This *is the way to do it. These monuments can coexist, honored heritage beside honored heritage, recognizing the complex intricacies of history. Adding to the story, not subtracting, excising, or erasing. "And," not "either/or."*

Primary voting was going on that day, so the State House grounds were busier than usual. A few old white guys—well, not much older than me—carrying Rebel battle flags stood at the base of the Confederate monument. When I gave them a simpatico nod, one handed me a flyer in support of Trump's presidential campaign, ugh, and another complimented me on my black Western drover.

They thought they recognized a brother, I suppose. As you know by now, since you've read this far in this prickly, partisan polemic, they had and they hadn't.

As I left the State House grounds, I walked between a little clutch of Rebel-flag bearers and a little clutch of black folks, one of them resembling an adult version of my nephew. Though each group eyed the other warily, I felt a commonality and empathy for both, the Rebel crew for reasons detailed above, the black group because, as a gay man, I too am a member of a minority, and because, quite often, homophobes are also racists. My dominant emotion, though, was sadness for us all. I thought of the last paragraph of Poole's "Lincoln in Hell":

> A bitter irony lies at the heart of these struggles. Economically disenfranchised African-Americans are the natural allies of the white working class, sharing with them similar concerns regarding access to quality education, fair and equitable law enforcement, and the proper distribution of public services to rural communities. Rather than viewing one another as allies, they have often been locked in acrimony... (141)

25.

WHILE CITIES LIKE New Orleans have chosen to remove Rebel monuments, other communities have had more intelligent reactions to the controversy over all things Confederate. One, as we've seen, is Columbia. Another is Franklin, Tennessee.

After touring Civil War sites in Franklin back in 2015, I became a member of an organization called "Save the Franklin Battlefield." I've donated money to them every year and receive their newsletter.

The August 2018 issue reprinted "Three preachers and a historian tell 'fuller story' by proposing Civil War monument, markers," a long article by Kerri Bartlett that first appeared in the August 14, 2018 issue of the *Williamson Herald*. "With a desire to quell any onset of mounting racial tensions following the Charlottesville tragedy and to understand how Civil War monuments impact a community," Bartlett explains, "four men—a white historian, two African-American preachers and one white preacher—started a year-long conversation." "'We didn't want anything like Charlottesville to happen in Franklin,'" said Eric Jacobson, "the chief executive officer of the Battle of Franklin Trust."

As a result of that conversation, the town plans to erect four historical markers that "would tell the story of African American soldiers and slaves" on Franklin's Public Square, near "Chip," the statue of a Confederate soldier who's stood there since 1899. They also plan to erect "a United States Colored Troops (USCT) soldier at an undecided location in Franklin to honor those soldiers who fought for their freedom." "'Instead of taking something away, we can add to it,'" Jacobson said. A town Alderman, Bev Burger, said, "'On the square it's to honor the dead, not really politics or ideologies but people.'"

26.

THE AMERICAN CIVIL War Museum's logo is "Confederacy * Union * Freedom." According to its website, its mission is "to be the preeminent center for the exploration of the American Civil War and its legacies from multiple perspectives: Union and Confederate, enslaved and free African Americans, soldiers and civilians" ("Our Mission"). It has three branches, two in Richmond, at the White House of the Confederacy and at the site of the old Tredegar Iron Works, and another in Appomattox. If you tour the Tredegar museum, you'll see the above logo physically embodied: you can go through the exhibits in three different ways. One, "Confederacy," tells you the story of the war from the Southern perspective. Another, "Union," gives you the Northern viewpoint. Another, "Freedom," details the African-American struggle. This arrangement is ingenious and inclusive, exactly right.

Human existence is about pain and struggle, but war is most especially. Only the solipsistic, narcissistic, immature, and deeply neurotic play the game I call "Pain-o-Meter," in which someone who hears another's tale of woe responds with, "You think *that's* bad? That's nothing! Let me tell you about the awful time that I…"

Suffering isn't a competition, and struggle's ubiquitous. So often, anguish and loss can isolate, but shouldn't they create understanding, unity, and compassion instead, since all mortal beings suffer? Everyone suffered in the Civil War: Yankees, Confederates, and slaves. When I ask that Rebel monuments and emblems be respected, I'm only asking that everyone's suffering should be honored, including my ancestor's, his fellow soldiers, and the land he fought for. You don't need to erase my people's story in order to tell your own.

You would see yourselves in

our hefty flesh.

scrapple

(for Suzanne Franks)

A TASTE FOR WHAT'S SOLID, WHETHER it's a man or a meal, that's the inheritance, how you'd recognize me across centuries of distance, you forebears who left Baden-Württemberg, crossed the Atlantic, struggled up the Shenandoah, then higher into the hills of what would be West Virginia, bearing your proverbs, your recipes, your love for well-tilled farms and expansive barns.

You would perhaps think little of me—the time I spend reading and writing, tapping on this glowing keyboard, every poem mere wisp, flimsy whimsy compared to a plow or a finely sown garden, a closely scythed field. I certainly imagine you glowering darkly, shaking your heads, brows wrinkled with outrage and piety, were you to see me watching gay porn videos to while away a puffing half-hour on the stationary bike, trying to fight your metabolic legacy, this Teutonic density (the phrase these days is "running to fat").

No, you'd have to focus on more simpatico scenes in order to recognize your descendant. "Frugality," say the books describing German settlers in

America, "a fear of debt," "a lust for land, the more the better," and certainly the saying, "Good feeding is time well spent" (Mitchell 4). Oh, yes, I am all of that, thanks to my father, thanks to his Hilldale grandparents, hill-farmers I never met, who tapped the maple trees, cleared the stony fields, harrowed the earth, raised all they needed, split wood, drove cattle, baled hay, chopped cabbage for kraut, in November slaughtered pigs for ham and sausage, using the porky leftovers to mix with broth and cornmeal and pat into loaves of scrapple.

You would see our kinship in the lip-smacking delight with which I bend over a pastry cart or sort through the small-town produce stand, how I peel a potato, heat carefully hoarded bacon grease to flavor green beans and pintos, to dress wilted lettuce (what you would know as *Verwelkter Kopfsalat mit Specksosse*), to grease biscuit dough or braise onions and sauerkraut.

Farms or food, so much of what I savor is due to you. Here's ancestry in this glass of Riesling, in this dense dumpling steaming atop chicken soup, in the way my body thickens and hardens, coarse with fat and hair, muscle and musk, cuddling against a man shaped very much the same.

You would see yourselves in our hefty flesh. My husband and I, we're brawny as foundation posts, rooted deep, built to last, our bulks well fed today with eggs I've fried, then slid atop skillet-browned scrapple. Broken, the golden yoke melds with the tastes of liver, buckwheat, cornmeal, pork. This breakfast is your world—Germany, West Virginia, the nineteenth century. Passion's chaff. The simpler loves, seated dually in the belly and the heart, are how bloodlines continue, appetites more durable than art.

> *My small-town tongue*
>
> *had never encountered*
>
> *anything like that.*

muslim food

> "Food and clothes must the farer have, the man from the mountains come."
> —*The Poetic Edda*, trans. Henry Adams Bellows

Appalachia

TODAY, I'M BROWSING COOKBOOKS and recipes, and I'm starting a grocery list. In a few weeks, my friend Lizzy, a brilliant MIT graduate, is visiting. She's driving down from the Philadelphia suburbs to my little mountain town in southwest Virginia, and I want to make sure we share a few good meals.

"Southern hospitality" is a cliché because it's so often true. At least it's true of many members of my generation; I gather that the majority of millennials don't know how to cook. "Appalachian hospitality" is a cliché too, at least for those of us familiar with or native to the Highland South. Loyal Jones, in his famous essay "Appalachian Values," includes neighborliness and hospitality in his list of Appalachian folks' best qualities. "It was necessary to survival for everyone to be hospitable on the frontier," he says, suggesting rural isolation as an initial motivator.

I've never lived in rural isolation (despite a lifelong, misanthropic desire to do so), but as a small-town dweller, I think Jones' statement about the frontier makes a lot of sense. Both my hometown of Hinton, West Virginia, and my present home of Pulaski, Virginia, are far distant from the multitudinous options of urban areas. Such small towns have very few restaurants, so if you're accustomed to good food—as I am, having grown up around my father and paternal grandmother, both excellent country cooks—and if you want a good meal, you pretty much have to make it yourself (self-reliance being another Appalachian trait that Loyal Jones lists). If I have guests visiting, I'm much more likely to make them a meal than take them out to eat.

Here's an international far-from-Appalachia aside: isolation as the root of hospitality also makes sense to me as a fan of Norse and Celtic mythology and literature. In both bodies of medieval writing, hospitality's a cardinal virtue. In that Icelandic collection of proverbs and advice, *Hávamál*, a lengthy section of *The Poetic Edda*, quite a few stanzas focus on the importance of hospitality, and it's also stressed in many Icelandic sagas. Having traveled in the Scottish Highlands, Norway, the Orkneys, the Hebrides, and Iceland, I have a good sense of how remote many farmsteads are there today. Imagine how much more remote they would have been in the distant past.

Back to my own version of hillbilly hospitality. Were I a typical mountain man (and "typical mountain man" itself would be difficult to define), I'd be making Lizzy the Appalachian food I grew up on, dishes that make me feel safe, comfortable, and at home. It's a cuisine with many influences, including Native-American, English, Scottish, Irish, German, and African. Some of y'all reading this might have no idea what Appalachian cuisine is, so prepare to be educated. Off the top of my head, here are just a few regional delights.

Brown beans (usually pintos), cornbread, and chowchow (a combo that I call the unofficial West Virginia State Meal). Cabbage rolls and stuffed peppers. Greens: creecy, kale, collards, mustard, turnip, beet, or poke. Biscuits with sausage gravy, or apple butter, or topped with mayonnaise and a fresh slice of tomato. Ramps fried with potatoes and/or scrambled eggs. Fried cabbage, fried potatoes, fried apples, fried okra, fried corn, fried green tomatoes, sautéed squash or squash casserole. Potato salad, country ham with redeye gravy. Wilted lettuce, deviled eggs, new peas and potatoes. Fried chicken, or chicken and dumplings. Half-runners cooked with ham hock or bacon grease. Pickled beets, bread-and-butter pickles, lime pickles, corn relish. Fried apple pies, fruit pies, or cobblers. (If any of the above appeals, check out *Appalachian Home Cooking: History, Culture, & Recipes* by Mark F. Sohn or *Victuals: An Appalachian Journey, with Recipes* by Ronni Lundy.)

Had Lizzy asked for mountain food, I'd plan to make one or several of the aforementioned dishes. But she didn't. When I asked her via e-mail what she was hankering for, encouraging her to choose any cuisine she craved, she picked Persian, probably as a bit of a challenge to see if I could really follow up. How many Caucasian Appalachian guys with Northern European ancestry know how to cook Persian food?

Well, I can. I have a huge bookcase of cookbooks, covering one wall of my dining room, and the specific cookbooks I've been leafing through are *In a Persian Kitchen: Favorite Recipes from the Near East* by Maideh Mazda and *New Food of Life: Ancient Persian and Modern Iranian Cooking and Ceremonies* by Najmieh Batmanglij. I prepare Middle Eastern food and other international cuisines with some regularity for several reasons. One, something restless inside me is easily bored and has all my life craved variety, whether it be cultural, culinary, or sensual. As much as I love my native Southern Appalachian cooking, I don't want to eat it all the time. Second, I'm literate, which is to say, I can read a cookbook. I've never understood folks who claim an inability to cook. (Hell, pick up a cookbook and read a recipe. It ain't that hard.) Third, like many gay bears, I love to eat. It's one of my top hedonistic joys. If I crave a certain kind of food, I'll make it myself. Back to Appalachian self-reliance. There's a kind of freedom in not needing anyone to do things for you.

For Lizzy's visit, though, I'm especially glad that she chose Persian, because I'm always poised to give the religious right, Republicans, and other conservative assholes a great big Fuck-You finger in any way possible, public or private, big or small. Trump, that loathsome troll, has been pushing his Muslim bans lately, so cooking the cuisine of a country that's largely Muslim gives me great satisfaction. It also reminds me of how I, a country boy from a provincial town in West Virginia, first came to discover international cuisine, in particular the wonderful food of the Middle East.

Iraq

OUTSIDERS WHO ENTERTAIN uninformed preconceptions about my native region might not know this, but Appalachia has a decent amount of ethnic diversity these days. I know many black Appalachians, including my Summers County in-laws; there's even a group of writers in the region who call themselves Affrilachians. I've known Appalachians who trace their ancestry to Mexico, China, Lebanon, Palestine, Italy, Russia, Poland, the Czech Republic, Serbia, and Hungary, and I've certainly known some Jewish Appalachians.

Back in the 1970s, however, when I was attending grade school, middle school, and high school, Summers County was predominantly white, though there were small black communities in the county's only two towns, Hinton and Talcott (home of the John Henry legend). The local Caucasian bloodlines were pretty much like mine—English, German, Scottish, and Irish—and the local cuisine in both white and black communities was the Appalachian version of peasant food or poverty food, composed for the most part of the dishes I've listed above. Many people, including my family, saved money by cultivating large vegetable gardens and canning their own food. Others brought home venison and other wildlife during hunting season.

International cuisine? Well, there was a Pizza Hut in Hinton, a Taco Bell in an adjoining county, and, at Kroger, La Choy products in cans. Once in a rare while, when I spent a weekend with my grandmother in the country, she'd cook me up—well, heat me up—the latter. I can still remember what an exotic treat it was, gobbling that store-bought chow mein, with the crunchy little noodles sprinkled on top and doused with soy sauce. About once a year, I still eat La Choy, despite the high sodium content, just for the sake of nostalgia.

Then, unexpectedly, a family from far overseas entered my family's life, along with their fantastic food. It was a surprise and a blessing, and it opened up my adolescent country-boy mind to worlds beyond West Virginia.

For political, social, and economic reasons I don't comprehend but that have no doubt been studied by some scholar somewhere, in the 1970s quite a few medical doctors from foreign countries began practicing in Appalachia. In Summers County alone, a Latino doctor, a Filipino doctor (whose sister married into my extended family), and an Iraqi doctor bought homes, and their children attended the county schools.

That was how my sister met Leyla Ahmadi, a little girl with black hair and dark, sad eyes. Leyla's father was a doctor who'd recently joined the staff at Summers County Hospital. In 1970, the Ahmadis had fled their native Iraq (that's pronounced "Eye-rack" in my native hillbilly) for reasons that I never knew, though my guess is that they were members of several aristocratic families persecuted by the latest regime. Their escape from the country was painfully suspenseful. In order to avoid suspicion, Dr. and Mrs. Ahmadi left the country separately, the father with Leyla, the mother with their two sons. It was only when they met in London that they knew that all five of them had gotten out. After that, they ended up in the Washington D.C. area, and then—how this happened I have no earthly idea—in Summers County, West Virginia. Long damned way from Baghdad!

After so many displacements and relocations, Leyla was traumatized, but the effects of that trauma were the very reason that my family and hers got to know one another. In school, she wouldn't speak, either to the teacher or to her fellow classmates. This could have had all sorts of unfortunate consequences, but then she started interacting with my little sister, Amy. Something about Amy's friendliness and kindness encouraged Leyla to open up, to speak to someone outside her home. The Ahmadis were so delighted by this change that they invited my father, mother, Amy, and me up for dinner. Their hospitality was impeccable. Over the next several years, our two families spent quite a few pleasant evenings together, and it was during those visits that I got my first tastes of home-cooked international food.

All of it was wildly exotic, and all of it was delicious. The Ahmadis' coffee was scented with cardamom. Their Arabic hamburgers were tender with flour and flavored with allspice and turmeric. Their green-bean casserole was rich with ground beef, spicy with crushed red pepper, and topped with green peppers and tomatoes. Their rice was fluffy, and at the bottom of the pot, one found the luscious *tahdig*, a golden-brown crusty layer that everyone wanted a piece of. Most exotic of all were the desserts they served: apricot fruit paste in delicate sheets, or a rosewater pudding, sprinkled with pistachios and cardamom. My small-town tongue had never encountered anything like that.

One among many preconceptions about Appalachians is that we're clannish and suspicious of outsiders. My father called it tribalism, which I suspect is innate in our species. Such assumptions about mountain people are sometimes true. I myself certainly possess a clan mentality, by which I mean that I'll do just about anything for family members and close friends, but the rest of the world is cordially invited to leave me alone and stay the hell out of my way. In my nastier moods, I've been known to mutter under my breath, like some *Deliverance* hillbilly, "Y'all ain't from around here, are you?" I've also been known to growl about city-dwellers, the entitled wealthy, and Yankees, and I have a positive hatred for Christian fundamentalists and conservative Republicans, the natural enemies of an openly gay guy like myself.

That said, my educated and agnostic parents raised me to be curious about difference rather than fearing it. I assume that many Summers County Southern Baptists, had they ever seen the Koran on the Ahmadis' living room table, might have recoiled in horror. My response, like the rest of my family's, was curiosity. I wanted to ask, "What is this book, what is this religion? What is this language, written out in such beautiful, curving, flowing script?" but I was too young, polite, and shy. Now I wish I'd asked. It's absurd for a man as well-educated as I am to know so little about Islam. What with the state of globalism in the twenty-first century, and the state of religious intolerance everywhere, it might be time to make a class in Comparative Religion a required part of every curriculum.

I headed to WVU in 1977, and, after several years in Summers County, the Ahmadis moved to California in 1978. In Morgantown, my inquisitive, ravenous backwoods appetite discovered restaurants with international offerings: Szechuan beef, sweet and sour pork, and eggrolls at The Great Wall of China and burritos at Wings and Things. At Ali Baba's, my favorite, I battened as often as I could afford on Mediterranean treats like hummus, baba ganoush, tabbouleh, pita bread, and kebabs. I was both poor and lonely then, so good food meant a lot to me: it was proof that life was worth living despite all the things lacking in my life. Since I was single, with no one around to cook for me, I also began learning how to make the Appalachian food I'd grown up on.

In 1988, a lesbian buddy and I drove cross-country from Morgantown to San Francisco, and after Laura and I parted, I took a train to Fullerton, where the Ahmadis had moved. Their children had grown up and gone off to college, but Dr. and Mrs. Ahmadi looked much the same, meeting me at the train station and whisking me up to their beautiful house in their Mercedes. Their property, in a swank neighborhood high on a hill, sported palms, hot tub, and pool. It occurred to me only then that they must be fairly well-off to live in such accommodations, but they treated me—an English instructor with a paltry income—like a beloved cousin. During my few days there, they cooked me all my old favorites, and I wrote the recipes down on note cards for future reference.

I thought of them all again during the Gulf War in 1990-91, the 9/11 attacks, and the Iraq War of 2003-2011. So many Americans were busy hating Iraq, hating Iraqis, and condemning all Muslims as murderous terrorists. Had I not met the Ahmadis in my youth, would I have shared that hate? I don't think so, considering the way my parents raised me, but who knows? What I realized—as I worried about the Ahmadis, the only Iraqis I knew, and wondered about their daily lives in California, how much American anti-Arab sentiment might impinge on them, despite their status as United States citizens—is that there are both advantages and disadvantages to becoming friends with folks from other parts of the world. Yes, you learn to appreciate their culture, your mind is broadened, and, if you're lucky, your belly filled, but fondness and empathy open you up to others' pain and the turmoils of their native places.

What had I cared, a country boy growing up in Summers County, isolated and insulated, about what went on across the globe? Such faraway conflicts felt irrelevant, until I met the Ahmadis, and then distant politics slowly began to take on personal relevance. As is obvious to anyone open-minded, familiarity with those who are different can make for fellowship and understanding, which can erode tribalism, xenophobia, homophobia, and racism. Having black in-laws and a biracial nephew have certainly made the Black Lives Matter movement a personal concern for me, in the same way that having friends from the Middle East makes me detest Trump's Muslim bans, and having Mexican students makes me detest Trump's proposed Border Wall.

Iran

I WENT THROUGH a brief phrase of being ferociously nationalistic and getting my "Kill-them-Ay-rabs" redneck on, back in the late 1970s, though my simple rage was mixed with more confusing feelings.

The Iranian hostage crisis began in November 1979, my junior year in college, and continued until January 1981, a few months before I graduated. Photo after photo appeared in newspapers and the national news, of blindfolded Americans surrounded by a host of Iranian men, many of them university students like me. Images like that swamped me with savage tribalism and the nastier kinds of patriotism. I was young, I was hot-headed, and I had anger-management issues. (Only one of those has changed in the intervening years.) I wanted to kill those bastards, those crazy, fucking Islamic fundamentalists, those dark-haired, dark-eyed, dark-bearded demons humiliating and terrorizing U.S. citizens. But there was a complication: my inner sadist lusted after them. Those dark eyes, dark hair, and dark beards made me salivate, partly with patriotic hatred and partly with erotic hunger. Surely each one of them was sporting a furry chest, belly, and butt beneath those nondescript clothes. The mountain redneck in me wanted to blow their brains out, but the kinky mountain queer wanted to blow something else, to see every captor turned captive, every one of them stripped naked, blindfolded, bound and gagged, each made my own houri/hostage/house-boy/sex slave, ready to serve, eager for punishment.

Fantasy rarely translates into reality, and homosexual lust is rarely practicable, especially when it's sadistic and especially when it's set in Appalachia, where I have never found sufficient play-partners. Had I met a hairy, bearded Iranian-American willing to submit to me, someone to work over, first with cruelty and then with tenderness (that combo sums up most of us leather men), there would have been deliciously violent yet entirely harmless catharses, after which I would have untied him, lounged in bed with him, luxuriating in his body hair, and then no doubt asked him about his native culture and cuisine.

As you might imagine, this never happened. Instead, the best I could do, after too much rum at parties or at the local gay bar, was to make lewd jokes. "You talkin' 'bout Eye-ran? Y'all jus' need to air-lift this ole boy into Tayyy-ran and drop me behind enemy lines, and I'll give it to those hot fuckers for Old Glory!" I'd slur, while vigorously pumping my hips. Liquor made me a stupid show-off, as it does many young men.

Years later, a real Iranian entered my life, and any rancorous generalizations I might still have been carrying around fell to pieces. I was an emotional mess, recovering from the loss of a lover I now call The Mythical Thomas, when Hastee took my freshman comp class in Spring Semester 1992 at Virginia Tech. She was strikingly attractive, with an aquiline nose, full lips, dark eyes, mocha complexion, and long, wavy black hair. She could have been a fashion model. If I'd been straight, I'd have discreetly lusted after her. Luckily, we were both spared that embarrassment.

She had an unusual first and last name, so I asked her what Appalachians almost always ask someone they've just met: "Where you from?" Her parents, it turns out, were from Iran, though she'd grown up in the Northern Virginia suburbs, near D.C. "Iran?" I thought. "Wonder how close their cuisine is to that luscious stuff the Ahmadis used to make me?" Curious, desperate for any kind of distraction from my pathetically lovelorn state, I special-ordered from the local bookstore, Printer's Ink, the Persian cookbook by Maideh Mazda I've mentioned earlier. I lent it to Hastee and asked her to recommend dishes. She did, making a list on a sheet of lined notebook paper I still have tucked into that cookbook.

I had those few recipes I'd garnered from the Ahmadis in the late 1980s, and now I had an entire cookbook of Middle Eastern delights. Lonely, sad, eager to avoid empty evenings, I'd invite English Department friends over for dinners featuring international cuisine. Sometimes I made dishes from *Betty Crocker's International*

Cookbook, which contained simple recipes from innumerable countries. Other times I made Iraqi or Persian food: those Arabic hamburgers I'd savored in the seventies, or *khoreshe fesenjan*, chicken with pomegranate sauce. I developed the habit of putting a little check mark in pencil beside every new recipe I'd made: it gave me a small sense of accomplishment, as if each dish I marked were a country I'd traveled to, an adventure I'd experienced.

Hastee was pleased that I found her native cuisine so interesting, and several times she gifted me with delights from Persian food stores, including the obscenely tasty *zoolbia*, deep-fried, translucent pastries with saffron and syrup, and *bamieh*, grooved doughnuts flavored with rose water. What a gold mine of gastronomic pleasure for a bereft bachelor like me! That semester, for reasons I don't recall, Hastee and I were both in the D.C. area one weekend, so we had dinner at a Persian restaurant in Bethesda. I was the envy of every man in the room, walking in with such a beautiful young girl by my side. While they stared at her, I stared at the menu, and soon I was happily devouring *chelo*, fluffy Persian rice just like the Ahmadis had made, and ground meat kebabs, *kabab-e kubideh*.

That evening, any lingering anti-Iranian hostility I might have carried from the late 1970s evaporated. After experiencing that meal, If I'd had my druthers, I would have gladly headed home every evening to a furry Iranian man dressed in nothing but slave collar, jock strap, and work boots, who would have prepared me a Persian feast before submitting to me in bed all night. Hell, I'd do that now, if I had the chance.

As it is, here in Southwest Virginia, if I want Persian food, I have to prepare it myself. Well, with one memorable exception. In the late 1990s, my favored watering hole in Blacksburg was the Café at Champs, and I got to know the owner, a gorgeous lady named Roya, who'd grown up in Iran. (Straight men, envy me: I seem to meet only the most beautiful Persian women.) As you might imagine, I revealed to her my lust for Persian food, and we used to discuss recipes.

Then, in 1997, the year I met my husband, John, my poetry manuscript *Bliss* won the Stonewall Chapbook Competition. In the summer of 1998, Brickhouse Books published it, much to my preening delight. It was my first book, a short collection of poems about The Mythical Thomas. I decided to throw a party at Roya's café, and, since she ran a catering business on the side, I asked her to cater it.

"What sort of cuisine would you prefer?" she asked, with notepad in hand.

"Your native food, loveliness."

"Persian? But what if people don't like it?"

"Screw 'em," I said, scowling. "It's *my* party. I'll serve what I please. If they don't like it, that leaves more for me."

And so, the crowd battened on herb *kuku*, Persian chicken salad, kebobs, fragrant rice, global good will, and the glory of my little chapbook. In 2006, Roya hosted a Persian cooking class at her new business, Gourmet Pantry, and the participants watched her prepare a big Iranian meal and then got to sample it. I left replete with cosmopolitan cuisine (one of my favorite states) and bearing recipes for Iranian allspice (*advieh*), saffron steamed basmati rice, Persian rice with green beans, saffron ice cream, and eggplant *khoresh*.

In 2010, I was invited to be part of an international student mentoring program at Virginia Tech, and I chose Amir, an Iranian student in engineering. We met for coffee several times. He was surprised to know that I was a Persian-food aficionado, and we chatted about cuisine. One day, he brought in a beautiful photo book featuring the ruins of the palace of Persepolis. Over it, we laughed about Mahmoud Ahmadinejad, the president of Iran at that time, and his ignorance: in 2007, during a speech at Columbia University in New York City, he'd stated that there were no homosexuals in Iran. "A country without queers is a country without air or earth," I said, rolling my eyes. It was clear to me that Amir held his country's president in as much contempt as I did. Important lesson, especially these days, with that tangerine cretin in the White House: you can't always judge a people by its leaders.

Breaking Bread

I DIDN'T KNOW such a thing existed, until Lizzy told me she'd ordered one for me. She'd been introduced to the remarkable device by her Iranian friend, Esteri. A few days before Lizzy arrived in Pulaski, a big box was delivered to my doorstep. I cut it open and, with gratitude and wonder, lifted out a Pars Persian rice cooker.

I've made *chelo* from scratch only once. The recipe in Mazda's cookbook, to my dismay, had eight steps. It came out pretty well, reminiscent of the Ahmadis'—very fluffy, with a crunchy golden-brown layer on the bottom—but it was a pain in the ass. I was prepared to essay it again for Lizzy's sake, but, with the gift of the rice cooker, she's made that difficult process obsolete.

And so, at last, our Persian feast. Lizzy and I prepare *borani bademjan*, fried eggplant layered with garlicky yogurt; *khoreshe bagali*, a thick stew made of beef, onions, curry power, yogurt, and baby lima beans; and *yakh dar behesht*, rosewater custard. For the *chelo*, we rinse basmati rice until the water runs fairly clear, then mix the prescribed proportions of rice, salt, water, and vegetable oil in the cooker, put on the lid, and let everything simmer. Fifty minutes later, to our delight and relief, the rice is perfect, just like the rice the Ahmadis made my teenaged self so long ago. Feeling victorious, we each take a big chunk of *tahdig*, top it with *khoresh*, and enthusiastically partake.

Sated after dinner, we relax in the living room, enjoying the gas fire's warmth. I'm piddling around on the electronic piano, slipping into and out of Joni Mitchell songs I've played for decades. My playing's semi-automatic; my mind's on other things.

Playing "Woodstock," I'm thankful for Persian and Iraqi cookbooks and restaurants, because I'm pretty sure that I'll never travel in the Middle East. Male homosexuality is illegal in Kuwait, Egypt, and Syria. In Saudi Arabia and Iran, it's punishable by death. It's legal in Iraq, but I've read too many stories about Iraqi vigilantes and crazy ISIS motherfuckers throwing gay men off roofs. Does such knowledge make me Islamophobic? Hell, no. I detest Islamic extremists, not Muslims. Any kind of religious fundamentalism scares the shit out of me. I've spent my life quietly afraid of the conservative Christians that surround me in Appalachia, and I vote against the politicians they support any chance I get.

Playing "Both Sides Now," I'm remembering those hairy men from 1979 Tehran, student radicals I wanted to beat and fuck, now men as old as I, their midnight beards no doubt as gray as mine. I'm thinking of their sons or nephews or grandsons, one of whom—statistics insist despite Ahmadinejad's 2007 claims—is grunting with rapture beneath another man, or on his knees before his beloved, head happily bobbing. He loves black beards and hairy chests as wildly as I, and, sick with fear and sick with longing, he's making love despite the law, despite the possibilities of prison or execution.

After the lovers are done, they lie together, sweaty, weary, eye on the clock, drapes drawn, door locked. One feeds the other dates or this same rosewater custard I serve in Virginia, kisses him and tastes the sweet lingering on his lips. Even as they touch, they're aware of possible tomorrows. One future's slicing a lash across a back, another's tightening a noose around a neck, another's hurling stones at a head, another's aiming rifles at a heart.

Playing "Shine," I'm thinking about the grim state of the world, the anxiety, disgust, and dread I'm feeling with that egregious moron in the Oval Office, but I'm trying to count my blessings, reminding myself to be thankful for the kin and friends who've blessed my life and the many meals we've shared. I'm thinking about Hestia, Greek goddess of the home and hearth, and the Dagda, Irish god of the ever-replenishing cauldron, and how the heat of cookfires or cookstoves serves as the symbolic heart of a dwelling, from ancient Greece through medieval Scandinavia to now. I'm remembering Muslim friends—the Ahmadis, Hastee, and Roya—their hospitality, their kindnesses, the delicious feasts they've treated me to. And I'm contemplating the connotations of that old-fashioned expression, "breaking bread."

The phrase is a fine reminder of important truths. Sharing good food can create community, gratitude, and cross-cultural understanding, and it can banish a fear of the other (in this case what I've jokingly begun to call "those scawy Muslims"). Meals remind us of that earthy commonality all animals share, human or otherwise: the necessity of nourishment; the sense of satisfaction, safety, and comfort that the enjoyment of food can bring; and the ubiquity and recurrence of bodily appetite. Cooks like me might not be able to save the world, but we can bring people together and keep life going. That's a small, daily reality I intend to cling to in tough times, when I find myself both cleaning my gun and flipping through cookbooks, looking for the next new recipe to check off.

> "Leather bears and drag queens and bull dykes, oh my!" the three of us often chanted, a triumvirate of inverts that any self-respecting Christian fundamentalist would, we hoped, find sinister, sordid, and horrifying.

a ferocious drag queen

ONE OF MY FAVORITE MEMORIES of Okey is from April 2016. He drove us in his junky old car north along the Ohio River to Lesage, where we had lunch at the infamous Hillbilly Hot Dogs. It's a place I visit every time I get to Huntington, West Virginia, Okey's stomping grounds; we scions of the Mountain State are hot-dog connoisseurs. The roadside wiener joint is a deliberately dilapidated mess, an amalgam of shacks with old school buses as dining areas. The indoor space is claustrophobic with kitschy decorations, and neither Okey nor I are small men, so after ordering our dogs, we wedged ourselves back outside to eat at picnic tables by the parking area. Above us, big box elders were leafing, that fragile green-gold that Robert Frost's thinking of in his poem, "Nothing Gold Can Stay." Across the road, the wide river flowed south towards the Mississippi and the Gulf of Mexico.

I don't remember what we talked about as we sipped our iced tea and devoured our dogs. I probably bitched about other Appalachian writers, ones whose work gets more attention than mine, either because they're straight or they've pretended to be straight.

(I'm eaten up with professional envy about 98% of the time.) Okey probably complained about his poorly-paid, heavy workload as a gypsy instructor, teaching four or five sections of Intro to Sociology at Mountwest Community College and/or the Proctorville branch of Ohio University. I probably told him about a short story I was finishing up, one about the Greek hero Hercules and his many, many male lovers. He probably told me about the memoir he was working on, *Rainbow in the Mountains*, a book about his life as an Appalachian drag queen, and about his plans to apply to the low-residency M.F.A. program in creative writing at West Virginia Wesleyan College. Perhaps, looking out over the river, I told one of my favorite jokes—"What's the difference between a hillbilly and a son of a bitch? The Ohio River!"—before explaining that I was actually pretty fond of "O-Hi," as I pronounce it. Afterwards, we drove back to Huntington for the first of two professional gigs I had at Marshall University. That evening, I served as a respondent to scholar Allison Carey's presentation on "LGBTQ Literature in Appalachia." The next night, I read from my works in the student center.

Of all the memories I have of Okey, why does this one stand out? I wrote in my journal about that lunch, "Nice to be w/ a gay man who enjoyed the rural setting as much as I did." So many gay guys I've known would have recoiled from such a down-home/redneck establishment deep in the boonies, but Okey and I were at home there, out in the country, enjoying the spring air, watching scruffy locals come and go. Hell, *we* were scruffy locals, albeit queer ones.

That combination in my journal entry, "gay" and "rural," was the crux of our connection. We were both West Virginians, he a defiant drag queen, I a contrary leather bear. He'd grown up in remote Wayne County, "out Wayne," as they say there, and I'd grown up in equally remote Summers County. Both of us had struggled over the years, coming to terms with and learning to accept our gay and Appalachian identities. Both of us had mastered that struggle, saying "Fuck You!" to queers who didn't like country hillfolk and "Up Yours!" to hillfolk who didn't like queers. We were both pagan, he an acolyte of Artemis, Athena, and other warrior goddesses, I a follower of battle-gods like Thor and Odin and horny/horned deities of nature and the manly erotic like Cernunnos. We were two halves of the same eccentric hillbilly-homo coin. How could we not have become tribesmen and comrades-in-arms?

IN FALL 1977, I was eighteen years old, beginning my freshman year at West Virginia University. I was a shy, insecure bear cub, lumbering around in my first black-leather jacket, just beginning to cultivate a decent beard and a sparse crop of chest hair, and trying hard to figure out how to reconcile my lust for men with the traditions of Appalachian masculinity I'd been brought up around. Seeing drag queens at the Fox, the local gay bar, blew my country-boy mind. I was both flummoxed and fascinated by their wildly colorful and shameless "gender non-normativity," as scholars would put it these days.

Miss Jerry and I were introduced by mutual lesbian friends. He cared not a whit for the conventional manhood I was enamored of and bent on emulating. Instead, he was an outrageous, flamboyant creature who prided himself on resembling the blonde actress Suzanne Somers when his drag transformation—chrysalis to butterfly—was complete. One wintry evening, in a trailer in rural Osage, I watched him prepare for one of the big parties we young queers lived for in the late 70s. The wigs! The jewelry! The bevy of spangly dresses! "Look here now, honey," he said, using Scotch tape to bunch up his pecs and create cleavage. "This here's how you make yourself some titties."

Once, he and Bill, a butch lesbian buddy of ours, took me to Pittsburgh for my first visit to a big-city gay bar, The Venture Inn. As we stood on a street corner outside the place, Miss Jerry pointed at nearby landmarks and regaled me with tales of his erotic exploits. "Honey," he confided breathlessly, "I've sucked dick there, and there, and there, and there!" I was still an idealistic naïf, looking for love, not sexual adventure, so I was probably embarrassed and horrified by his storied promiscuity. Now, I can only grin. Good for him! Carpe diem!

Time spent with Miss Jerry taught me that a drag queen would say or do most anything. This unpredictability was mildly frightening to a sheltered kid who'd grown up in a small, conservative town. When, one night at the bar, Miss Jerry's cohort, Miss Leroy, gave me an indignant cussing over God knows what small slight, I was mortified, intimidated, and thoroughly chagrined. I was also educated: never, *never*, <u>*never*</u> piss off a drag queen…unless you enjoy being publicly humiliated.

When, on Halloween night 1978, Miss Jerry and Miss Leroy came into the bar in full drag, complete with parasols and humongous floppy hats, had a few stiff cocktails, and then sashayed out the bar door and up Pleasant Street, I was flabbergasted at the courage such a public display must have taken. Addicted I might have been to the valor of mythical Greek and Roman heroes, Arthurian knights, and Confederate soldiers, but I knew I would never be as brave as those two furbelowed drag queens stalking the nighttime streets of Morgantown.

Years later, during my graduate-school days at WVU, I had an affair with a close friend of Leroy's, an older man who lived in South Park, the old-money neighborhood of Morgantown. Briefly, Emery was my sugar daddy, treating my poverty to fancy meals of London broil and crab casserole and teaching me how to enjoy getting topped, but just about the time I got used to such luxurious treatment, he dumped me for a more cosmopolitan grad student in theater.

Soon after, to my surprise, I received a fancy party invitation from Leroy in the mail. At the party, I roused myself from my bereft moping long enough to grab Leroy by the arm and stammer out a few words. "H-Hey, thanks for inviting me. I was kinda surprised to get the invitation. I, I know you and I don't know one another all that well, and I, uh, know you and Emery are pretty close. Maybe you don't know this, but, uh, he broke up with me. He probably wouldn't be pleased to know that you invited me here."

Leroy tugged at the scruff on my chin. "Darling, I heard about that sad soap opera. That's why I invited you. I thought some party company would do you good. And I don't care if Emery finds out that you were here. He doesn't tell me who my friends are. Now stop pouting and have another drink. Try the spinach dip. It's divine."

That's when I discovered the magical quartet of qualities that just about every drag queen I've ever known has owned. Not only are they fearless, ferocious, and funny, they're also kind. Who could resist such a combination?

MEETING SOMEONE WHO will prove to be very important to you is just like meeting someone whom you'll never see again or care to see again. On a day apparently like every other day, you encounter a new face, a new name. You smile and shake hands, with no sense of coming consequence, with no knowledge of what's in store.

Okey and I met in Spring 1999, at the Appalachian Studies Association (ASA) Conference, held that year at the Southwest Virginia Center for Higher Education in Abingdon, Virginia. Both of us spoke on a panel focusing on Denise Giardina's work, and both of us discussed gay characters in her novels. "Amazing," I thought, listening to his frank and lively presentation. "I get to meet another mountaineer queer!" Okey, a big-built, balding guy in his thirties, was a sociologist connected with Marshall University.

In 2005, Ohio University Press published my collection of memoir and poetry, *Loving Mountains, Loving Men*, and, soon after that, I spoke about gay and lesbian issues at another ASA conference. In between sessions, Okey and I had several very welcome simpatico chats. When he was younger, he told me, he'd been a drag queen named Ilene Over. In those days, he'd encountered such homophobic violence in Huntington that he carried a brick in his purse. I thought that juxtaposition was downright delicious and often took vicarious pleasure in the thought of a big, ferocious drag queen beating the hell out of hapless homophobes. On the other hand, Okey was so large and impressive that he made me—a fairly brawny, bulky guy—feel small. I don't think he ever really needed the brick.

A few years later, when I encountered Okey at ASA again, he told me he'd had a heart attack. Cardiac woes weren't unusual in his family, he explained, and he knew that smoking and being overweight hadn't helped. Still, he said, he'd quit smoking, and he was recovering nicely, even contemplating the resurrection of his drag career as Ilene Over. It was a move I enthusiastically encouraged. As much as he'd referred to his drag past, I'd never seen Ilene perform.

That changed in March 2014 at another ASA conference in Huntington. There, I moderated "LGBT in Appalachia: A Queer Quartet," a panel composed of my good friend and political theorist, Cindy Burack; Carol Mason, a lesbian author; Richard Parmer, a hopelessly handsome young gay scholar; and myself. Right after our panel, Cindy and I hurried off to another, much anticipated session: Okey was performing in "Diary of an Appalachian Drag Queen."

There he was, in an over-crowded Marshall University classroom, with elaborate makeup, towering turban, flowery house dress, furry pink bedroom slippers, and elegant cigarette holder *sans* cigarette. His mixture of humor, social and political commentary, and autobiography was spot-on. Everyone loved him. Afterwards, I congratulated him on his triumphant return to drag.

That summer, Okey's drag persona inspired my writing. I was working on new fiction about my ongoing vampire alter ego, Derek Maclaine. I'd created Derek back in the summer of 2002, writing "Devoured," a novella, which appeared in a Kensington Books collection, *Masters of Midnight: Erotic Tales of the Vampire*. I'd continued Derek's adventures in a series of short stories published in erotic anthologies and eventually collected in *Desire and Devour: Stories of Blood and Sweat*. Now, fueled by my hatred for mountaintop-removal mining in West Virginia, I was planning a full-length novel about Derek called *Insatiable*. I already had a big cast of queer characters: my leather-bear vampire protagonist, his lesbian cohort (based on Cindy, of course), a lesbian werewolf, a bear-cub werewolf, and Derek's harem of bearded, hairy human thralls. But someone else was needed to lend Derek magical aid and add a little levity. How about a witch? How about a drag-queen witch?

Excitedly, I e-mailed Okey, asking for permission to fictionalize him and wanting suggestions for that depiction. Here's his response.

> *Hello my friend,*
> *I've thought about your questions and here is what came to me.*
> *The drag name should be something funny. Mine was Ilene Over. You could go with anything that is funny or saucy like Anita Mann. Her real name should be just a regular old Appalachian name like Randall Jones or something like that. Those in the gay community will always refer to her by her drag name (in or out of drag). In fact, many would not even know her "boy" name.*
> *As far as what she would wear. Imagine Delta Burke as Suzanne Sugarbaker (off stage in drag) and Phyllis Dilleresque clothing while onstage (with many kaftans and dusters). Her dress as a boy would be sloppy comfortable (sweatshirt and sweats or shorts and t-shirts). For a big convocation of fangs, she would be in high drag. She would wear something like a sequined and bugle beaded dress, lots of glittery jewelry and her hair in an updo. Imagine elegance incarnate. Perfect hair, nails, shoes, clutch purse, and a $5000 or more dollar dress (of course it would be black and blood red, with deep red lips*

and deep red nails, and black fishnet hose, which would show from the slit in the dress). Is this a good start?

My God, I thought, *what the fuck are bugle beads? I am out of my element!* I googled them, then carefully copied and pasted Okey's e-mail message into my notes for the novel.

OKEY FIRST CAME to Hinton in December 2014. John and I had bought my family home there the previous summer, so now we're fortunate enough to own two roomy houses in which to entertain friends: our main residence in Pulaski, Virginia, and that home in Hinton.

Same-sex marriage in Virginia became legal on October 6, 2014, and in West Virginia on October 9, 2014. John and I arranged a trial-run wedding in West Virginia before the legally recognized one in Pulaski, where we officially reside, and Okey drove down to Hinton to officiate, since I wanted a pagan-style ceremony. I've described that wedding elsewhere: a wonderfully diverse gathering of three lesbians, two Jews, my Appalachian father and sister, my biracial nephew, and the grooms, two gay bears. Okey wore a purple robe, with a striking necklace made by a Shoshone acquaintance of his in Idaho, and the ceremony he'd written—one that called the four elements and the four quarters, as do most Wiccan rituals—was perfect.

He came down to Hinton many times after that, for those gatherings I came to call Big Queer Convocations (also described earlier), weekends complete with lots of wine, booze, and country cooking. Cindy often joined us, bearing with her delicious desserts from Just Pies in Columbus, Ohio. "Leather bears and drag queens and bull dykes, oh my!" the three of us often chanted, a triumvirate of inverts that any self-respecting Christian fundamentalist would, we hoped, find sinister, sordid, and horrifying.

Our BQC conversations were always passionate and entertaining, and Okey was a natural storyteller. One of my favorite tales concerned his encounter with a Hollywood star. "Honey, one time I was sashaying down the street there near the Black Sheep, right across from the Marshall campus, and I turned the corner, and a jogger ran right into me. You'll never guess who it was. Matthew McConaughey! He was in town filming *We Are Marshall*. Honey, he bounced! He bounced right off me like a rubber ball. I had to help him up off the pavement. And gurrrrl, he stank! He smelled like funk. That boy was just rank! I didn't know whether I should ravish him right there or throw him into the Ohio for a good warshing."

Like Miss Jerry before him, Okey was fond of recounting his erotic exploits, though he tended to save those bawdy tales for late-night discussions the two of us had after Cindy and John headed up to bed. Like me, when he went into storytelling mode, his accent thickened and he peppered his tales with regional expressions.

"Gurrl, Miss Todd and I used to drive down to Charleston on a Saturday night to hit them wicked-naughty erotic bookstores, 'cause we needed to *feed*!"

"Feed?" I'd say, sipping Drambuie and acting naive.

"Feed! You don't fool me, Butch. You want it as much as I do. Cock!"

I grinned. "Cock? Why, Ah wouldn't know what to do with such a thing. Which is to say, *hell*, yes! The more, the better, though I'm more of a tits-and-ass man myself."

"Not this gurl. I needed to feed! To gobble up a man, right down to the marrow, and then spit out the bones! One night, I got into a knock-down drag-out with an old cooter of a queen who wouldn't leave the erotic video cubicle I wanted to use. She stuck out her finger and poked me hard in the chest and said, 'Git out of here, you whore,' and I rared back and backhanded the bitch, and she fell against the wall and started to squall like a wildcat in heat! She run right outta there! It was like a scene off *Dynasty*! So then I was free to feast on the man of my dreams."

Not all our conversations were as colorful or as blithe. When I snarled, "All my life, I've been saying to the right, 'Screw you! Don't tell me how to live and how to think!' and now I'm having to say the same to the left," Okey understood absolutely. Caught between political extremes, we worried about the ways that West Virginia was turning more and more Republican-red, at the same time that we complained about the oversensitive sanctimony of young queers, especially the transgender thought police, who not only want to control what language we use but to abolish drag as somehow transphobic. Okey was particularly angry when Glasglow's Free Pride tried to bar drag acts at their 2015 festival, and he got into savage fights on Facebook with politically correct queers over this issue. He was a terror on Facebook, abso-fucking-lutely not to be crossed. He sent all sorts of folks packing with his dry "Get lost, you gobshite. Buh-Bye, Felicia."

We chatted about pagan pantheons those late nights in Hinton, how to invite the energy of certain deities into our lives. Sometimes I read from my works-in-progress; to my pleasure and relief, he heartily approved of the way I'd fictionalized him in *Insatiable*. Sometimes, he'd read to me, wonderful excerpts from books he was working on: a gay werewolf novel set in France; his memoir, *Rainbow in the Mountains*; and his drag-queen romance, *Make Me Pretty, Sissy*. We talked comic-book movies: my love of the X-Men and the Avengers, my crush on Marvel role models Captain America, Thor, and Wolverine; his life-long role model, Wonder Woman, his ecstatic delight over Gal Gadot in the 2017 *Wonder Woman* film. We talked *Lord of the Rings*: I always wore my Aragorn ring when I knew he and I would be spending time together, and he often wore his Galadriel ring. One year, I bought him Arwen's evenstar necklace as a Yuletide present. Trump to us was Sauron, a poisonous glare blighting the national landscape. Once in a rare while, I'd play the piano. Karla Bonoff's "Goodbye, My Friend" was his favorite. "Lord, honey, that's beautiful," he'd say. "I've heard that at so many funerals…friends who died of AIDS." Okey often talked about his years of political activism in the Huntington area, the conservatives he'd offended, the city officials he'd pissed off, the LGBT group he'd helped organize at Marshall, acts of real courage and citizen resistance that he knew would have negative consequences for him but which he carried out anyway. Other times he'd tell me about his estrangement from his homophobic, conservative Christian mother and father in Wayne County, but how much he adored his grandmother, how unmoored he would feel when she died. Many times, I shared with him my struggles with depression, and Okey theorized that I was having difficulty moving from the Thor-stage of my life to the Odin-stage as I aged. He helped me understand my own paganism, my own warrior mentality, and he was hugely supportive when I suffered a series of sharp career disappointments at Virginia Tech, patiently listening to me rant on and on about assorted pit-viper colleagues. When I told him that what I'd really needed at a certain M.F.A. Committee meeting was a knife, he got me to laugh despite my wrath by declaring, "There! That should be your drag name! Ahneeda Kniph!" "Hmm, really?" I said, going with the joke. "But don't all West Virginia drag queens have 'St. Clair' as their last name? I was thinking 'Gorgopotamus St. Clair.' Or 'M'Orbesity St. Clair.' Or 'Rantarella St. Clair.' Or 'Tyrannosaurus Rexapotamus St. Clair.' Or even 'Fertilizante St Clair.' Urrr, I mean...'Santa Clara?'" "Lord, where'd that come from?" "A sign I saw in the gardening section of Walmart." "Oh, no, gurl, not that one. You're not a Latina. That would be cultural appropriation. Heaven forfend. No, no, Ahneeda Kniph it is."

Most helpfully, every time I asked, "Why the fuck do I keep writing? Who the fuck cares? Why the fuck should I bother?" he gently convinced me of the worth of my publications and the need to be resilient and to persevere. In encouraging me to continue, he liked to refer to two of his favorite authors. One was a sociologist hero of his, Patricia Hill Collins, who says in *Black Feminist Thought*: "Oppressed groups are frequently placed in the situation of being listened to only if we frame our ideas in the language that is familiar to and comfortable for a dominant group. This requirement often changes the meaning of our ideas and works to elevate the ideas of dominant groups" (ix).

"The reason mainstream folks resist or ignore or refuse to recognize your work is because you're not framing your ideas for them, you're not trying to make them comfortable," he'd explain. "You're not packaging your publications for straight people by creating polite, sanitized, tasteful little stories with inoffensive gays and funny-faggot best friends. Instead, you're writing for other queers, and that's a good thing, an important thing. There's sex in your books, kinky sex, there're men who use their dicks, who rim ass and lick armpits and fuck butt. Keep it up! Don't be silenced! No more of that 'love that dare not speak its name' bullshit."

Another favorite was Starhawk, a Wiccan author, priestess, and political activist we both admired. "You're telling the stories of the oppressed. Starhawk says that's a revolutionary act. Fuck a tight-assed mainstream audience. You got more important things to do. Write for hillbillies and queers. Telling the stories that you feel compelled to tell's an act of rebellion and resistance."

The book of mine that he enjoyed the most was *Cub*, a novel I'd set in Summers County in the early 1990s, so when he visited Hinton, I often gave him "*Cub* Tours" of the novel's settings. I took him to our family farm at Forest Hill, where my sister now lives, and the family graveyard. We drove down to Brooks Falls and Sandstone Falls, and over to Kirk's, where we sat on the patio overlooking the New River and ate hot dogs just as Travis and Mike, *Cub*'s main characters, had done. One winter day, we had barbeque sandwiches and sweet iced tea in the Bluestone Dining Room at Pipestem State Park, and, despite the amazing view over the Bluestone River Gorge and the mountains beyond, both of us fixated on and fell desperately in love with the same man, a fellow diner. The guy was young, tall, and burly, with a big blond beard, dressed in jeans, cowboy boots, and flannel shirt and carrying a guitar.

"Ummmm," I growled, "I'd like to strip that boy down and keep him trussed and gagged in my bed for a few days. Who knows what cruel uses I'd put him to?"

"Honey, I shudder to think, preee-verse leather bear that you are. Me, I have a simple need to feed. What a morsel."

"Damn right. Yum. Grade-A beef. I'll bet he has golden fuzz all over his chest and belly, and a big, round, furry ass…skin pale as the flesh of a McIntosh apple and tasting just as sweet…"

"Mercy, Mr. Mann! Stop! You're a'rilin' Mama up! Big-built boy like that has got to have a prodigious tallywacker."

"Let's take him," I said, sinking my teeth into more available meat, i.e., my barbeque. "We can divvy up the haul, so to speak. I get that pretty bearded mouth, his nipples and butt, and—"

"And I get the pecker. Deal?"

"Deal."

This concurrent salacious fascination was to occur again and again over the years: a broad-shouldered, ponytailed waiter at Draper Mercantile; a lean, black-bearded Middle Eastern waiter at Virginia Tech's Skelton Inn; various goateed, firm-rumped redneck boys on the streets of Hinton. Both keen connoisseurs of male beauty, Okey and I would spot something toothsome, then catch each other's eyes with a look that meant, "I'd climb all over that." I'd grin and tongue a canine tooth, imitating my vampire alter ego, Derek Maclaine, Okey'd arch an eyebrow, mutter, "Gurrrrrrrrrrl…" and then, palpitating with lust, we'd shift our glances back to our innocent and unknowing would-be prey. We were ruthless erotic predators, if only in our own minds…though Okey was bolder and sometimes acted in ways I've always been too shy, sheepish, and downright afraid to. I still remember how puffed up with concupiscent triumph he was, telling me how he'd chatted up a hot cop serving as crowd control at a political protest Okey'd attended and promptly seduced him. "Honey," he said, in response to my disbelieving gape, "sometimes you gotta grab life by the balls…and I mean that literally."

As a writer, I've gotten little to no help from older or more recognized authors. They haven't offered, and I've been too proud to ask. This lack of nourishing networking has had a profoundly negative effect on my career, so I've done my best to give to other writers and artists what I rarely got, arranging opportunities and making connections for them in any way I can. As supportive of my writing as Okey was, the least I could do was talk him up and encourage folks to invite Miss Ilene to perform. I managed this twice, finagling him gigs with honoraria at Virginia Tech in October 2015 and again at VT when the university hosted the ASA Conference in March 2017.

Here's the promotional material he gave me to share with potential sponsors.

> Miss Ilene Over is a sassy (and single) gal born in Appalachia—a true mountain Queer. The illegitimate love child of Carol Burnett and Leslie Jordan, she was raised in West Virginia and graduated in 1999 with a Master's Degree in Sociology. Ilene has been doing drag since 1989.
>
> One of the organizers of the first Lesbian, Gay, Bisexual and Transgendered Pride event in West Virginia, she has been active in the fight for LGBT equality and civil rights for twenty-five years on the local, state, and national level.
>
> In 2014, Ilene decided to create a show, *Rainbow in the Mountains: Growing Up Gay and Fabulous in Appalachia*. The show drew upon her experiences growing up gay in Appalachia and as a Sociology professor. The result was a show that premiered at the Appalachian Studies Association Annual Conference at Marshall University in Huntington, WV that year. The

show was a hit—standing room only.

After some fine tuning the next few years, Ilene created her new show: *Gay and Fabulous in Appalachia: Confessions of An Appalachian Drag Queen.* Ilene shares some of her personal stories and analysis as a sociologist. She brings her own style of storytelling, comedy, and education to her audience. Really, how many sociology professors can look this fabulous, be this funny, and give good lecture?

Currently, Ilene resides in Huntington, WV, where she teaches sociology and is working on her long-awaited memoir.

Okey's October 2015 show at VT was a classic. He stayed with John and me in Pulaski, and I went into my usual Southern-hospitality mode, pouring lots of wine, whipping up bucatini with Amatriciana sauce for dinner and baking buttermilk biscuits for breakfast. His show was scheduled in Shanks Hall, the English Department building, so we'd planned for him to change in my office. As we approached Shanks, me lugging a big trunk full of outfits and other drag paraphernalia and him carrying his wild umber wig on a mannequin head, a woman left the building.

"That's an odd thing to be carrying," she said, nodding at the bodiless, bewigged head as she passed.

"Not if you're a drag queen," Okey said, without missing a beat. I didn't quite keep a straight face but did resist the urge to slap my knee and guffaw.

In my office, I got to witness the complex hour-long preparations that transformed a three-hundred-something-pound man into a drag queen: stage makeup, powder, the big wig, the caftan, the flashy costume jewelry.

"I'm so sorry. I'm getting powder all over your desk and floor," Okey said, patting his cheeks.

"Hell, I don't care. This is fascinating. But soooo much trouble."

"You're telling me. That's why I don't do this anymore unless people pay me. Would you hand me my breastesses, Mr. Mann?"

I picked up the big bags he indicated, shook them, and passed them to him. "What's in here? Cat litter?"

"Ah, one of the most arcane secrets of drag: it's bird seed," he said, strapping said breastesses on before slipping into a golden caftan.

"Now the hairrrssss." He combed out the umber wig and secured it to his head. Next he rummaged in the trunk and pulled out a transparent plastic case of fake fingernails. "And now…the claws! If you'll help me. I can do one hand, but once those nails are on, I can't do the other."

"Do you mean I'll be able to add 'drag technician' to my résumé? Sure."

Okey showed me how to apply a tiny bit of glue, center the nail, press it down, and hold it in place till the glue dried. When we were done, he was indeed beclawed, with long, blood-red nails.

"'Nature red in tooth and claw,'" I said, quoting Tennyson.

"Exactly. Didn't Shakespeare have a line about…"

"'Could I come near your beauty with my nails?'"

"Right. Well, Butch, if you see any of those hateful colleagues of yours in the audience tonight, point 'em out to me and I'll claw 'em a comeuppance."

When you invite a writer or performer to campus, you can pour as much energy and money into publicity as you'd like, but you still don't know whether or not you'll have a decent audience. But the fliers I'd posted and the e-mails I'd sent worked. To my relief, 370-380 Shanks Hall was standing-room only. Ilene Over was a huge hit. In fact, you can watch that performance on YouTube (you'll find the link address under the Works Cited).

Miss Ilene was as frank and bold in her show as I try to be in my publications. She talked about reconciling mountain and gay identities, all the names she'd been called over the years—sissy, queer, fag, cocksucker, pervert—the wedding dress she tried to wear during grade-school dress-up, and her passionate love of Wonder Woman. Reminiscing about her coming-out days in college, she brought down the house with the priceless statement, "I wanted *cock*. I craved it, I wanted it, I needed it, and I went and got it," which I'm sure has never been announced in a Virginia Tech classroom in the entire history of that institution. I wanted to yell, "Testify, sister!" but thought better of it.

IN APRIL 2016, we enjoyed that memorable trip along the Ohio to Hillbilly Hot Dogs. The next day, we had lunch at a Huntington institution, Jim's Steak and Spaghetti House, with my Marshall hostess, the aforementioned Allison Carey, who's composing a much-needed book about LGBT writing in Appalachia. In a crowded corner of the restaurant, we three battened on pasta, meat sauce, and garlic bread while Okey loudly held forth with many an off-color tale.

Years later, Allison was to confide in me, "I don't think I've heard anyone use the word 'dick' that many times in any one conversation. The really notable thing to me was the juxtaposition of dick-dick-dick within the context of Jim's Steak & Spaghetti—I recall that from our table, we could see the table where President Kennedy once sat, and the photo of Kennedy sitting in that booth, and we were surrounded by those waitresses in their crisp white dresses. And Okey's talking volubly about dicks!"

What could I do but smile? Okey never gave a shit about who overheard what or what people thought. I don't think I've ever met anyone so fearless.

IN SEPTEMBER 2016, my father died at age 95. The only silver lining to that was that he didn't live to see Trump elected, a horror that definitely would have killed him. In November 2016, Okey drove to Hinton for the memorial service my sister had organized. I walked with him from our Hinton house to the service, held in the old McCreery Hotel. It was the distance of one block. Okey had to pause to catch his breath about every ten steps.

"Mr. Mann," he panted, "I'm tired of shuffling around like an old woman with all this extra weight. I've got work to do, trouble to stir up, and books to write. I'm turning my life around. I talked to the doctors: I'm getting my stomach stapled next month. And I'm starting that West Virginia Wesleyan M.F.A. program in January."

That's what happened. The next time he came to Hinton, in January 2017, he'd lost fifty pounds. He'd joined a gym, he explained, and was burning up fat on a treadmill. He brought along a box of protein shakes to serve as breakfast and lunch, and I made sure that the dinners I made were all low-fat and low-carb, though he did allow himself during our chatty cocktail hour(s) one glass of the sweet wine he savored —Moscato or Sangria. The next time I saw him, in February, he'd lost another twenty-five pounds. His diabetes had receded, and his breathing was much better, though at night he still used a CPAP machine. When Miss Ilene performed at the ASA Conference that March, the room was packed, and she was lively, lip-syncing, dancing, moving around, though at one point she nearly lost her pink-furred bedroom slipper, saying, "Lordamercy, I almost threw a shoe."

And Okey was writing. He flourished in that low-residency M.F.A. program, making many friends and impressing many people, both with his boisterous, friendly presence and his fine fiction and creative nonfiction. He did share a few sharp words with me about certain instructors who assigned an egregious amount of reading material and certain egotistical and/or neurotic visiting writers. "Honey," he said of a vaunted male essayist, "she's a cunt." Of a vaunted male poet, "She's ashamed to be where she's from. What a sad mess. And homely as a bedbug, bless her heart."

Okey had started a podcast on iTunes too. He interviewed

authors Martin Hyatt, J. B. Stilwell, and me. His greatest coup was interviewing someone really famous: Del Shores, the writer and director of one of our favorite films, *Sordid Lives*. Okey also posted a hysterical mock commercial, complete with manic banjo music, on YouTube.

This program is sponsored by Wide Load Drag Discount Warehouse, bringin' big girls big clothes for thirty-five years. Girls, do you have an ass the size of a truck? Do you need sparkle and shine and just can't find the drag to fit that ass? Then Wide Load Drag Discount Warehouse is for you! We can fit any girl, regardless of just how wide that load is. Come on down and see us. We're here on Highway 903. And remember, don't let that wide load keep you off that stage. Let Wide Load Drag Discount Warehouse help!

Okey was in even better shape when he came down to Hinton in October 2017 for our annual tradition, moseying through the street fair during Railroad Days, a festival my hometown's hosted for over fifty years. There was a cacophonous children's choir we both scowled at and hordes of out-of-town visitors. As I recall, Okey limited himself to a bowl of brown beans, a dish just about every West Virginian savors, while I threw myself at my usual trio of fattening pleasures: a hot dog with everything, a pulled-pork barbeque sandwich, and a country ham, egg, and cheese sandwich, followed by an unsuccessful search for decent fried apple pies.

On the stroll back to the house, our attentions were absorbed by a hot young guy escorting his girlfriend. The combo of beard, buzz cut, tight T-shirt, broad shoulders, small waist, and a great butt beneath cargo pants had us both horned up.

"Mr. Mann, will you look at that? I'm verklempt. I might swoon right here."

"Mmmmmmmm, yes. I'd tie that to a chair. Talk about the perfect slave-boy."

"And holding a girl's hand, of course. What a tragic waste. *Where* is my next husband? *What* is he waiting for? *When* will he come?"

"Jesus fucking *Christ*, whatta rump. I'd eat that ass for a good hour." Back at the house, I buried my face in one of the season's last pink roses.

IN 2017, OKEY started to get published. First was "Dave," an essay about an old friend who'd died of AIDS. It appeared in *Unbroken Circle: Stories of Cultural Diversity in the South*, edited by Julia Watts and Larry Smith, an anthology in which I'd placed an essay of my own, "Big Queer Convocations," about our Hinton weekends. Later came "Dancing in the Dirt," an essay in *Electric Dirt*, a queer Appalachian journal edited by an acquaintance of his.

Along with Julia Watts, and thanks to Allison Carey, we read together from *Unbroken Circle* at Marshall University in January 2018. One of the settings in my vampire novel, *Insatiable*, is a gay bar in Columbus, Ohio, called Club Diversity, so in March 2018, Okey and I read there as well, to a room full of enthusiastic lesbians Cindy and her housemate Felon had encouraged to attend. Plus, Julia and I were co-editing, for WVU Press, *LGBTQ Fiction and Poetry from Appalachia*, and we eagerly accepted Okey's "Come to Jesus Meeting," a segment of his novel-in-progress. By June 2018, during another visit to Hinton, he told me that he'd just about finished both the gay werewolf novel and the drag-queen romance, books that my publisher, Steve Berman of Lethe Press, was interested in obtaining.

THERE'S A LOCAL produce stand down the hill from me, the kind of place you'll never find in a highfalutin town like Blacksburg but which is common in little country towns like Hinton or Pulaski. On July 17, 2018, I discovered, to my gastronomic excitement, fresh crowder peas there. The next morning, I shelled them. I had them simmering on the stove with a dollop of obligatory bacon grease when the phone rang.

It was Susan, a friend of Okey's in Huntington. She called to tell me that he'd died the night before, apparently of a massive heart attack. "He called 911 and told them he was having trouble breathing, but by the time they got there, he was gone. They couldn't resuscitate him." At some point soon, she explained, she and other friends of his would organize a memorial service, and she hoped I'd be able to attend.

Stunned, I hung up. Stunned, I stirred crowder peas. I knew I'd just entered a grim new era of my life. Older family members of mine had died, and much-cherished pets, but never before a friend. *Who's next?* I thought. *This attrition, this diminishment will continue, one by one, until it's my turn to go.*

In times of grief, I go numb and get efficient. I headed up to John's office and told him. I e-mailed Cindy. I called my sister. I called my publisher, who suggested that I write an essay about Okey. My focus was far too shattered to write anything yet, so I read, *The Viking Spirit* by Daniel McCoy and *Secret City* by Julia Watts. I cooked a lot over the next week: Trisha Yearwood's vegetable pie, the Two Fat Ladies' summer pudding with tomato and fresh basil, white asparagus au gratin, Caprese salad. When you cook, process distracts you. When you cook, you're nourishing life.

The memorial service was scheduled for Sunday, July 29, in B'Nai Sholom Temple in Huntington. The setting of a Jewish synagogue wasn't a complete surprise. The last time I'd seen Okey, he'd told me about accompanying a Jewish friend to a service there and being very impressed with the rabbi. He'd met with her several times afterwards to discuss the Jewish faith. *You bastard*, I'd thought, *if you convert to Judaism, I'm going to be pissed. You're my only pagan friend.*

I drove up to St. Albans, West Virginia, early that Sunday of the service. Debbie, an old forestry friend from my undergrad days at WVU, lives up the Coal River with her wife, Billie, and they'd offered to put me up for the night, since St. Albans is only about fifty minutes from Huntington. Billie, an embodiment of Appalachian hospitality if there ever was one, had prepared a huge, complex salad for lunch, plus a plethora of fruit. Afterwards, we relaxed and caught up, and I got to know Molly, their beagle, and Jay, their animated schnauzer. He took to me in a big way, lounging with his head in my lap, sensing, Billie suggested, my emotional fragility.

Then it was time to get ready for the service. In their guest room, I tugged on dress clothes, something most country boys passionately resent, including me. "In July, for fuck's sake," I grumbled, buttoning the too-snug pants. "Ugh. Stuffing sausage into sausage casing. Miss Ilene would probably prefer me in denim overalls." But my Virginia-bred mother had raised me to be a Southern gentleman, and a gentleman wears dress pants, dress shirt, and blazer to a funeral, though I did forego a detestable tie.

The Huntington synagogue was beautiful, full of light, with a high ceiling and stained glass. I'd never been in a Jewish temple before, other than a few unconsecrated ones in Prague that served as museums or memorials to Holocaust victims. I found it difficult to chat with the few folks who recognized me—social interactions with people I don't know well are a strain even in my most emotionally stable times—though I did get to meet a handful of Okey's friends I'd heard about. Susan, the friend who'd called me with the news, was passing out a limited number of Wonder Woman armbands and, wet-eyed, I claimed and wore one, then took a seat at the end of a pew, as far away from everyone else as possible. I had no desire for strangers to witness my grief.

Most memorial services I've attended have, to be blunt, griped my ass. They're sentimental and full of clichés, or, worse, turn into attempts by the Christian minister to convert the audience. That kind of service makes me snarl and bristle like a wolf. But the service for Okey was perfect. His friend and former classics professor, Charles Lloyd, played masterfully haunting piano beforehand, and the rabbi was understated, concise, dignified, warm, and elegant. She gave a short interpretation of a Bible passage, one in which God says to a complaining Moses, "You have so much." That hit me hard. For a while now, it's been clear to me that I focus far more on what's lost or what's missing than on all I have. That kind of ingratitude surely offends the gods.

Three of Okey's close friends, possessing self-control I never would have had in such circumstances, gave short tributes to him. When one mentioned Wonder Woman, how Okey's courage matched his favorite heroine's, I got shaky. When she mentioned the scene in the 2017 film where Wonder Woman strides under heavy fire across No Man's Land, I was wrecked entirely. It took a lifelong dedication to the ideals of male stoicism not to sob.

The rabbi took the podium again, long enough to mention Okey's passionate commitment to social and political change. She exhorted us to follow in his footsteps, to keep creating, writing, and fighting. The service ended with the singing of the Christian hymn, "Amazing Grace," and the chanting of the Jewish Mourner's Kaddish.

When folks rose and began to file down to the basement for a reception, I fled. Outside, I pulled off my blazer, unbuttoned my shirt, climbed into my truck, and, windows down, took the long way back to St. Albans, along Route 60, breathing in twilit July, passing wooded hills and small towns, thankful for having had the friends I've had, thankful for being in West Virginia.

That evening, I had little appetite, so Billie fixed me up a simple plate of fruit and made me a peculiar cocktail, Fireball whiskey with sour mix, which tasted just right. Debbie started a fine blaze in their back-yard firepit, and the three of us sat outside with their dogs in the dark, feeding wood to the fire, drinking, telling stories, and watching the full moon rise. I woke the next morning to a gift from Thor—a sweet summer thunderstorm—and a gift from Cernunnos—frightened of the thunder, their beagle had climbed up onto my bed to cuddle with me. Billie made a huge country breakfast of biscuits, organic sausage, fried potatoes, scrambled eggs, and fruit. They sent me home with garden-fresh tomatoes, cucumbers, zucchini, leftover biscuits, and a little jar of moonshine.

God damn, *I love the Mountain State*, I thought, driving home. *The gods send what consolations they can.*

A few weeks later, an odd thing happened. John brought in the mail with a confused look on his face. He handed me an envelope, one with images of dancing woodland fairies and a Harvey Milk stamp. It was from Okey. The postmark was "02 AUG 2018," but he'd died July 18th. How it was mailed after his death I don't know. Inside was a card from Tree-Free Greetings, with another elaborate forest fairy on the cover. Inside that was a handwritten note.

> *Jeff and John,*
> *Just a note to tell you how much I value your friendship and how much I appreciate your encouragement and support! See you soon.* Okey
> aka Ilene Over

THE AFTERMATHS OF loss are always sorrowful. Sometimes they're also bitter.

A few weeks after Okey's death, the editors at WVU Press told me that we'd have to remove his contribution to *LGBTQ Fiction and Poetry from Appalachia*. He'd signed a contract, but his death made that contract void. Because he'd died intestate, his estate's controlled by his parents. In the last months of his life, he'd made some peace with them, but as of this writing, I have no idea if they'll allow his manuscripts ever to be published. I'm dubious, considering the many stories he told me of how embarrassed they were by his homosexuality and his drag. To think that he worked so hard and so long on those bold, brave, and provocative books only to have them consigned to oblivion…it's an intolerable thought. It makes me want to horsewhip someone.

I have a few things left of his generosity, gifts he gave me over the years. In Hinton, watercolor paintings of Pan and the Green Man, a bolline for inscribing candles and gathering herbs, and a leather-bound journal with a metal pentagram on the cover. In Pulaski, a miniature erect cock made of crystal, resting on the bookshelf in the guest room. An Odin's raven necklace I sometimes wear. Most amazing of all, a necklace made of beads and bear claws, its woven pendent adorned with a bear-paw design, still faintly scented with the smoke that Okey's Shoshone friend used to consecrate it in Idaho.

In October 2018, I gave a reading at Empire Books and News in Huntington, an event that Okey had set up. Several friends of his were in the small audience, so I read a scene from *Insatiable* in which Ilene Over appears. To my pleasure, they said they could hear Okey's voice in the character. I was glad to have done his colorful self justice. It was the first time I'd been in Huntington without him to hang out with. His ashes are buried on his family's property back in Wayne County, beneath a newly planted tree. I might get there one of these days, though I might not, if such a visit involves interacting with his parents. I was in the mood to honor the dead, though, so the next day I visited Spring Hill Cemetery to see the memorial to the members of the Marshall football team who'd died in that awful 1970 plane crash when I was still a child.

After that, I drove up to Columbus to spend a few days with Cindy and Felon. We enjoyed lots of good talk by Felon's fireplace, a long walk in the woods at High Banks, tasty tacos at an unpretentious Mexican joint, and great country-fried steak at Tee Jaye's Country Place, a blue-collar restaurant no academic snob would be caught dead in. After battening on a lunch of pirogi and cucumber salad at North Market, I chatted with a beautiful, hipster-bearded, plump-rumped boy at the spice store there, a guy I know Okey would have salivated over as much as I did. When I headed back to Pulaski, I took the slower route down the Ohio River once I got to West Virginia. In Lesage, belly growling, I stopped at Hillbilly Hot Dogs. Just another bearded mountain man in a pickup truck, ready for lunch and trapped in time.

When I'd last been to that roadside dive, I'd been there with

Okey. I sat beneath the same box elder trees, but they weren't lush with spring's green-gold. Instead, their leaves were brown and dry with autumn. I had a "West Virginia dog"—with chili, mustard, onions, and slaw—watched the broad Ohio roll by, and thought of Edwin Arlington Robinson's "Mr. Flood's Party." In that poem, a drunk old man with a jug of liquor looks down on a town in the moonlight, melancholy with the knowledge that he's outlived all his friends. Here's how the poem ends: "There was not much that was ahead of him, / And there was nothing in the town below— / Where strangers would have shut the many doors / That many friends had opened long ago."

Well.

Annie Proulx's "Brokeback Mountain" ends with this: "If you can't fix it you've got to stand it." This is true. The Viking ethos I admire is all about courage, honor, and dignity in the face of fate, loss, and death, even in the grim face of Ragnarök. Having known someone who personified toughness and courage—a ferocious drag queen—the least I can do is emulate Okey's mountaineer-queer orneriness and endure. I'll play "Goodbye, My Friend" on nights when I'm drunk and nostalgic. I'll watch *RuPaul's Drag Race* to get my drag fix and root for the big girls. I'll get briny-eyed when I rewatch *Wonder Woman* or see the upcoming *Wonder Woman 1984*, a film Okey was very much looking forward to.

At the same time that I'll do my best to celebrate all that's left, I'll face the facts. The things I love are passing from the earth, and there's no way to slow or stay them. I'm not like the Irish Dagda, with a club that kills with one end and resurrects with the other. But I can do this. I can write. I can honor and I can commemorate, again and again and again, until I myself disappear.

> "One hundred rounds?" I thought. "That'd bring down a helluva lot of religious conservatives, if I could ever get skilled enough to plug them."

watch out! that queer's got a gun!

I.

They're very simple machines. I'm inept with most technology, but even I can tell that. When I take them apart to clean them, they have only five sections: the magazine, the frame, the slide, the recoil spring, and the barrel. Up till now, I've had romantic taste in weaponry: swords, daggers, dirks, Bowie knives, and *sgian-dubh*. These new weapons aren't romantic. They're practical, efficient, and deadly. Nevertheless, I've felt compelled to name them after figures of legend. The larger is "Valkyrie," a version of the Old Norse *Valkyrja*, "chooser of the slain." The smaller is "the Morrigan," the Irish crow-goddess of death and battle.

II.

When I was younger, I was insulated from national and world news, because I was either too poor to own a television or subscribe to a newspaper, or I simply chose not to keep up with current events. Facebook changed all that, Facebook and my fear of the growing power of the Republican party and Christian conservatives. With millions of people, I watched Christine Blasey Ford speak before the Senate Judiciary Committee in September, 2018. When she said, "I'm terrified," the statement brought tears to my eyes. I was terrified for her, and I was terrified for myself and my clan and all the folks—women, queers, people of color, immigrants—that Trump's contemptible regime disdains.

After Dr. Ford's testimony was ignored by Republicans (and by a supposed Democrat, Joseph Manchin, from my home state of West Virginia, a man I'll detest till the day I die), and after Kavanaugh, that snarling, entitled pig, was confirmed, I was swamped with fear, dread, and disgust. On Facebook Messenger, I engaged in an intense back-and-forth with three women friends, Cindy, Felon, and Lizzy. Lizzy had this to say: "So, dark thoughts before I turn in for bed, having just read Paul Krugman's editorial in *The New York Times*. If the Republicans retain control of both houses of Congress in this midterm election, is it time to start putting an escape plan into action? And if so, is there anywhere to actually escape to?"

Hurriedly, I looked up the link Lizzy included and read Krugman's essay, "The Paranoid Style in G.O.P. Politics," published October 8, 2018. "Many people are worried, rightly, about what the appointment of Brett Kavanaugh means for America in the long term," he begins. He ends with this:

> ...the G.O.P. is an authoritarian regime in waiting, not yet one in practice. What's it waiting for?
>
> Well, think of what Trump and his party might do if they retain both houses of Congress in the coming election. If you aren't terrified of where we might be in the very near future, you aren't paying attention.

"Terrified." There's that word again. An escape plan, Lizzy mentioned. Like the Jews fleeing Europe as Hitler's power waxed? I love Scotland, Iceland, and Norway. Come to think of it, Germany would be sweet, or the Netherlands, or Wales. Someplace isolated and quiet, like the West Virginia small town I grew up in, or the southwest Virginia small town I've made my home.

Hell, no. To leave the U.S. would be to run from a fight.

Only those closest to me know how inordinately emotional and sensitive I am, qualities that often prove to be exhausting and inconvenient, especially in a culture that values male stoicism. I've been trying to toughen myself up since I was a tender teenager, with only moderate success, hoping to be resilient enough for the many difficulties life hurls at us and, more recently, needing to be strong for the people I care about. For four decades, I've been reading ancient epics and medieval sagas and watching films full of heroism, all in an attempt to emulate and incorporate courage, as if bravery could be learned if it's studied hard enough.

There's no goddamned way I'm going to flee this country. That would be cowardly, and if I thought myself a coward, I'd despise myself. At any rate, Appalachians hate to leave their native hills, and there's no way I could afford to move to another country anyway. I'm staying, despite Trump and Pence and McConnell and Franklin Graham and Pat Robertson and all those other vicious jackals. My response to Kavanaugh's confirmation and Krugman's article wasn't to contemplate expatriation, it was to clean my guns and load my magazines. I did it all in the guest room, with the door closed, so as not to make my husband nervous.

III.

IT'S AMAZING HOW many profound internal changes you can undergo if you live long enough. I vaguely remember arguing once with a high-school classmate in geometry class, objecting to his army aspirations and to the United States military. As an idealistic pacifist, I had no use for weapons of any kind. When my entire high school had to attend a mandatory all-day gun-safety class in the auditorium, I was seriously peeved. I was indifferent to firearms, even though my home county of Summers was and is full of hunters and gun owners. In fact, Hinton High School classes were usually cancelled during the first week of deer-hunting season, because the school administrators knew that almost no male students would show up if classes were held. My father had been a hunter in his youth, but by the time he'd had children, fairly late in life, he'd long since given up hunting, so it was not an enthusiasm I picked up, though I do remember once shooting a rifle under his tutelage near our family graveyard, trying to hit a row of bottles. I can't imagine that I was any good, though I do imagine that, young and small as I was, the rifle's recoil must have bruised my shoulder.

Killing any kind of animal has never appealed to me, especially after I embraced paganism and began to respect the divinity in nature, both flora and fauna. In fact, I go out of my way to rescue animals from harm, whether it be the cuddly sort that most people approve of or those critters that many find repulsive. I'm regularly catching wasps, spiders, and stinkbugs in the house and escorting them outside, or stopping my truck to make sure a turtle gets across a road. A few years ago, I extricated with a broom handle a four-foot-long blacksnake lounging in the basement, and, more recently, I demanded that my intensely ophidiophobic husband help me free another blacksnake from garden netting it had gotten trapped in. I held it by the head and tail while he carefully cut it loose. (He's never gotten over it. As soon as I'd tossed it into the woods behind our house, he rushed to Facebook and posted, "I touched a *snake*!!!")

Though I can understand someone hunting in order to supplement his larder, as do many of my fellow Appalachians, the egregious waste of life caused by wildlife poaching and safari hunting leaves me nauseated. I would rather shoot poachers or big-game hunters, dismember them, and feed them to their would-be prey. I take special delight in reading Internet articles about bull elephants or lions "accidentally" killing hunters. As far as I'm concerned, *Homo sapiens* is a nasty species, with many notable exceptions.

Though I never shared my fellow country boys' love for gunfire, I certainly began considering how to protect myself once I realized I was gay, especially after a homophobic punch to the face in high school. In college, I began lifting weights and took a series of Phys Ed classes involving the martial arts: self-defense, karate, and aikido. I'm pretty uncoordinated, so I wasn't much good at any of them. Manual skills come very slowly to me, only after lots of repetitive practice. In this regard, I like to say that my brain's smart but my body's stupid.

In my forties and fifties, I began to collect the aforementioned knives and swords in response to several eccentric passions: pride in my Scottish ancestry (a dirk and *sgian-dubh* accompany my kilt), my love of certain films (*The Lord of the Rings* epics and *300*), my research into the Civil War and my Confederate ancestry, and, most recently, my interest in Vikings. These handsome blades are, for the most part, merely martial decoration. Only twice have I had them at hand for self-protection.

The first time is a tale I've already told in "Southern (LGBT) Living," included in my essay collection, *Binding the God*. Someone at a party began to pelt my mailbox with stones in the middle of the night, and I went out to confront him with Aragorn's elven hunting knife concealed in my drover, just in case (Mann 91-95).

The second time occurred one windy, bitterly cold January night three or four years ago, when my husband was out of town. Around three in the morning, our house alarm woke me, its beeping an indication that someone had broken into the house.

My response wasn't fear but anger. I rolled out of bed naked and pulled on the pair of button-up desert camo pants I often wear during the winter months. Bare-chested, barefoot, my face set in a snarl, I headed downstairs, flipping on light after light. From its wall plaque, I slipped the elven hunting knife mentioned above, a very sharp curved scimitar. I stalked from room to room, ready to slice or stab any intruder I found. I went back upstairs to check all the bedrooms; I headed down to the basement, examining every corner.

Nothing. I almost went back to bed but thought I'd best err on the side of caution, so I dialed 911.

"Stay on the phone, sir, till the officers arrive," said the dispatcher.

"Yes, ma'am, I will," I said, scimitar in hand.

"Sir, do you have a weapon?"

"Yes, ma'am, I do. A great big ole knife."

"Sir, before you answer the door, please put your knife down."

I snickered. "Yes, ma'am. My father and sister are both lawyers, so I'd already kinda figured that'd be a good idea."

Looking down, I realized that, in my haste, I'd left my fly open, so I figured another good idea might be to button up before I answered the door and inadvertently flashed the officers with my Prodigious Hillbilly Meat. (It was a cold January night, as I've said; nothing prodigious was present.)

As it was, the officers found nothing amiss in the house or on the property. They explained that they'd already had three earlier calls of the same kind that evening. Apparently, very cold, windy nights tend to trigger house security systems.

In such situations, one's always grateful for anticlimaxes and false alarms. As I climbed back into bed after the night's drama, it occurred to me that an intruder would be more likely to carry a gun than a knife. If someone really had broken into the house, my handsome elven hunting blade probably would have been useless.

IV.

"IF TRUMP'S ELECTED, I'm buying a gun," I told close friends and family again and again in the months leading up to the 2016 election.

I think I said it so many times just to make sure I'd follow up and do what I said I'd do.

I'd never before had the slightest desire to own a firearm, even though, as a gay man, I've learned to move through the world with a certain kind of caution, aware of potential hostilities all around me. (Up this caution by one hundred percent, and you'll get, I suspect, the kind of anxious attentiveness that women must possess in order to stay safe.) A former student of mine who'd been in the Marines described such a stance as "situational awareness" and was surprised that a university professor like me displayed it. Luckily, my brawny, tattooed daddy-bear look makes me resemble other mountain men and discourages potential confrontations. Big shoulders, biceps, and pectorals are a fine preventative, thus my decades of weightlifting. Also—and I think this is true of many—as I've aged, I've achieved a firm sense of self that I didn't have when I was younger. Assholes can generally sense such solidity in others and are able to gauge, probably on a subconscious level, that it'd be unwise to fuck with such folks, because we'll stand our ground and throw that hostility right back, rather than cowering or fleeing.

For most of my life, learning how to use a gun seemed unnecessary, one aspect of native Appalachian country culture I had no enthusiasm for, much like the local variations of conservative Christianity that I find so threatening and distasteful. But watching Trump as he campaigned and studying his cronies and supporters alarmed me to my core, as it did so many other liberals, Democrats, and marginalized folks. In one respect, the man really is remarkable, in that he manages to combine all the nastiest qualities of my sex into one bloated package: pride, narcissism, a prickly ego, a craving for adoration, a suspicion of those different, and a contempt for women.

The xenophobia, racism, misogyny, and homophobia he and his allies evinced convinced me that danger unlike any I'd experienced in my lifetime was imminent, and I had a very strong gut sense of how things would go if he were elected. Since that election, nothing he and his kind have done has surprised me, though

I am surprised at the number, the virulence, and, in particular, the shamelessness of his supporters, many of them my fellow Appalachians and Southerners. In fact, despite my considerable regional pride, for several days after the election I truly wished that I were not a Southerner or an Appalachian. I find his popularity in West Virginia, my home state, particularly nauseating, since I well remember what a staunchly Democratic state West Virginia was in my youth.

Thus the determination to purchase a gun. One of my patron gods is Thor, the protector of humankind, and I intend to follow his example and protect those I love. In times as grim and perilous as these, an elven hunting knife and Strider's ranger sword are insufficient.

The day after the election, I was numb and fearful, as were so many I knew. Did I think that gay-bashers would attack me on the street as soon as Trump was sworn in? Did I expect gay-hating mobs to storm my house? No. But feelings aren't reasonable, by definition. I was and I am feeling, to use a term popular among the delicate members of Generation Z, "unsafe," and not just because I encountered a "microaggression" or wasn't coddled with a "trigger warning." Having grown up in a rural gun culture, I suppose it was reflexive, even inevitable, for a country boy like me, feeling at risk, to purchase a firearm.

I knew jack-shit about guns, so what kind of gun should I get? Fortunately, I knew just the person to ask.

A few decades ago, Everett and I were infrequent fuck buddies. These days, we chat seldom, maybe every couple of years. He's a gay country boy/mountain man/leather bear like me, and he's a gun collector. Everett, I figured, of all the folks I knew, would be the one to introduce me to firearm options. Having bribed many a man with my cooking skills, I dropped him an e-mail message in late November of 2016, offering to drive up the mountain to his deliciously isolated log-cabin home and make him a meal if he'd give me some gun tips.

So he did. I'd teased him for years about his gun collection, his semi-conservative politics, and his survivalist attitudes, but now he sensed that he might have a convert on his hands and seemed downright delighted to give me advice. He pulled weapon after weapon out of his gun safe: rifles, shotguns, revolvers, semi-automatics. I handled a few. Some memories born of that mandatory gun-safety class from the mid-seventies kicked in: never point a gun at anyone. Others did not. "Keep your finger out of the trigger guard," Everett kept saying. "You shouldn't touch the trigger until you're ready to shoot." Most revolvers only have five or six rounds, he explained, but semi-automatics have over twice as many.

By evening's end, I'd decided to buy a semi-automatic. *I can't imagine that I'll ever be a really good shot*, I thought to myself, handling Everett's Glock 17 and recalling my ineptitude when it came to things manual. *If I ever need to use a gun, I'll probably need as many rounds as I can get.*

"So, before you buy a gun, you need to ask yourself something," Everett said, putting his deadly toys back in their cases. "Are you really ready to defend yourself? Forget all that shit on television about shooting them in the shoulder or the knee. That takes precision. The best way to stop an attacker is to shoot them in the trunk. That's the widest target, the easiest area to hit. You prepared to do that? You prepared to kill somebody if necessary?"

I hesitated for about three seconds, imagining some vicious prick attacking my sister, or my husband, or my friends, or myself.

"Yes, I am. Absolutely."

"Full speed ahead then," Everett said, opening a bottle of red wine, while I set up some cheeses and crackers as appetizers, then headed to the cabin's kitchen to make Salisbury steak with mushroom and cream sauce. Nothing like feeding your friends after choosing which instrument might most effectively finish your foes.

V.

I REFUSED TO watch a minute of the inauguration, but I could hear it in the background, on a television set somewhere in the store. I'd deliberately chosen the day of Trump's swearing-in as the day to purchase a gun. We writers enjoy symbolic gestures.

You can buy guns all over southwest Virginia. I'd had only to drive six miles, up over scenic Draper Mountain, to find a sporting goods store offering a wide assortment of weapons. In early December, I'd visited the place, handled a few guns, picked up a copy of the slick Glock Buyer's Guide catalog, then headed home and cogitated, trying to gauge my own resolve, trying to determine if buying a gun was the right move.

The Glock catalog was oddly erotic, at least to me. In one color photo, a handsome young man with a trimmed brown beard—just my type!—looks intent and threatening while aiming his Glock 19 Gen4 MOD. In another color photo, set inside the back cover, two young men sit half in shadow in the background, their hands apparently cuffed behind their backs—subdued criminals? bondage bottoms? In the foreground, a burly, big-bearded, hairy-chested daddy bear—just my type!—in a sleeveless flannel shirt, Glock holstered at his hip, badge hanging around his neck, biceps thick and tattoo-covered, forearms muscular and plastered with fur—undercover cop? bondage top?—studies a small notebook. *Too bad men like that don't come with the gun purchase*, I thought, half-aroused.

I returned to that sports store on Inauguration Day and asked to see a Glock 19, a gun more compact than Everett's Glock 17, holding fifteen rounds. "For home defense," I explained.

The friendly proprietor nodded. "Yes, sir. Here you go." He removed a Glock 19 from beneath the glass-topped counter and handed it to me. In retrospect, I'm sure the way I handled it screamed "*Novice! Novice! Never shot a semi-automatic before!*" but what did he care? I was about to charge a little over six hundred dollars to my Visa card. At least I had the common sense not to point it at anyone.

"It's a great gun," he said. "Pretty easy to conceal, lots of rounds, no recoil to speak of. From Austria. One of our bestsellers."

"Yep, I'll take it." I *did* like the size and light weight of it, the way it fit in my hand, before passing it back to him. "Along with some 9mm bullets for target practice."

"You bet, sir. This box of Blazer Brass is pretty cheap. Will you be needing a holster too?"

I had no idea. He no doubt could tell I was new to gun ownership and probably decided to sell me as much as he could. "Uh, sure." I felt keenly aware of my relative ignorance and wished I had a big-built, bearded, leather top like Everett at my side to give me advice.

"How about some paper targets?"

I nodded. "Please." Those I knew I needed. I wanted to ask if he had any with photos of prominent homophobes on them but thought better of it.

What would he have said if I'd explained that I was a gay man freaked out over the rise of the alt-right in this country and looking for an effective way to defend himself? Having been the target of erroneous stereotypes and false assumptions, I try not to assume much of anything about anybody, but I was indeed assuming that the proprietors of a small gun store in southwest Virginia were Republicans and homophobes. If I'd come out, he might have surprised me with a friendly grin. Or he might have expressed high dudgeon and asked me to leave. The most likely probability is that he'd have curled his lips, choked back his opinion about queers, sold me the gun, been pleased at a six hundred dollar sale, and muttered unpleasant things once I'd left. (I confess here to a big streak of paranoia that's sometimes reasonable, sometimes not.)

"Great," he said. "First of all, I'll need your driver's license."

I handed him my license, very curious to see what would happen next. I couldn't help but be familiar with the national controversies over firearms, and such topics had been vividly on my mind since the April 16, 2007, shooting at Virginia Tech. (I teach there, but I hadn't been on campus that day.). I should have done some online research before gun-shopping, but I hadn't. I figured it would be more interesting to discover in person what a guy had to do to purchase a gun in Virginia. My guess was that it would be pretty easy in the rural South.

"Thanks." He handed the license to a waiting coworker, then placed a pile of papers on the counter. "If you'll fill out these forms, we should be set."

There were five or six sheets of paper, questionnaires with many blanks to fill in and boxes to check. I don't remember the questions, but for the purposes of this essay, I've looked them up online at the Virginia State Police's "Firearms Purchase Eligibility Test" site. Here are just a few.

> Are you under indictment for a felony offense?
>
> Are you the subject of an active misdemeanor or felony arrest warrant from any state?
>
> Is there an outstanding protective or restraining order against you from any court that involves your spouse, a former spouse, an individual with whom you share a child in common, or someone you cohabited with as an intimate partner?
>
> Are you an unlawful user of, or addicted to, marijuana, or any depressant, stimulant, or narcotic drug, or any controlled substance? The Federal Gun Control Act defines an addicted person, or unlawful user, as a person who has a conviction for use or possession of

a controlled substance within the past year or persons found through a drug test to use a controlled substance unlawfully, provided that the test was administered within the past year.

Have you ever been acquitted by reason of insanity? ("Firearms Purchase")

Well, fuck me, I thought, dutifully checking boxes. *If I needed to, I could lie about any of this. This is way too easy. Shit, can anyone buy a gun in this state?! This process has been as convenient and congenial as buying an anniversary gift at a jewelry counter.*

"Here you go," said the clerk, returning my license before bagging up the ammunition, targets, and holster. My new gun he nestled inside its case, upon gray foam lining. "Here's the bore brush, here's the cleaning rod, here's an extra magazine, here's the owner's manual, here's the magazine speed loader, and here's the cable lock," he explained, pointing to each of the case's contents before snapping it closed. I resisted the urge to ask, "What the hell's a magazine speed loader?" and "How the hell do I use the bore brush to clean the gun?" Instead, I nodded knowingly. Most men feel obliged to look confident, even when they're not. I'm no exception.

"So how do I get a concealed-carry license in Virginia?" I said. "I hear there's an online class you can take. And a gun-safety class at New River Community College."

"That community-college class is pretty good. Don't bother with the on-line class. A high-school kid could pass it. If you really want to learn, try this guy."

I took the colorful business card he offered. It was, to my surprise, a local evangelist's. I scanned phrases like "Protect the Children Programs," "Training the Church, Protecting the Body of Christ," "Christian Ministries," and "Concealed Carry Instructor."

I almost laughed out loud. *Ah, the American South,* I thought.

Concealed carry and Christ, all in one package. How can I resist this? How delicious would it be to have a fundamentalist Christian teach me how to defend myself against homophobes?

"Thanks, man. This looks helpful," I said, maintaining a straight face. I shook his hand, gathered my purchases, and, suppressing a snicker, walked out into the January day. Gripping the case's handle, I studied its square-shaped hard plastic. *My God*, I thought, *it looks like a purse. I'm carrying a gun purse. That was all too easy. Walk in, sign a few papers, slap down a credit card, and walk out with a killing machine. No background check? No wonder crazy motherfuckers are shooting people right and left all over this nation.*

What I didn't discover until months later, when I bought my second gun at the same store, is that the owners had indeed run a background check, feeding my driver's license number into their computer. From the Virginia Arms Co. site:

> There is no "waiting period" in Virginia to buy a firearm. There are state and federal forms to be filled out. A background check must be submitted once those forms are completed and signed. When the background check is approved, the firearm may be transferred. Many background checks are approved within a few minutes, but many are delayed for a few minutes, an hour or two, or even overnight. ("FAQs")

So, I'm relieved to say, the folks at the sports store only sold me the gun after their electronic research made clear that I wasn't crazy or criminal. Knowing that now makes me feel better about the process.

When I got home, there was the small matter of informing my husband that a gun now shared our house. John's a Yankee who grew up in towns and urban areas, not in the rural Southern gun culture of which I'm so much a logical product, so I was worried about his reaction, even though he'd heard me say again and again that a gun was in my (our) future if that "orange shitgibbon" moved into the White House. (For interesting background on the classic insult "shitgibbon," check out Ben Zimmer's article, listed in the "Works Cited" of this book).

In a September 2016 *Edge Media Network* interview with Kilian Melloy, "Jeff Mann on *Country*," I'd said, "If Trump becomes president—heaven forbid—and if that leads—as it most certainly would—to an increase in homophobic violence, well, then, I want to be prepared. If that means buying a gun, so be it…though I would, like Melville's Bartleby the Scrivener, 'prefer not to,' since my husband might just up and divorce my ass."

I wasn't really afraid that John would divorce me, but I knew he wouldn't be pleased. Rather than tell him, I chose a less direct way: I put the unopened "gun purse" on the coffee table in my study where he'd see it sooner or later.

Within a few hours, he'd noticed it. Our conversation was laconic. He strolled into the kitchen, looking serious, while I was preparing dinner.

"You bought a gun," he said.

"I did," I said.

He hesitated, nodded, and starting mixing martinis. After dinner, I took the gun purse up to the guest room and hid it under the bed. The gun wasn't coming out of its little nest until I'd learned how to use it.

A few weeks after the Trump inauguration, the Katz Jewish Community Center in Cherry Hill, New Jersey, received a bomb threat (Woods). The children present were evacuated to a nearby Jewish ladies' retirement home that I'd visited a few times. My publisher's mother lived in an apartment adjoining the Center—a lady I downright adore. I was furious. The incident brought the national shitstorm home, so to speak; which is to say, someone I personally knew and cared about was endangered by the vile, racist, anti-Semitic nutcases Trump had enflamed with his virulent rhetoric. If I'd had any doubts or regrets about buying a gun, they evaporated. I've read *The Men with the Pink Triangle* (Heger and Fernbach). I've been to Buchenwald. I know what kinds of folks ended up in the concentration camps with the Jews: queers like me.

VI.

I OWNED "VALKYRIE," as I'd christened the Glock, for months before I finally got around to learning how to use her. I had problems contacting the evangelist, so I visited New River Community College in the summer of 2017 and got information about their gun safety class. Due to low enrollment, the September class was canceled. The October 2017 class ran, on a Tuesday and Thursday from 6 p.m. till 9 p.m. It was conveniently timed right after my 4 p.m. fiction workshop at Virginia Tech and conveniently located just down the road in the New River Valley Mall in Christiansburg, Virginia.

The last time I'd been a student was my final semester of graduate school, Spring 1984, when I completed my M.A. in English at WVU. I've been teaching full-time, with only a handful of semesters off, since Fall 1984, so it was a huge change of pace to be a pupil again. There were only four of us in the class, three men and one woman; the instructor was the head of security at the New River Community College main campus in Dublin, Virginia.

I know something about pedagogy, so I can confidently say that he was a great teacher: relaxed, approachable, methodical, understandable. He opened by showing us a video compilation of people mishandling guns, all of which made me wince. (Google "Stupid People with Guns" and experience the same horror and humor I did.). He gave us a pile of helpful handouts and went over them one by one: NRA Gun Safety Rules, photos of various kinds of handguns with their parts labeled, and a lengthy printed-out Power Point presentation on handgun safety. I was the good student I used to be: eager to learn new things, assiduous at paying attention, taking notes, and studying. I passed the final test with ease (it was, admittedly, not difficult: everyone passed), and then the instructor handed me a fancy certificate: an "Award of Completion Given this 19th Day of October 2017: Concealed Carry, Handgun Safety Attendance, 6 Contact Hours."

There was only one disappointing element to the experience. As the class dispersed, the instructor invited us to join him that following Saturday at a shooting range run by the Pulaski County Police Department. I really wanted some hands-on experience—the class had all been theoretical—but I'd made other plans. That weekend was Railroad Days in my West Virginia hometown, and a good friend was driving down from Huntington to stay with me in my Hinton house. My visitor that weekend was Okey Napier, that ferocious and infamous drag queen. I can't imagine that a lot of hillbilly boys like me have had to choose between time at a shooting range and time spent with a delightful drag queen, but who knows? I chose the drag queen.

As confident, take-no-shit and fierce as Okey was, I imagine he would have been very effective on a shooting range. Hell, his alter ego, that burly Wonder Woman, Miss Ilene Over, used to carry a brick in her purse in case homophobes got nasty. One time, outside a gay bar, when she was attacked by three homo-hating guys, one of them with a baseball bat, she swung said weighted purse. She brought one down, knocking him senseless; his cowardly buddies fled. "Gurrrrl," said Ilene, telling me the tale, "I stood there a minute, trying to decide if I should lift my skirts and piss on him. Then I decided that wouldn't be ladylike." (I regret that decision. If I'd been her, I would have soaked the little bastard.)

A side note: as detailed earlier in this collection, Okey died unexpectedly in July 2018, and I miss him badly. I do take comfort, though, in a Viking vision of us in the afterlife: Miss Ilene's in full drag and I'm in my country-boy camo clothes and leather jacket, and we're mowing down hordes of homophobes with handguns, assault rifles, and good old-fashioned swords and axes, then repairing to the mead hall for a Norse feast, followed by vigorously intimate naked nights with long-haired, scruffy warriors resembling Chris and Liam Hemsworth. Let's hear it for queer Valhallas.

VII.

I'D BEEN TO the Pulaski County Circuit Court's office once before, in December 2014, when John and I applied for a marriage license. I entered that room with some trepidation, not sure what to expect. To my relief, everyone there was friendly and polite.

Being a gay Appalachian, I'm used to paradoxes, tensions, and apparent contradictions. When I entered that same office in January 2018, I wondered if I were the first homosexual hillbilly to have applied there for both a marriage license and a concealed-carry license. Who knows? We Are Everywhere. Still, I was aware of the Love/Death irony: a license to marry a man and a license to carry a small machine with which I might end attackers. For some, that juxtaposition might seem insane. It made perfect sense to me: protect those you love, even if it means destroying those who menace them. That form of death-bringing is rooted in love. Turning the other cheek has never appealed to me. I am, after all, a Heathen, not a follower of "the White Christ," as Vikings contemptuously referred to Jesus.

I presented the clerk with my gun-safety class "Award of Completion," I filled out a form, and about a week and a half later, my concealed-carry card came in the mail, a square of plastic small enough to fit into my wallet. I was honestly amazed at how easily I had gone from a gunless innocent to a man with no shooting practice who could walk around in public places with a gun hidden on his person. The politically conscious part of me thought that the process should have been more difficult; the selfish part of me was pleased at how simple it had all been.

The next step was getting some target practice on a firing range. The gun was useless, even a danger to myself, if I didn't know how to shoot it. Before I could try to contact the evangelist again, a more convenient opportunity presented itself. A friend of mine told me that her son, Aidan, a Virginia Tech cadet, gave shooting lessons, fifty dollars for two hours. She gave me his e-mail address, and I dropped him a note, expressing interest. Aidan and I settled on a date in mid-February, planning to focus on "basic marksmanship fundamentals," as he put it.

I'd need "basic" and "fundamentals," not having shot a gun since that afternoon my father took me out for target practice in my teens. As glad as I was to have a shooting session set up, I was also anxious, imagining how profoundly incompetent I might prove to be. No man wants to look inept in front of another man. There's a lot of talk about women who're addicted to male approval. Well, lots of men are addicted to male approval too. As critical, dominating, and difficult to satisfy as my father was, I can't help but be that kind of addict.

I often turn anxiety and other disagreeable emotions into humor, so as I contemplated just how foolish I might appear my first time on a firing range, I remembered two scenarios that cropped up again and again in the television entertainments of my youth, situations in which a helpless, fearful woman ends up with a gun. In one version, she holds the gun out, hands shaking uncontrollably, as the villain inches toward her. "D-Don't come a-any c-c-c-closer!" she pleads. Then— (to borrow from *The Simpsons*) *Yoink!*—the villain's snatched the weapon away from her and she's easily subdued. The second version is even more ludicrous: trembling, she aims at her adversary, then, with a hysterical screech—"*Yeeeeeeeee!*" (to borrow from Florence King's *Southern Ladies and Gentlemen*)—she shoots with such frantic inaccuracy that she brings down a chandelier or chunks of ceiling plaster. (Delta Burke does something like this in one of my favorite films, *Sordid Lives*.)

Would the brawny bear's hands shake? Would he bring tree limbs down on his instructor's head while squealing girlishly, then lumber red-faced from the range? Would he piss himself? I didn't think so, but such mental pictures were absurd and campy enough to make me laugh, and I'll create any laughter I can, even if it's at my own expense. If you don't have a sense of humor about yourself, you're fucked.

VIII.

FOR FEBRUARY 9TH in my *Witches' Datebook 2018*, one word is written: "ammo."

"As far as ammo is concerned," Aidan had advised on e-mail, "I would get a small box of hollow points to use when at home or carrying concealed should you decide to (which hopefully you only need to ever buy once,) and then a bunch of the cheapest ammo you can find for range work (it's significantly cheaper if you buy in bulk.) I will go ahead and plan out a course and give you a specific round count well in advance of the range day so that you have time to get enough. It shouldn't be a huge amount."

As I entered the sports store again, I tried to imagine what my late mother and father would think were they to see their son— once a gentle, intellectual, pacifist nerd—shopping for ammunition. In fact, I wonder even more how my high-school self would have responded, had he seen the future. Would he be horrified? Disappointed? Disgusted? What a failure, to have fallen so far from rosy ideals into harsh reality, austere necessity.

Well, I had no further use for that boy. The world was darkening, the Thor's hammer tattooed on my right forearm was as much a commitment as a decoration, and I had loved ones to safeguard. I followed Aidan's advice, buying more cheap ammo, an ear-protection device (shooting ranges are noisy, noisy places), and a box of twenty-five Hornady Critical Defense hollow points.

These were pricy bullets meant not for practice but for use in the sort of dire situation I was trying to prepare for. These were meant to finish an attacker as efficiently as possible. On the side of the box was a grim little illustration of how the bullet would expand, making a bloody hole as big as possible.

From *Wikipedia*:

> When a hollow-point hunting bullet strikes a soft target, the pressure created in the pit forces the material (usually lead) around the inside edge to expand outwards, increasing the axial diameter of the projectile as it passes through. This process is commonly referred to as *mushrooming*, because the resulting shape, a widened, rounded nose on top of a cylindrical base, typically resembles a mushroom.
>
> The greater frontal surface area of the expanded bullet limits its depth of penetration into the target, and causes more extensive tissue damage along the wound path. ("Hollow-point bullet")

I met Aidan on a warm mid-February afternoon, at the edge of the Virginia Tech campus. The last time I'd seen him, he was a child. Now, to my astonishment and chagrin, he was taller than I, a lean, well-built, good-looking young man, luckily too clean-cut and blond to stir up my daddy-bear libido. We shook hands, climbed into his enviably humongous pickup truck, drove up into the university parking garage to fetch my "gun purse" from the toolbox of my own significantly smaller truck (yes, size comparisons are inevitable), and then headed out of town and into the mountains to the west.

The Blacksburg Shooting Range is located in the Jefferson National Forest, down Craig Creek Road, at the base of Sinking

Creek Mountain. In other words, in the sort of place I feel perfectly comfortable, out in the relative middle of nowhere, where there are more trees than people. Maintained by the Forest Service, it's isolated, scenic, and, unlike many ranges, free.

Aidan and I climbed down out of his Magnificent Macho Mobile (the kind of behemoth I've always craved but could never afford to buy or to feed), and he led the way up an asphalt path ascending the forested slope, toward the POP-POP-POP of gunfire. At the top of the slope, a field opened up and leveled out, surrounded on all sides by woods, at its far end grading into an earth bank angling up the side of the mountain. A long, narrow roof shadowed the lanes and shooting benches; only a handful of other folks were present.

At the entrance to the range, a slatted bin held a pile of cardboard boxes. Aidan grabbed a couple, then walked down to the unoccupied far end. I followed, pleased to get as far away as possible from aficionados who might recognize what a rookie I was. (Men who were once high-school outcasts bear a keen fear of mockery.) Beneath my feet, thousands of spent casings covered the ground. *Each one a potential death sentence*, I thought, an observation both overdramatic and accurate.

Aidan laid out several of his guns and some cleaning products on the nearby benches, then checked his wristwatch. "Perfect timing," he said. "I'll set us up some targets." Waving at the folks at the other end of the lanes, he shouted, "Cold!" They nodded, gave us a thumbs-up, and put down their weapons.

"So what was——?" I began, but then Aidan pointed to placards tacked up on wooden posts supporting the roof. They announced that every half-hour, the range went cold, meaning there was a ceasefire so that folks could safely walk out onto the range and set up more targets or fetch their targets.

Aidan affixed paper targets to the two cardboard boxes, strode out onto the field, set the boxes different distances away, then returned. He eyed the other folks. They nodded. He yelled, "Hot!" and the POP-POP-POP resumed.

Aidan was a natural teacher, calm and patient, unfazed by my ignorance. At age twenty-one, he exuded confidence in his speech and his movements, the kind of self-assurance I still haven't achieved at age fifty-nine. Like Everett, he kept coaching me to keep my finger off the trigger till I was ready to shoot (a dangerous habitual tendency of mine, I've come to discover). He showed me the proper way to hold the gun, how to stand, how to pull the trigger steadily and evenly, how to load, how to use the magazine speed loader, and how to manipulate the slide stop lever and the magazine catch, both of which gave me trouble.

During those two hours, I fired a decent number of rounds, and, to my amazement, actually hit the closer target several times. (The field's ammo-furrowed mud probably swallowed all the bullets I aimed at that farther target.) My Glock had no recoil, as the sports-store proprietor had promised. I wasn't unnerved by the guns or the gunfire, my hands didn't tremble, I didn't shriek like a drag-queen denied a pageant crown, and I didn't bring down any tree limbs on anyone's heads `a la Delta Burke. In other words, I wasn't as bad as I feared I'd be. In fact, I liked learning new skills, I enjoyed Aidan's company, and I savored the woodland setting, despite the bullet ruckus. After Aidan cleaned our guns and fetched my nearer target for me to keep as a souvenir, we packed up, I wrote him a check (with a big tip), and we headed down the mountain. I already knew I'd want to come again.

IX.

THERE ARE VIDEOS for just about anything on the Internet. I discovered this between my first session with Aidan and my second. If I needed reminders on how to hold a Glock 19, there were instructors online. If I needed reminders on gun safety or how to load and unload my gun, there were instructors online ("How to grip," "How to load").

I needed those reminders. As I've suggested earlier, I'm pretty impractical, though I can cook, clean the kitchen, do laundry and play piano, guitar, and Appalachian dulcimer. That's about it. I used to be able to change the oil in my truck and split wood in a half-assed way, but I've gotten too old or lazy for either. The only way I was going to get even halfway competent with my gun was to handle it again and again and again.

If visits to the shooting range, a good hour away from my house, were inconvenient in the middle of an overly busy semester, fumblings with an unloaded gun in the guest room while my husband was out of town were convenient indeed. I practiced holding it. I practiced pulling the slide back and releasing it. I fooled with the troublesome slide stop lever and magazine catch, getting my thumb sore in the process. Both gestures reminded me of something I'd learned in those long-ago self-defense classes at WVU: how hard it is to make a perfect gesture, a precise movement. The difference between manipulating the magazine catch successfully and manipulating it unsuccessfully was minute, and the same was true of the slide stop lever. *If I ever have to use this gun in an emergency*, I thought, *knowing how to make these tiny gestures correctly might become a matter of life or death.*

The private practice paid off. I was a little more confident and competent at that next shooting session, a little more in my element. It was mid-May, and the national forest's tulip trees were in full leaf. The Appalachian woodlands were scenic, as were several sexy tattooed boys in tank tops. I got to shoot Aidan's rifle, finding the sights super-hard to line up, and even shot his assault rifle, the infamous AK-47. The first was quiet, the second was loud, but neither had any recoil to speak of. Aidan went over how to clean guns, recommending several products to use, among them CLP cleaner and a bore snake. We talked a little about holsters, in case I decided to carry a concealed gun in public. I already had a belt holster, but Aidan showed me his shoulder holster.

"Then there's this option," he said, pulling his T-shirt up a few inches to reveal his lean midriff, then tucking his handgun into the front of his waistband. I was just as unnerved to be admiring the treasure trail of a guy I'd first met when he was a little boy as I was to be seeing the gun's proximity to his crotch.

"Just make sure it doesn't go off there," he said casually.

I blanched. "Think I'll stick to the belt option," I said, suppressing a shudder.

As we drove down the hillside, taking in the wonderful green-gold of a mountain spring, I felt an odd pleasure, one I rarely feel, one I've analyzed and have come to recognize. In college psychology, I learned about cognitive dissonance. To adapt that phrase, all my life I've suffered from what I can call regional and community dissonance, meaning that sometimes I feel like I fit into Appalachia and sometimes I don't, and sometimes I feel like I fit into the gay community and sometimes I don't. (Interestingly, I've felt more at home in Appalachia and less at home in the queer community as I've aged. This I blame on alt-left political correctness and prickly transgender extremists, those prescriptive and hypersensitive pests that have hijacked the entire LGBT movement.)

Usually, I feel like I don't belong anywhere, that I'm a perpetual outsider, an odd amalgam of traditional regional traits, higher education, idiosyncratic enthusiasms, liberal politics, gender non-normativity, and erotic peculiarities that are anomalous everywhere. That gets very tiring. When I can feel, for however short a time, that I fit in, it's pleasurable, and I can forget, or at least ignore, the continuous dissonance I live with. Riding down that mountain road through the spring woods after time at a shooting range, I felt very briefly as if I belonged, as if I'd laid down the burdens of complexity, conflict, and contradiction and become simpler, even serene, a typical Appalachian man instead of the multifaceted freak that I am. There was illusory comfort in it.

Later that week, I told a colleague about my visit to the shooting range. "All I'd really need to do now to become the perfect redneck stereotype is to turn straight and become a fundamentalist Christian."

We both guffawed. "Yeah, right. That ain't gonna happen," I said, rolling my eyes and heading down the hall to teach creative writing.

X.

WE'RE THE PRODUCTS of our histories: personal, familial, regional, national, and global. That the latter two have lately been nudging me more and more toward developing gun proficiency skills may, ultimately, be pointless, but the process allows me to be active, not passive. It allows me to feel a little safer.

On June 19, 2018, officials in Washington D.C. announced that the United States was leaving the United Nations' Human Rights Council (Morello). The next day, my husband conveniently absent on a business trip, I cleaned my Glock, using recently purchased CLP, the bore snake, and the remains of a ratty wife-beater that had once been cut off me during a BDSM knife-play session. I also used the magazine speed loader to fill one of my magazines with hollow-points. Once again, minute movements were important to doing it right…well, doing it at all. I'd been aware for a while that my Glock was useless if someone broke into the house and I had no magazines loaded, so I rectified that situation. The Glock's like an electric battery: the gun's one charge, and the loaded magazine's an opposite charge. Apart, they're harmless, useless. Put them together—pop the loaded magazine into the gun—and immediately you possess the power to protect yourself.

Later that summer, several photos showed up in my Facebook feed, close-ups of gay men—acquaintances of acquaintances—who'd been bashed in several U.S. cities. In August, up came a news report about Armenian gay activists being attacked by homophobes ("LGBT Activists"). That reminded me of news stories I'd seen over the years about gay men being thrown off rooftops in Middle Eastern countries by Muslim extremists ("ISIS"), and that reminded me of news reports I'd read online about Chechnya, horror stories about disappearances, tortures, concentration camps, and anti-gay purges ("Anti-gay purges").

In early August, on a trip to Memphis, I visited the National Civil Rights Museum. Among the exhibits, a quotation by Ida B. Wells caught my eye. Here's the expanded version of that quotation that I found online.

> Of the many inhuman outrages of this present year, the only case where the proposed lynching did not occur, was where the men armed themselves in Jacksonville, Fla., and Paducah, Ky., and prevented it. The only times an Afro-American who was assaulted got away has been when he had a gun and used it in self-defense.
>
> The lesson this teaches and which every Afro-American should ponder well, is that a Winchester rifle should have a place of honor in every black home, and it should be used for that protection which the law refuses to give. When the white man who is always the aggressor knows he runs as great a risk of biting the dust every time his Afro-American victim does, he will have greater respect for Afro-American life. The more the Afro-American yields and cringes and begs, the more he has to do so, the more he is insulted, outraged and lynched. ("Southern Horrors")

The weekend after we returned home, a right-wing rally occurred in Washington D.C. The day after that, I drove back to the sports store and spent another six hundred dollars. I'd been browsing that aforementioned erotic Glock catalog, I'd been contemplating how many isolated back roads I drive in rural red counties with two Obama stickers on the back bumper of my truck, and I'd been thinking about the national hatefulness that right-wingers seem so adept at enflaming. My new gun was a sub-compact Glock 26, also a 9mm, with ten rounds, small enough to fit into the black-leather backpack that goes just about everywhere I go. I drove home from the store along a scenic country road with wide views over summer meadows and the Blue Ridge Mountains beyond—the world's life at its seasonal height—sharply aware that the purpose of what I'd just bought was to save life by causing death.

XI.

I FINALLY GOT hold of that evangelist, or, rather, his scheduler, who signed me up for the shooting class. A few days after the Ford/Kavanaugh hearings, I drove four miles around Draper Mountain to a little Baptist church set picturesquely among green fields, with another Blue Ridge backdrop. I took both Glocks, one hundred rounds of ammo, and two magazines, as the scheduler had advised. *One hundred rounds?* I thought. *That'd bring down a helluva lot of religious conservatives, if I could ever get skilled enough to plug them.*

The gun instructor/evangelist turned out to be a good-looking, nicely built man with a graying beard like mine, someone I would've chatted up in the more simpatico settings of a bear or leather bar. His two assistants resembled me a bit, too: middle-aged guys with country accents, salt-and-pepper beards, and stocky-running-to-fat physiques. As I chatted with them, I felt again that old dissonance. Was I a clever queer passing as straight so as to infiltrate the enemy—fundamentalist Christians—and learn from them skills that I might in future use against their kind? Or was I a rural Southerner chatting with other rural Southerners, fluent in Good Ole Boy because one of my many selves *is* a Good Ole Boy? As usual, the answer was both.

There were eight other students, all of them women, which

I found significant, considering the Kavanaugh hearings and the Me Too movement. In the big meeting room adjoining the church, we all watched a National Rifle Association video about situational awareness and the three mental states people operate in—unaware, alert, and alarmed—before the class divided up into beginning students and advanced ones. Since I'd already had a concealed-carry class, the scheduler had signed me up for the advanced class, and I'd agreed. What was I thinking? I'd only been on a range twice.

While the handsome evangelist stayed inside to speak to the beginners, his two assistants led us three "advanced" students outside into the bright September day. We all drove our trucks down the slope to a meadow, where we pinned paper targets to clotheslines and set out our gear.

The next two hours were pretty intense, and my innate incompetence asserted itself, or at least my lack of experience. I'm lucky that I'm not one of those men whose dick's so tiny that he can't stand being outperformed by women, because I was way out of my league. My two fellow students definitely had been on a shooting range more than twice. Luckily, I'm a big fan of strong, independent, proficient women, having had close lesbian friends since high school, and the two instructors were consistently helpful rather than mocking. They timed us for many of the exercises, deliberately creating an atmosphere of anxiety to somewhat mirror crisis situations in which a gun would be called for. After some regular target practice, they tipped card tables up to serve as barricades around which we shot. Unfortunately, they demanded that we shoot with both the right and the left hand! Hell, I hardly knew how to shoot with my right hand, much less my left. I was no damn good, having to be carefully coached on how to hold the gun and pull the trigger with my left index finger. Thank God the instructors were patient. I also turned out to be painfully slow at loading a magazine. Had the crisis been real, I would've been fucked. At the session's end, when we tallied up the holes in our respective targets, my total was by far the lowest.

Well, I had a lot of learning yet to do. I already knew that. I chatted with one of the instructors while everyone else packed up and left, he gave me a couple pointers about my stance and gripping the gun, I asked him to let me know when classes were offered again, so that I might take the beginner's course, then I packed up and drove off, past a field where folks were mowing a late crop of hay. The wicked thrill of passing and infiltrating I'd expected to enjoy wasn't there. None of them—the evangelist or his assistants—had done any proselytizing or even mentioned religion at all. In fact, they were all friendly, laid-back country guys I liked…or would've liked if I weren't fairly sure that, as Baptist fundamentalists, they were conservatives, Republicans, and homophobes. If I were a different kind of queer, the more detectable kind, the afternoon might have gone quite differently.

XII.

AS I'VE MENTIONED throughout this collection, I have a wonderful friend I've known since 1979, Cindy Burack, an author and political theorist who teaches in the Women's Studies Department at Ohio State University. Cindy met me when I was twenty years old, so she's been around to see my many changes. Over the last couple of years, I've been sharing with her the "gun odyssey" delineated above. (My husband doesn't want to hear about it.)

A few months ago in Hinton, while I made preparations for dinner, we chatted about white supremacists, the alt-right, neo-Nazis, and other scum who worship at the Altar of the Orange Shitgibbon. I told her about buying my second gun, the Morrigan, and my experiences with Aidan on the national forest's shooting range.

"You're not alone in this," Cindy said, always immaculately informed about current events. "After Trump's election, gun sales went up among two groups, African Americans and queers." I've since found confirmation of this assertion, in "Gun sales have dropped since Trump's election, except among people scared of his administration," an article published in *The Washington Post*, March 5, 2017 (Shapiro and Zezima).

"I'm a statistic again," I sighed, waving a kitchen knife as if it were Aragorn's reforged sword. "Dammit! I've always wanted to feel exceptional."

Cindy smiled, long used to my narcissism. "You know they'll always have more guns and ammunition than we will, right?"

"Yep." I nodded, sipping my martini and stirring a pot of German-style sweet-and-sour red cabbage, one of her favorites. (I'm a little like the Irish father-god, the Dagda, possessor of a killing club and a magical cooking pot.) "But at least I can take some of the bastards down with me as I go."

Inside that image is embedded the way that I, a tales-of-heroism addict, would most want to leave this world: dying in the process of successfully defending my clan. The way I would most want *not* to leave this world would be dying in the process of unsuccessfully defending my clan.

These hypothetical scenarios remind me of an essay I used to teach in freshman composition, "The Ignored Lesson of Anne Frank." Its author, Bruno Bettelheim, survived the Buchenwald concentration camp and so was in a better position than most to question the Frank family's response to Nazi persecution. His thesis is that "Anne Frank's fate demonstrates how efforts at disregarding in private life what goes on around one in society can hasten one's own destruction" (615). He suggests that "the main principle of their planning was continuing their beloved family life—an understandable desire, but highly unrealistic in those times," and he points out that they didn't arm themselves with weapons in their hiding place and didn't choose one with multiple exits that might have allowed for escape (616).

Most relevant for the purposes of this essay is the following:

> Had they had a gun, Mr. Frank could have shot down at least one or two of the "green police" who came for them. There was no surplus of such police, and the loss of an SS with every Jew arrested would have noticeably hindered the functioning of the police state.... The fate of the Franks wouldn't have been very different, because they all died anyway except for Anne's father. But they could have sold their lives for a high price, instead of walking to their death. Still, although one must assume that Mr. Frank would have fought courageously, as we know he did when a soldier in the first World War, it is not everybody who can plan to kill those who are bent on killing him, although many who would not be ready to contemplate doing so would be willing to kill those who are bent on murdering not only them but also their wives and little daughters. (616)

In contrast, Bettelheim describes groups of resistance fighters that relatives of his joined in Hungary. He says that "[many] of these groups survived intact. Furthermore, they had also equipped themselves with small arms, so that if they were detected, they could put up enough of a fight for the majority to escape while a few would die fighting to make the escape possible" (619).

As a priest of Thor, Odin, and the Dagda, I much prefer this active response to danger.

XIII.

I'D NEVER HEARD of the Pink Pistols until Kilian Melloy referred to them in his 2016 interview with me, mentioned above. There, he said that "the Pink Pistols claim[ed] a spike in new members after the Orlando shootings," meaning the notorious massacre at Pulse, a gay nightclub, in June 2016.

I looked them up. To quote from their website, they're a national organization "dedicated to the legal, safe, and responsible use of firearms for self-defense of the sexual-minority community" ("About the Pink Pistols"). Unfortunately, I live in an area without a Pink Pistols chapter (the nearest is nearly three hours away, in Charlottesville, Virginia), but a quotation from their webpage speaks to me.

> *We teach queers to shoot. Then we teach others that we have done so.* Armed queers don't get bashed. We change the public perception of the sexual minorities, such that those who have in the past perceived them as safe targets for violence and hateful acts — beatings, assaults, rapes, murders — will realize that that [sic] now, a segment of the sexual minority population is now armed and effective with those arms. Those arms are also concealed, so they do not know which ones are safe to attack, and which are not...which they can harm as they have in the past, and which may draw a weapon and fight back.
>
> The Pink Pistols are the ones who have decided to no longer be safe targets. They have teeth. They will use them. ("About the Pink Pistols")

"HELL, yes!" I wanted to shout, reading the above. As Cindy said, it looks like I'm not alone in this.

XIV.

IN THE PAST few weeks, as I've safely sat in my study and worked on this essay, a crazy Trump supporter sent pipe bombs to prominent Democratic politicians, another crazy bastard killed eleven Jews in a Pittsburgh synagogue, another crazy bastard killed two women in a Florida yoga studio, and another crazy bastard killed two black folks in a Kentucky parking lot after trying unsuccessfully to get into a predominantly black church, no doubt eager to slaughter as many people as possible. Meanwhile, in Tanzania, the largest city's governor has "vowed to begin mass arrests" of gays, and has asked citizens, "If you know any gays…report them to me" (Fitzsimons).

Yesterday, Election Day 2018, I felt compelled to start reading a book I've owned since 1991 but never made time for, *The Pink Triangle: The Nazi War Against Homosexuals*, by Richard Plant. This morning, CNN's announced that the Democrats have taken back the House of Representatives. Women, Muslims, Latinas, and queer candidates have been elected, including a Native American lesbian from Kansas.

My sense of impending doom has lessened, even though the loathsome Morgan Griffith, a Trump-supporting Republican, has, to my disgust, held onto his position as Representative for my congressional district, Virginia's ninth, and West Virginians voted solidly red, once again going against their own best interests. (I don't consider that re-elected prick Manchin a real Democrat.)

"We *are* in Republican Land," John said, in response to my snarling and fuming over Griffith's re-election.

Well, yes, we are, I thought, locking the door behind John after he left for a brief business meeting. He and I met in 1997, and in 1998 he graduated from Virginia Tech with a Ph.D. in Instructional Technology. He could have gone anywhere; he seriously considered a position in Rochester, New York. But he stayed here, in my native region, first in Charleston, West Virginia, and now here in Pulaski. He stayed in Republican Land to be with me, so the least I can do is to be prepared to ward off what potential hostility I can. As I'm sure I've made very clear, small-town Appalachia's a place that feels like home to me and also vaguely dangerous. This is why, as I type this, "the Morrigan" and a loaded magazine rest in a bookcase three yards from me.

Tonight, after John's gone up to bed, I'm going to check the locks on the front and back doors, as I do every night. Cautious as I am, I'll probably check them twice. Whenever I do that, I think of author Jack Donovan. He upset a lot of folks in the queer community back in 2006, when he published, under a pseudonym, "Jack Malebranche," *Androphilia: A Manifesto*, in which he suggested that "there is ample opportunity for those critical of gay culture to found a new subculture based on masculinity, not as a mere subset of gay culture but in tribute to the rich history of masculine culture itself" (Malebranche 21). Despite its unfortunate anti-feminist stance, I could relate to a lot of material in *Androphilia*. Much gay culture is too urban for me; it seems superficial and trivial, and I have little use for it.

These days, Donovan's gotten way too conservative for me, as Maureen O'Connor made clear in her article, "The Philosophical Fascists of the Gay Alt-Right," where she describes him as a "skinhead icon and right-wing extremist." Uck. But something he says in his 2012 book, *The Way of Men*, is directly connected to my gun ownership and my compulsive securing of the house. "The first job of men in dire times has always been to establish and secure 'the perimeter,'" he says (12). A few pages later, he adds, "It all comes down to you, the guardians, because you know that if you fail at your jobs there can be no human happiness, no family life, no storytelling, no art or music. Your role at the bloody edges of the boundary between *us* and *them* supersedes any role you have within the protected space" (14-15).

He's no doubt speaking to men here, most likely traditionally masculine men, but I'm thinking more inclusively. I'm thinking about warriors of all kinds. The most ferocious warriors I've ever known have been lesbians and drag queens. If I can serve as any kind of homo-hillbilly daddy-bear Thor to their Wonder Women and Athenas, I'll count myself lucky. If becoming proficient with my Glocks makes me better able to protect my people and stand by the side of other bellicose and determined queers, so be it. May the grimmest necessities pass us by, but, if not, may we be prepared to meet them.

Works Cited

"About The Pink Pistols." *Pink Pistols*, 14 June 2016, www.pinkpistols.org/about-the-pink-pistols.

Anderson, Courtney. "Base of Jefferson Davis statue removed from downtown Memphis." *News Channel 3 WREG Memphis* (28 July 2018). Television.

Anderson, Maggie. *A Space Filled with Moving*. Pittsburgh: University of Pittsburgh Press, 1992.

"Anti-Gay Purges in Chechnya." *Wikipedia*, Wikimedia Foundation, 19 Mar. 2019, en.wikipedia.org/wiki/Anti-gay_purges_in_Chechnya.

Arnow, Harriette. "Adjusting." *Voices from the Hills: Selected Readings of Southern Appalachia*. Ed. Robert J. Higgs and Ambrose N. Manning. 2nd ed. Dubuque, Iowa: Kendall/Hunt Publishing Company, 1996.

Bageant, Joe. *Deer Hunting with Jesus: Dispatches from America's Class War*. New York: Three Rivers Press, 2007.

Bartlett, Kerri. "Three Preachers and a Historian Tell 'Fuller Story' by Proposing Civil War Monument, Markers." Save the Franklin Battlefield, Inc., Aug. 2018, www.franklin-stfb.org/2018August_STFBNewsletter.pdf.

Bettelheim, Bruno. "The Ignored Lesson of Anne Frank." *Fields of Writing: Readings Across the Disciplines*. Ed. Nancy R. Comley, David Hamilton, Carl H. Klaus, Robert Scholes, and Nancy Sommers. Second Edition. New York: St. Martin's Press, 1987.

Burack, Cynthia. *Because We Are Human: Contesting US Support for Gender and Sexuality Human Rights Abroad*. Albany, New York: SUNY Press, 2018.

Catton, Bruce. *The Civil War*. Boston: Houghton Mifflin, 2005.

Cohen, Dov, Richard E. Nisbett, Brian F. Bowdle, and Norbert Schwarz. "Insult, Aggression, and the Southern Culture of Honor: An 'Experimental Ethnography.'" Simine Vazire, Ph.D., http://www.simine.com/240/readings/Cohen_et_al_(2).pdf.

Collins, Patricia Hill. *Black Feminist Thought: Knowledge, Consciousness, and the Politics of Empowerment*. New York: Routledge, 2008.

Crawford, Jackson C., translator. *The Poetic Edda: Stories of the Norse Gods and Heroes*. Hackett Publishing Company, 2015.

Donovan, Jack. *The Way of Men*. Milwaukie, Oregon: Dissonant Hum, 2012.

Douglas, Henry Kyd. *I Rode with Stonewall*. St. Simons Island, Georgia: Mockingbird Books, 1987.

Dressler, Muriel Miller. "Appalachia." *Wild Sweet Notes: Fifty Years of West Virginia Poetry, 1950-1999*. Ed. Barbara Smith and Kirk Judd. Huntington, West Virginia: Publishers Place, 2000.

Edgar, Alfred Mallory. *My Reminiscences of the Civil War with the Stonewall Brigade and the Immortal 600*. Charleston, West Virginia: 35th Star Publishing, 2011.

"FAQs." *FAQs*, Virginia Arms Co., 2019, www.virginiaarms.com/faq.
"Firearms Purchase Eligibility Test." *Virginia State Police - Firearms Purchase Eligibility Test*, Virginia State Police, 2009, www.vsp.state.va.us/Firearms_PurchaseEligibility.shtm.
Fitzsimons, Tim. "'Report Them to Me': Tanzanian Official Asks Residents to Help Hunt Gays." *NBCNews.com*, NBCUniversal News Group, 1 Nov. 2018, www.nbcnews.com/feature/nbc-out/report-them-me-tanzanian-official-asks-residents-help-hunt-gays-n929741?fbclid=IwAR13oyqf5ebhni1Kzmmp Y59C978YTvobUk7kc6EsZWu2emHFi8F7GJtD0K0>.
"General Order No. 28." *Wikipedia*, Wikimedia Foundation, 26 Sept. 2018, en.wikipedia.org/wiki/General_Order_No._28.
Giardina, Denise. *Storming Heaven*. New York: Ivy Books, 1988.
Graham, Paul C. *Confederaphobia! An American Epidemic*. Columbia, South Carolina: Shotwell Publishing, 2017.
Held, Amy. "Shrouds Pulled From Charlottesville Confederate Statues, Following Ruling." *NPR*, NPR, 28 Feb. 2018, www.npr.org/sections/thetwo-way/2018/02/28/589451855/shrouds-pulled-from-charlottesville-confederate-statues-following-ruling.
Handgun World Podcast. "How to Grip a Glock or Any Pistol." *YouTube*, YouTube, 18 July 2010, www.youtube.com/watch?v=hy00qD4ivgA.
Heaney, Seamus, translator. *Beowulf*. New York: Norton, 2000.
Heger, Heinz, and David Fernbach. *The Men with the Pink Triangle: The True Life-and-Death Story of Homosexuals in the Nazi Death Camps*. Boston: Alyson Books, 1994.
"Hinton, WV." *Data USA*, datausa.io/profile/geo/hinton-wv/.
"Hollow-Point Bullet." *Wikipedia*, Wikimedia Foundation, 9 Mar. 2019, en.wikipedia.org/wiki/Hollow-point_bullet.
Homer. *The Iliad of Homer*. Trans. Richmond Lattimore. Chicago: University of Chicago Press, 1961.
Horton, Alex. "Tennessee Lawmakers Punish Memphis for Removing Statue of Confederate and KKK Leader." *The Washington Post*, 18 Apr. 2018, www.washingtonpost.com/news/post-nation/wp/2018/04/18/tennessee-lawmakers-punish-memphis-for-removing-statue-of-confederate-and-kkk-leader/?utm_term=.f13f3a617d34.
Horwitz, Tony. *Confederates in the Attic: Dispatches from the Unfinished Civil War*. New York: Vintage Books, 1999.
"ISIS, Many of Their Enemies Share a Homicidal Hatred of Gays." *CBS News*, CBS Interactive, 13 June 2016, www.cbsnews.com/news/isis-orlando-shooting-gays-execution-torture-ramadan/.
Jones, Loyal. "Appalachian Values." *Voices from the Hills: Selected Readings of Southern Appalachia*. Ed. Robert J. Higgs and Ambrose N. Manning. 2nd ed. Dubuque, Iowa: Kendall/Hunt Publishing Company, 1996.
Jones, Loyal, and Billy Edd Wheeler. *Laughter in Appalachia: A Festival of Southern Mountain Humor*. Little Rock, Arkansas: August House, 1987.

Krugman, Paul. "The Paranoid Style in G.O.P. Politics." *The New York Times*, 8 Oct. 2018.

Kula, Cheryl. "To Remotest Ages." *Now and Then: The Appalachian Magazine* 30.1 (Summer 2014): 35-36.

Litten, Kevin. "A Year after New Orleans Confederate Monuments Came down, Questions Linger." *NOLA.com*, 23 Apr. 2018, expo.nola.com/erry-2018/04/476a19f1324154/new_orleans_confederate_monume.html.

Lofstead, Becky. "Defending Our Right to the Past." *West Virginia University Magazine*, Summer 2017, magazine.wvu.edu/stories/2017/08/06/defending-our-right-to-the-past.

Malebranche, Jack. *Androphilia: A Manifesto*. Baltimore: Scapegoat Publishing, 2006.

McKinney, Irene. *Vivid Companion*. Morgantown, West Virginia: West Virginia University Press, 2004.

McPherson, James M. *For Cause and Comrades: Why Men Fought in the Civil War*. New York: Oxford University Press, 1997.

Melloy, Kilian. "Jeff Mann on 'Country.'" *EDGE Media Network*, 7 Sept. 2016, boston.edgemedianetwork.com/entertainment/books/news/203355/jeff_mann_on_.

Mitchell, Patricia B. *German Cooking in America*. Chatham, Virginia: Mitchells Publications, 2003.

Morello, Carol. "U.S. Withdraws from U.N. Human Rights Council over Perceived Bias against Israel." *The Washington Post*, 19 June 2018, www.washingtonpost.com/world/national-security/us-expected-to-back-away-from-un-human-rights-council/2018/06/19/a49c2d0c-733c-11e8-b4b7-308400242c2e_story.html?utm_term=.ea13106795d1.

MrEk78. "How to Load and Unload a Glock Pistol." *YouTube*, YouTube, 26 Apr. 2013, www.youtube.com/watch?v=H-FzwKjxQrk.

"Nathan Bedford Forrest Monument." *Wikipedia*, Wikimedia Foundation, 27 Nov. 2018, en.wikipedia.org/wiki/Nathan_Bedford_Forrest_Monument.

O'Connor, Maureen. "The Philosophical Fascists of the Gay Alt-Right." *The Cut*, 30 Apr. 2017, www.thecut.com/2017/04/jack-donovan-philosophical-fascists-of-the-gay-alt-right.html.

"Our Mission." *American Civil War Museum*, acwm.org/about-us/our-mission.

Over, Ilene. "Ilene Over at Virginia Tech - October 2015." *YouTube*, YouTube, 24 Oct. 2015, www.youtube.com/watch?v=s3xzXOhwBOU.

Pancake, Breece, D'J. *The Stories of Breece D'J Pancake*. New York: Holt, Rinehart and Winston, 1983.

Poole, W. Scott. "Lincoln in Hell: Class and Confederate Symbols in the American South." *National Symbols, Fractured Identities: Contesting the National Narrative*. Ed. Michael E. Geisler. Lebanon, New Hampshire: University Press of New England, 2005. 121-148.

Rfe/rl. "LGBT Activists Reportedly Attacked In Southern Armenia." *RadioFreeEurope/RadioLiberty*, RadioFreeEurope/RadioLiberty, 4 Aug. 2018, www.rferl.org/a/lgbt-activists-reportedly-attacked-in-southern-armenia/29412726.html.

Rich, Adrienne. *Blood, Bread, and Poetry: Selected Prose 1979-1985.* New York: Norton, 1986.

--. *Your Native Land, Your Life.* New York: Norton, 1993.

Rife, Luanne. "W&L Will Remove Confederate Battle Flags from Lee Chapel." *The Roanoke Times*, 8 July 2014, www.roanoke.com/news/virginia/w-l-will-remove-confederate-battle-flags-from-lee-chapel/article_a13cae23-4367-56c5-9861-8ffd90e673e1.html.

"Robert E. Lee Monument (New Orleans, Louisiana)." *Wikipedia*, Wikimedia Foundation, 5 Jan. 2019, en.wikipedia.org/wiki/Robert_E._Lee_Monument_(New_Orleans,_Louisiana).

Robertson, Jr., James I. *Soldiers Blue and Gray.* Columbia: University of South Carolina Press, 1998.

Scott, J. L. *Lowry's, Bryan's, and Chapman's Batteries of Virginia Artillery.* Lynchburg, Virginia: H. E. Howard, 1988.

Sexton, Anne. *Transformations.* Boston: Mariner Books, 2001.

Shapiro, T. Rees., and Katie Zezima. "Gun sales have dropped since Trump's election, except among people scared of his administration." *The Washington Post*, 5 Mar. 2017, https://www.washingtonpost.com/politics/gun-sales-have-dropped-since-trumps-election-except-among-people-scared-of-his-administration/2017/03/05/03f5b522-ff6a-11e6-8f41-ea6ed597e4ca_story.html?utm_term=.1f7a9ce98961.

Still, James. *The Wolfpen Poems.* Berea, Kentucky: Berea College Press, 1986.

tmh10. "Mike Foster/Confederate Sharpshooter." *American Civil War Forums*, 26 Apr. 2017, civilwartalk.com/threads/mike-foster-confederate-sharpshooter.83647/.

"'The Vacant Chair.'" *Music of The Civil War*, petersonhist127.weebly.com/the-vacant-chair.html.

"The Virginia Flaggers." *The Virginia Flaggers*, 1 Jan. 1970, vaflaggers.blogspot.com/.

Ward, Geoffrey, with Ric Burns and Ken Burns. *The Civil War.* New York: Vintage, 1994.

Wells, Ida B. "Southern Horrors: Lynch Law in All Its Phases." *Digital History*, 2019, www.digitalhistory.uh.edu/disp_textbook.cfm?smtid=3&psid=3614. (Original essay published 1892)

Wiley, Bell Irvin. *The Life of Johnny Reb: The Common Soldier of the Confederacy.* Baton Rouge: LSU Press, 2008.

"William Tecumseh Sherman." *Wikipedia*, Wikimedia Foundation, 25 Feb. 2019, en.wikipedia.org/wiki/William_Tecumseh_Sherman.

Woods, Brian. "Bomb threat made to Jewish center in Cherry Hill." *Burlington County Times*, 27 Feb. 2017, http://www.burlingtoncountytimes.com/50f2efa4-fd29-11e6-aa7c-076c0147066c.html.

Zimmer, Ben. "A New Breakthrough in the History of the 'S—gibbon': The Insult's Originator Steps Forward." *Slate*, 13 Feb. 2017, https://slate.com/culture/2017/02/the-origin-of-the-trump-insult-shitgibbon-revealed.html.

About the Author

Jeff Mann grew up in Covington, Virginia, and Hinton, West Virginia, receiving degrees in English and forestry from West Virginia University. His poetry, fiction, and essays have appeared in many publications, including *Arts and Letters, Prairie Schooner, Shenandoah, Willow Springs, The Gay and Lesbian Review Worldwide, Crab Orchard Review,* and *Appalachian Heritage.* He has published three award-winning poetry chapbooks, *Bliss, Mountain Fireflies,* and *Flint Shards from Sussex*; five full-length books of poetry, *Bones Washed with Wine, On the Tongue, Ash: Poems from Norse Mythology, A Romantic Mann,* and *Rebels*; three collections of personal essays, *Edge: Travels of an Appalachian Leather Bear, Binding the God: Ursine Essays from the Mountain South,* and *Endangered Species: A Surly Bear in the Bible Belt*; three novellas, *Devoured,* included in *Masters of Midnight: Erotic Tales of the Vampire, Camp Allegheny,* included in *History's Passion: Stories of Sex Before Stonewall,* and *The Saga of Einar and Gisli,* included in *On the Run: Tales of Gay Pursuit and Passion*; six novels, *Cub, Country, Insatiable, Fog: A Novel of Desire and Reprisal* (which won the Pauline Réage Novel Award), *Purgatory: A Novel of the Civil War* (which won a Rainbow Award), and *Salvation: A Novel of the Civil War* (which won both the Pauline Réage Novel Award and a Lambda Literary Award); a book of poetry and memoir, *Loving Mountains, Loving Men*; and three volumes of short fiction, *Desire and Devour: Stories of Blood and Sweat, Consent: Bondage Tales,* and *A History of Barbed Wire* (which won a Lambda Literary Award). With Julia Watts, he's co-edited *LGBTQ Fiction and Poetry from Appalachia.* In 2013, he was inducted into the Saints and Sinners Literary Festival Hall of Fame. He teaches creative writing at Virginia Tech in Blacksburg, Virginia. His website is jeffmannauthor.com

www.ingramcontent.com/pod-product-compliance
Lightning Source LLC
Chambersburg PA
CBHW030850170426
43193CB00009BA/561